Deliberative Democracy

It is sometimes assumed that voting is the central mechanism for political decision making. However, the contributors to this volume focus on an alternative mechanism – decision by discussion or deliberation. These original contributions include case studies based on historical and current instances of deliberative democracy, normative discussion of the merits of deliberation compared with other models of collective decision making, and studies of the conditions under which deliberation tends to improve the quality of decisions. This volume takes a realistic approach: rather than assuming that deliberative democracy is always ideal, the authors critically probe its limits and weaknesses as well as its strengths.

Jon Elster is Robert K. Merton Professor of Social Science at Columbia University.

Cambridge Studies in the Theory of Democracy

Edited by Adam Przeworski
New York University

"It is not current politics but democracy as a form of government that I seek to describe," James Bryce wrote in 1921. The goal of this series is to reinvigorate theoretical reflection about democracy by exposing it to the full range of historical experiences under which democracies have flourished or floundered. Our ambition is to understand what makes democracies work and endure. How do they promote normatively desirable and politically desired objectives, and how do they peacefully handle crises that occur when such objectives are not being fulfilled? We intend to ignore artificial divisions among different approaches, by drawing simultaneously on classical political theory, modern analytical methods, and comparative empirical research. We hope that our conclusions not only will offer some guidance for countries that are still in the process of developing democratic institutions, but also will provide a means of understanding the deficiencies of the well-established democratic systems.

Deliberative Democracy

Edited by

Jon Elster

CAMBRIDGE
UNIVERSITY PRESS

PUBLISHED BY THE PRESS SYNDICATE OF THE UNIVERSITY OF CAMBRIDGE
The Pitt Building, Trumpington Street, Cambridge, United Kingdom

CAMBRIDGE UNIVERSITY PRESS
The Edinburgh Building, Cambridge CB2 2RU, UK   http: //www.cup.cam.ac.uk
40 West 20th Street, New York, NY 10011-4211, USA   http: //www.cup.org
10 Stamford Road, Oakleigh, Melbourne 3166, Australia

First published 1998
Reprinted 1998, 1999

Typeset in Centennial

A catalogue record for this book is available from the British Library

Library of Congress Cataloguing-in-Publication data

Deliberative democracy / edited by Jon Elster.
p. cm. – (Cambridge studies in the theory of democracy)
Includes bibliographical references and index.
1. Democracy. 2. Decision-making. 3. Representative government
and representation. I. Elster, Jon, 1940– . II. Series.
JC423.D3892   1998   97-32111
321.8 – dc21   CIP

ISBN 0 521 59296 8 hardback
ISBN 0 521 59696 3 paperback

Transferred to digital printing 2002

Contents

Contents

Contributors

Joshua Cohen, Department of Political Science, Massachusetts Institute of Technology

Jon Elster, Department of Political Science, Columbia University

James D. Fearon, Department of Political Science, University of Chicago

Diego Gambetta, All Souls College, Oxford

Roberto Gargarella, Department of Law and Political Science, Universidad di Tella, Buenos Aires

James Johnson, Department of Political Science, University of Rochester

Gerry Mackie, St. John's College, Oxford

Adam Przeworski, Department of Politics, New York University

Susan C. Stokes, Department of Political Science, University of Chicago

Cass R. Sunstein, University of Chicago Law School

Preface and Acknowledgment

Most of the essays in this volume were first presented at a conference at the University of Chicago in April 1995. One paper discussed at the conference, "Modeling Deliberative Democracy" by David Austen-Smith, is not included in the volume because the author preferred not to submit a revised version. As will be clear from several of the chapters, his paper had a considerable impact on the debates.

I thank the University of Chicago for financial support of the conference.

J.E.

Introduction

1. Historical Background

The idea of deliberative democracy, or decision making by discussion among free and equal citizens, is having a revival. During the five months between the initial drafting of the present introduction and the completion of the final version, at least three new books were published on the topic in the United States alone.[1] Largely under the influence of Jürgen Habermas, the idea that democracy revolves around the transformation rather than simply the aggregation of preferences has become one of the major positions in democratic theory.[2]

This development represents, to repeat, a revival rather than an innovation. The idea of deliberative democracy and its practical implementation are as old as democracy itself. Both came into being in Athens in the fifth century B.C. Pericles, in his eulogy of Athens, said:

> Our public men have, besides politics, their private affairs to attend to, and our ordinary citizens, though occupied with the pursuits of industry, are still fair judges of public matters; for, unlike any other nation, we regard the citizen who takes no part in these duties not as unambitious but as useless, and we are able to judge proposals even if we cannot originate them; instead of looking on discussion as a stumbling-block in the way of action, we think it an indispensable preliminary to any wise action at all. (Thucydides II.40)

Yet Athenian democracy was also the birthplace of the tendency to debunk discussion as sophistry or demagoguery. Aristotle's *Rhetoric* is to some extent a handbook in political manipulation. Distrust of clever speakers was so widespread that orators found it useful

1

to stress their own artlessness and the slickness of their opponents.[3] Thus, from the very beginning, democracy by deliberation was viewed both positively and negatively. Some argued that discussion would improve decision making, others that it would lead to bad decisions. More recently, as we shall see, the argument has been made that deliberation essentially makes no difference – for neither the good nor the bad.

The Athenian government was based on direct democracy. Yet although *anyone* could speak and make proposals, not *all* could, because the assembly typically included several thousand citizens. In assemblies of this size, "deliberation" can at best mean discussion among a small number of speakers before an audience rather than discussion among all members of the assembly. The speakers, typically, try to persuade the audience rather than each other. They may talk *about* each other – to point out weaknesses in their opponents' characters or arguments – but not *to* each other. This procedure obviously falls short of what many proponents of deliberative democracy have in mind. Nevertheless, it may to some extent mimic the process of genuine deliberation where the aim is to persuade the interlocutor rather than an audience. The procedure of debating one another before an audience may be compared to adversarial proceedings in the courtroom, with the jury in the role of the audience, or to negative advertising, with consumers in the same role. If the audience is also the ultimate arbiter, the interchanges that take place before it can serve to weed out falsehoods and inconsistencies and thus enable it to make a good decision – assuming, of course, that it is not swept away by passion.

Athenian democracy came to an end in 322 B.C. With the reemergence of democratic government about two thousand years later – but now representative rather than direct – the nature of political deliberation changed.[4] In the Athenian assembly, the handful of orators who debated among themselves were constrained by the need to appeal to the audience. The orators in an elected assembly, by contrast, are usually not subject to this constraint. (But see my Chapter 4 in this volume for some exceptions.) The electorate, to be sure, exercises a constraining effect on the decisions reached by virtue of *anticipation of retrospective control* through voting. The representatives know that if they vote against the wishes of their constituents, they may not be reelected. Yet this control is obviously a very diluted one. The voting record of a politician during the preceding session of Parliament is only one of many factors that determine the chances of reelection.

The idea of *prospective control* of representatives by the voter – through the device of bound mandates – came up almost simultaneously in Great Britain, France, and the United States, and was consistently rejected as being incompatible with the deliberative nature of democracy. In his speech to the electors of Bristol in 1774, Edmund Burke told them that he would not be bound by authoritative instructions:

> Your representative owes you, not his industry only, but his judgment; and he betrays instead of serving you, if he sacrifices it to your opinion. . . . Parliament is not a *congress* of ambassadors from different and hostile interests; which interests each must maintain, as an agent and advocate, against other agents and advocates, but parliament is a *deliberative* assembly of *one* nation, with *one* interest, that of the whole; where, not local purposes, not local prejudices ought to guide, but the general good, resulting from the general reason of the whole.[5]

This speech remains, probably, the most famous statement of the case for deliberative democracy.

The delegates to the French Assemblée Constituante of 1789 expressed similar opposition to bound mandates. In the best-known argument for the need to deliberate, Sieyès claimed that the *voeu national*, the desire of the nation, could not be determined by consulting the *cahiers* of complaints and wishes that the delegates had brought with them to Versailles. Bound mandates, similarly, could not be viewed as expressions of the national will. In a democracy (a pejorative term at the time), he said, people form their opinions at home and then bring them to the voting booth. If no majority emerges, they go back home to reconsider their views, once again isolated from one another. This procedure for forming a common will, he claimed, is absurd because it lacks the element of deliberation and discussion. "It is not a question of a democratic election, but of proposing, listening, concerting, changing one's opinion, in order to form in common a common will."[6] In the debates over the revision of the constitution, d'André[7] and Barnave[8] similarly claimed that a constitutional convention with bound mandates from primary assemblies would be a betrayal of the representative system in favor of democracy. In Barnave's phrase, "A personal wish or the wish of a faction,

3

which is not illuminated by a common deliberation, is not a real wish (*un voeu véritable*)."

Although the issue of bound mandates was not raised at the American Federal Convention or in the *Federalist Papers*, it came up in the first Congress, where the representatives rejected a proposal to give the citizens, as part of the Bill of Rights, a "right to instruct their officials." Roger Sherman, in particular, argued as follows:

> The words are miscalculated to mislead the people, by conveying an idea that they have a right to control the debates of the Legislature. This cannot be admitted to be just, because it would destroy the object of their meeting. I think, when the people have chosen a representative, it is his duty to meet others from the different parts of the Union, and consult, and agree with them to such acts as are for the general benefit of the whole community. If they were to be guided by instructions, there would be no use for deliberation.[9]

In nineteenth-century political thought, John Stuart Mill was the foremost advocate of "government by discussion." He articulated explicitly an idea that was mostly implicit among eighteenth-century thinkers, that deliberation is justified on grounds of human fallibility. In Stephen Holmes's summary, Mill argued:

> The delegate model is objectionable because it implicitly rejects the epistemology of fallibilism. It implies that a representative has nothing important to learn from an uninhibited give-and-take with his fellow deputies. But this assumption is unrealistic. "If he devotes himself to this duty," a representative "has greater opportunities of correcting an original false judgment, than fall to the lot of most of his constituents." The decisive superiority of deputies over citizens lies not in higher intelligence, virtue, or education, but in the unusual nature of the legislative situation itself, which, according to Mill, fosters self-correction.[10]

"If he devotes himself to his duty": this assumption is crucial. Human fallibility is not limited to cognition, because representatives may also fail in their duty to promote the common good. This aspect of fallibility is at the root of another common idea of institutional design. According to Hume, "It is . . . a just *political* maxim, *that every man must be supposed to be a knave*; though, at the same time, it appears somewhat strange, that a maxim should be true in *politics* which is false in *fact*."[11] Whereas Mill thought

4

institutions should be designed to correct for cognitive deficits, Hume did not make the parallel argument that they ought to correct moral deficits. Rather, he thought they should be designed to limit the damage these deficits could do. As Morton White has shown, this idea was also central to the thinking of the Federalists.[12]

A Humean might grant that deliberation can make people change their mind on factual matters concerning the efficient realization of given ends, but not concede that it might have an impact on normative issues. If a representative is guided by factional or short-term interest, no amount of deliberation can induce the adoption of an impartial stance. "Reason is, and ought only to be, the slave of the passions."[13] In our century, this idea has been challenged by John Rawls and Jürgen Habermas, from very different perspectives. The Rawlsian idea of *reflective equilibrium* presupposes the possibility of moral deliberation. In Habermas, the *ideal speech situation* is intended to permit deliberation about ends as well as about means. Because each idea is embedded in a highly complex theory, one should beware of discussing them independently of the context. Yet the arguments advanced by Habermas and Rawls do seem to have a common core: political choice, to be legitimate, must be the outcome of *deliberation about ends among free, equal, and rational agents.*

2. Conceptual Background

Collective decision making by free, equal, and rational individuals need not take the form of deliberation. There are other modes of collective decision making, which can be assessed and compared with deliberation in terms of efficiency, equity, or intrinsic appropriateness. In Section 3, I survey how the contributors to this volume assess the advantages and disadvantages of the various modes. Here I shall try to state exactly which modes these are and what some of their properties are.

When a group of equal individuals are to make a decision on a matter that concerns them all and the initial distribution of opinion falls short of consensus, they can go about it in three different ways: arguing, bargaining, and voting. I believe that for modern societies this is an exhaustive list. In earlier times decisions could also be reached by duels, tournaments, and similar means, but these are not used today. Groups can reach a decision by using one of the three procedures, two of them in combination, or all three. Note

5

that arguing and bargaining are forms of *communication*, that is, they are speech acts, whereas voting is not.

This trichotomy is related to another. In a process of collective decision making, the preferences of the members are subject to three operations: aggregation, transformation, and misrepresentation. Aggregation of preferences, as I use the term here, is a synonym for voting. It includes vote trading, a form of bargaining. The transformation of preferences through rational deliberation is the ostensible goal of arguing. Misrepresentation of preferences can be induced by each of the three decision-making procedures. Voting can be strategic; bargainers often have an incentive to present themselves as less risk-averse or impatient than they actually are; and the impartial stance of those involved in deliberation may be a disguise for other motives. (See my Chapter 4, this volume, for some examples.)

A further trichotomy involves the motives of the members of the group. For my purposes it is convenient to distinguish among reason, interest, and passion. Reason is impartial, both disinterested and dispassionate. Arguing is intrinsically connected to reason, in the sense that anyone who engages in argument must appeal to impartial values. This appeal may, as I said, be a misrepresentation of the true motives, but that is another matter. Bargaining and voting can be motivated by, and present themselves as motivated by, any of these attitudes.

Let me give some examples of the three procedures. Pure argument is observed, or at least is supposed to be the rule, in juries, in which unanimity is required. Even here, some jurors may resort to tacit bargaining by virtue of their greater ability to hold out – that is, their lesser impatience to get out of jury work and back to their ordinary life. Because time always matters when a decision has to be made, and because the participants in the process usually discount the future at different rates, this case may in fact be typical.

Pure bargaining is illustrated by sequential "divide-a-dollar" games in which the parties make successive offers and counteroffers. The outcome is determined by the bargaining mechanism and the bargaining power of the parties – that is, the resources that enable them to make credible threats and promises.

Pure voting was Rousseau's conception of collective decision making. The citizens were to form their preferences in isolation from one another so as not to be contaminated by eloquence and demagogy. Because they would also cast their vote in isolation, vote trading would be excluded. In actual political systems this ideal is never realized. It may be illustrated, perhaps, by certain low-stake decisions, as in the election of members to a scientific academy the main function of which is to elect new members.

Mixed arguing and voting, without bargaining, can be illustrated by tenure decisions in a university department. These are supposed to be governed only by deliberation over the merits of the candidate followed by a vote. In good departments there is a norm against logrolling; and in the best departments this norm is actually adhered to: that is why they are the best.

Mixed arguing and bargaining, without voting, is illustrated by collective wage bargaining. When a union and a management are deciding how to divide the income of the firm, it might appear as if only bargaining is taking place. On closer inspection, however, there is always a substantial amount of arguing about factual matters, such as the financial well-being of the firm and the productivity of the labor force.

Mixed bargaining and voting, without arguing, is more difficult to illustrate. There may not be any such cases; in fact, the notion may be incoherent. Theories of n-person bargaining usually presuppose that the process breaks down unless the bargainers reach unanimity, and then voting is redundant.

Political decision making usually involves all three procedures. Again, this fact follows from the need to reach a decision sooner rather than later. Voting will tend to arise when an issue has to be decided urgently, so that the participants do not have the time to deliberate until they reach unanimity. More prosaically, they may not be motivated to achieve unanimity. As I mentioned, bargaining will tend to arise when the participants have unequal rates of time discounting. Bargaining also arises through logrolling, due to unequal intensity of preferences over the issues to be traded off against each other, and from a number of other mechanisms.

Earlier I said that arguing aims at the transformation of preferences. I also said that much arguing is about factual matters. These statements are not inconsistent with each other. Individuals have fundamental preferences over ultimate ends and derived preferences over the best means to realize those ends, the gap between the two being filled by factual beliefs about ends – means relationships. Arguments that affect those beliefs will also affect the derived preferences. (See my Chapter 4, this volume, for illustration.) In a decision-making process, unlike a scientific seminar, to change derived preferences is in fact the only purpose of arguing about factual matters. In addition, as I said earlier, decision making may involve deliberation about ultimate ends.

3. Defining Deliberative Democracy

The contributors to the present volume give explicit and implicit definitions of deliberative democracy that differ widely from one another. Yet I believe they are talking about the same object, at least in the sense that there is extensive overlap among the definitions. There is a robust core of phenomena that count as deliberative democracy in all of them. All agree, I think, that the notion includes collective decision making with the participation of all who will be affected by the decision or their representatives: this is the democratic part. Also, all agree that it includes decision making by means of arguments offered *by* and *to* participants who are committed to the values of rationality and impartiality: this is the deliberative part. These characterizations are somewhat rough, but I believe they capture the intersection of the extensions reasonably well.

The intensions diverge widely, however, especially with respect to what counts as deliberation. Susan Stokes, in Chapter 5, defines deliberation by its *outcome*: "the endogenous change of preferences resulting from communication." On this definition, propaganda as well as rational debate counts as deliberation. In Chapter 1, Diego Gambetta, citing Austen-Smith, defines the idea by features of the *process*: "a conversation whereby individuals speak and listen sequentially before making a collective decision." As far as this definition goes, deliberation need not have any impact on the outcome; indeed, it is an important implication of Austen-Smith's theory (discussed by Gerry Mackie in Chapter 3) that deliberation often makes no difference for the outcome. In Chapter 4, I focus on the deliberative *setting* as a set of institutional conditions that promote impartiality.

Joshua Cohen (Chapter 8) and James Fearon (Chapter 2) present two clear alternative conceptions. Cohen wants to go beyond the concept of discussion to consider the more ambitious idea of "free and public reasoning among equals." Fearon, by contrast, focuses on the more concrete idea of discussion. His aim is to investigate whether and when the empirically identifiable phenomenon of discussion has good results, rather than to define it such that it is intrinsically desirable. Whereas Cohen tries to develop the conceptual *implications* of deliberation, Fearon wants to identify the causal *consequences* of discussion.

The object of deliberation may be ultimate ends or beliefs from which, given ultimate ends, one can derive preferences over means. Of the essays in this volume, Cohen's places the most emphasis on deliberation about ends. Applying the principle of reflective equilibrium, he argues, for instance, that if I come to see that I should not harm another, the reasons for that conclusion may also constitute reasons for helping him. Most of the other chapters (see, e.g., Chapter 6 by Adam Przeworski) assume that deliberation is mainly about instrumental beliefs and induced preferences.

In his essay, Gambetta draws an analogy between political and scientific deliberation, arguing that they are sustained by similar processes and values. While not disagreeing with anything he says, I would also point to some disanalogies. In science, there is a *fact of the matter* that one can get right. In political deliberation, to the extent that it concerns ultimate ends, this is not obviously the case. To the extent that the object of deliberation is to get factual beliefs right, the analogy is closer. Yet even then the criteria for belief formation are less stringent in politics than in science. A better analogy might be engineering rather than science: the aim is to find an approximation that works rather than the truth. That difference is related to a further disanalogy, which is that political deliberation is constrained by the need to make a *decision*. Whereas scientists can wait for decades and science can wait for centuries, politicians are typically subject to strong time constraints, in two different senses. On the one hand, important decisions tend to be so urgent that one cannot afford to discuss them indefinitely. On the other hand, less important decisions do not justify lengthy deliberations. As I observed earlier, the importance of time in political life implies that, in addition to deliberation, voting as well as bargaining inevitably has some part to play.

4. Arguing over Arguing

Deliberative democracy rests on argumentation, not only in the sense that it proceeds by argument, but also in the sense that it must be justified by argument. It may not be obvious that arguing is the best way of making collective decisions. All things considered, bargaining or simply voting without prior communication might be superior. As James Johnson observes in Chapter 7, one must *argue* for arguing. I would add, however, that one must also argue against it. As observed by Gambetta and Fearon in their essays, the choice among different modes of decision making must be made by arguing about their relative merits. If the goal is to determine the procedure that yields the best outcomes, bargaining over arguing versus bargaining or voting simply does not make sense. The idea of voting over arguing versus voting or bargaining runs into an infinite regress, which can be cut short only by assuming that the first decision to decide by voting is reached by arguing. In this sense, arguing is logically prior to all other modes of collective decision making.

This argument does not prove, however, that arguing at the constitutional stage will yield the conclusion that arguing rather than bargaining or voting ought to be used at the postconstitutional stage. It might well be the case that the pathologies of deliberation, to use the title of Stokes's essay, are so severe that other modes are superior. The pathologies she identifies do not arise in debates among equals, however, but in the political system in a broader sense that includes politicians, citizens, and the media. This is also the case for the phenomena identified by Przeworski, notably the tendency for groups with more resources to impose the set of equilibrium beliefs that benefit them.

Other chapters, however, discuss pathologies that arise in deliberation-as-debate. In my chapter, I consider how publicity – which is often seen as part and parcel of deliberation – may have negative effects on the quality of debates and on the decisions that are made. In his contribution, Johnson suggests that if the discussion involves parties who seek to challenge one another at a fundamental level, it may lead to "intellectual war" – the escalation of conflict rather than its resolution. In such cases one may want to *ban discussion* by imposing "gag rules" rather than stimulate discussion.[14] Johnson also argues that in comparing deliberation with aggregation (voting), one should not stack the cards against the latter. If deliberative theorists can assume that participants are "reasonable," those who place their trust in aggregation should be allowed to assume that the preferences of citizens are similar enough that the paradoxes of aggregation do not arise.

Against these skeptical claims, several of the contributors argue for the virtues of deliberation, or rather discussion, in Fearon's sense. Cass Sunstein argues in Chapter 9 that in the context of risk regulation, deliberation is superior to aggregation when the latter reflects "interest-group pressures, selective attention, inadequate concern for incentives, inadequate information, no real process of reason giving, and little regard for side effects." Gambetta offers four arguments in favor of discussion; Fearon has six. Pooling their lists, they argue that discussion is (or can be) good because (or to the extent that) it

- reveals private information
- lessens or overcomes the impact of bounded rationality
- forces or induces a particular mode of justifying demands
- legitimizes the ultimate choice
- is desirable for its own sake
- makes for Pareto-superior decisions
- makes for better decisions in terms of distributive justice
- makes for a larger consensus
- improves the moral or intellectual qualities of the participants

As noted by Fearon, Cohen, and Johnson, the last argument does not stand on the same footing as most of the others. The impact of a particular decision-making procedure on the characters of the participants cannot be the main reason for choosing that procedure rather than another, although it may be a desirable by-product of choosing it. The argument from legitimacy may be vulnerable to a similar objection. Thus, Przeworski concludes his essay by arguing that if deliberation coordinates behavior on an equilibrium known to be Pareto-suboptimal, it will hardly command legitimacy.

Fearon's argument from bounded rationality rests on the claim that deliberation can be creative. Decision making is not only a process of choosing among given alternatives, but also a process of generating new alternatives ("brainstorming"). The private-information argument is more delicate. A speaker may have valuable private information, but not be able to communicate it credibly. If he has (and is known to have) a personal interest in the listener's believing a certain proposition, and then utters a statement asserting that proposition, the listener may discount the statement as uninformative. For instance, if a person applying for a job tells the employer that his ability is high, without further documentation and without putting down a bond to be forfeited if his ability turns out to be low, the employer may dismiss the statement as tainted at the source.[15] This insight, formalized in the theory of

11

"cheap talk,"[16] has also been applied to political debate – not to conclude that political communication is always devoid of content, but to argue that it often is. In his essay, Mackie offers a frontal attack on this line of reasoning, and on the related argument that because of the incentives for misrepresentation voting cannot be taken at face value as an expression of underlying preferences.

In his theory of discursive democracy, Habermas does not actually offer an argument in favor of this practice. Rather, he takes it for granted that in democracies problems are supposed to be resolved by argument and then tries to work out the implications of this fact. He shows, in particular, how implicit norms of propositional truth, normative rightness, and truthfulness are always presupposed in discussion. Cohen, in his essay, has a similar aim. Effective (as opposed to sham) deliberation presupposes public reasoning among free and equal participants. One might ask Habermas and Cohen whether their arguments have any purchase on actual political discussion. In his recent work, Habermas replies that although "the actual course of the debates deviates from the ideal procedure of deliberative politics . . . , presuppositions of rational discourse have a steering effect on the course of the debates."[17] Cohen, presumably, might offer a similar answer. The essays by Gambetta, Johnson, and myself argue that because of the Habermasian norms, even self-interested speakers are forced or induced to argue in terms of the public interest. As Fearon observes, this constraint may even prevent self-interested proposals from coming on the voting agenda. This "civilizing force of hypocrisy" provides a further, second-best argument for deliberation.

5. Dynamics of Deliberation

To provide a convincing argument for discussion as a problem-solving and conflict-resolving device, one has to have some idea about how it actually works. One mechanism could be the civilizing force of hypocrisy. Another is the conception of deliberation as analogous to negative advertising. Although the parties to the debates have no incentive to draw attention to the negative consequences of their own proposals, they have strong incentives to find flaws in those of their adversaries. In the ensuing contest, the truth will emerge as the set of propositions that have not been successfully challenged. In his writings on political manipulation and political rhetoric, William Riker has pointed to a number of devices that speakers can deploy in order to persuade an audience, including notably the strategy of pointing to the risks involved in the proposals of their opponents.[18]

The essays by Gambetta and myself focus explicitly on the conditions and dynamics of deliberation. Gambetta indicates how different cultures (or equilibrium belief systems) may promote or hinder deliberation. In what he calls "Claro!" cultures, the premium "on having strong opinions on virtually everything from the outset" (Albert Hirschman) works consistently against genuine exchanges of opinion. In more analytically oriented societies, where people do not have to fear that admission of ignorance on one issue will be taken as a sign of general ignorance, deliberation is more likely to occur. In my essay, I focus on contextual features, such as size and publicity, that determine where on the continuum from arguing to bargaining the proceedings will be located.

6. Alternatives and Supplements to Deliberation

Modern democracies may or may not be fully deliberative, but they are always representative. In systems based on both deliberation and representation, normative questions are not limited to the conditions for enhanced deliberation. As Roberto Gargarella emphasizes in Chapter 10, *who deliberates* is also an important issue. Bias and distortion can arise in the selection of representatives no less than in the proceedings of the assembly.[19] In my essay, I illustrate this point with the fact that the Frankfurt Constituent Assembly of 1848 – although elected by universal manhood suffrage – included no peasants, only a few small shopkeepers, virtually no manual workers, and no industrial workers at all. It is far from obvious that the goals of optimizing representation and optimizing deliberation always work in tandem. In fact, it would be wishful thinking to assume that this is always the case: it is only by accident that one institutional arrangement will maximize two different objectives. It would be foolish, for instance, to deny that education enhances deliberation and also foolish to assert that everybody could be equally well educated.

Gargarella also points to an ambiguity in the idea of a democracy that is supposed to be both representative and deliberative. If deliberation is the key to political decision making, what matters is the full representation of views rather than of individuals. Burke, he notes, "was concerned not with votes but with arguments." Even if there are ten times as many workers as capital owners, the idea of government by discussion provides no reason why the former should have more representatives than the latter, assuming – crucially – the internal homogeneity of each group. As long as all views are represented and decisions are made purely by rational argument, numbers shouldn't matter.

If there is internal heterogeneity, as there always is, this argument breaks down. It also breaks down for another reason, namely that deliberation is never used as the only procedure for making collective decisions. It is always supplemented by voting or bargaining or both, because of time constraints as well as for other reasons. In theory, one might establish a procedure of arguing followed by voting without any bargaining. To achieve this end, one could exploit the fact that a public setting precludes the overt use of promises and threats, and prevent the representatives from talking to one another in private. In practice, of course, this would hardly work. Alternatively, one might prevent representatives from engaging in vote bargaining by electing them with bound mandates – but then they would not be able to argue either. In practice, one cannot create the conditions for arguing without at the same time opening up a possibility for bargaining.

One might, however, aim at a system based on voting without either arguing or bargaining, by having all decisions made directly by voters who do not communicate with one another. This was Rousseau's conception of democracy. His reason for blocking communication was the fear that voters might be swayed by eloquence and demagogy. As far as I know, he did not mention that lack of communication would also have the effect of preventing deals from being struck. I believe, however, that from his perspective this effect would also be welcome. A somewhat different proposal would be to restrict deliberation to the local assemblies that elect deputies to the national parliament. In addition to electing deputies, these assemblies would instruct them to vote in specific ways on important issues. Such a system of bound mandates would be both deliberative and representative, although it would not involve deliberation among the representatives.

7. Case Studies

The volume contains two studies, by Cass Sunstein on risk regulation and by myself on constituent assemblies. Sunstein is concerned that risk regulation might be both insufficiently democratic and insufficiently deliberative. It would be insufficiently democratic if it ignored public opinion about risk and health trade-offs. It would be insufficiently deliberative if it took account of public opinion in its raw form, as simply an aggregation of individual preferences. I have already mentioned some of the reasons he cites for believing that mere aggregation might be inadequate. Using "raw" willingness to pay as a criterion for the importance people attach to health risks, for instance, is known to induce inconsistencies that could disappear in reflective equilibrium.

In my own study I focus on some early constituent assemblies: those in Philadelphia in 1787, Paris in 1789–91, Paris in 1848, and Frankfurt in 1848–9. On the one hand, these assemblies were under strong normative pressure to adopt deliberation rather than interest-based bargaining. The fact that they were legislating for the indefinite future forced them to put themselves "in everybody's place." On the other hand, the external circumstances of constitution making tend to be turbulent and even violent, a feature that is not exactly conducive to calm and impartial deliberation. The American framers succeeded largely because they managed to insulate themselves from these circumstances, yet that insulation also allowed them to engage in interest-based bargaining that would have been banned under conditions of publicity.

8. Some Further Questions

There is no single research agenda for the study of deliberative democracy. As the contributions to the present volume show, much depends on the definition of key terms. Also, normative and empirical studies address very different issues. The following list of questions, therefore, probably reflects my personal interests rather than any collective concern.

1. What institutional mechanisms could ensure that an agreement following deliberation is induced by argument rather than by inner or outer conformism?
2. Discussion as well as postdiscussion voting can take place in private as well as in public. What are the empirical and normative properties of the four cases that arise by crossing the two dichotomies?
3. To what extent are democracy and deliberation independent of

each other? Could conceptual analysis of democracy show that it implicitly presupposes deliberation and/or vice versa?

4. What is the relation between equal access to the deliberative process and the distribution of income? Does equality of access mandate a floor on incomes, a ceiling, or both?

5. Does the unequal distribution of education, information, and commitment pose a threat to deliberative democracy? Will deliberation produce all of its good effects if it takes place mainly within an elite that is self-selected because it knows more than others about public issues and is more concerned about them?

Notes

1. Bohman (1996); Gutmann and Thompson (1996); Nino (1996).
2. See notably Habermas (1984, 1987, 1996). Also see Bessette (1994); Cohen (1989); Dryzek (1990); Elster (1986); Manin (1987); Sunstein (1985).
3. Ober (1989: 165–77). For an analysis of one-upmanship in artlessness, see Perelman and Olbrechts-Tyteca (1969: § 96).
4. For an analysis of the transition from direct to representative democracy, see Manin (1997).
5. Cited by Kurland and Lerner (1987: 1: 391–2).
6. *Archives Parlementaires. Série I: 1789–1799* (Paris 1875–1888), 8: 595.
7. Ibid., 30: 68.
8. Ibid., 30: 115.
9. Cited after Sunstein (1993: 22). See also Wood (1969: 188–96, 379–82).
10. Holmes (1995: 181).
11. Hume (1963: 142).
12. White (1987).
13. Hume ([1740] 1960: 415).
14. For the notion of gag rules, see Holmes (1988). In a study of the gag rule on slavery in the House of Representatives in the 1830s, Miller (1996) shows, however, that because the rule had to be renewed in each session, and because it was often unclear whether a given petition fell under the rule, the attempt to stifle debate on slavery actually intensified debates in the House on this issue. As observed by George Soros in discussion, an attempt to take an issue off the agenda is likely to place it even more firmly on the agenda.
15. For a somewhat analogous problem in the context of bargaining, see Ross (1995).

16. Crawford and Sobel (1982); see also the more recent references cited by Mackie (Chapter 3, this volume).
17. Habermas (1996: 540).
18. Riker (1986, 1996: notably ch. 5, "The Utility of Negative Themes").
19. For bias in representation and remedies to it, see notably Ely (1980).

References

Bessette, J. R. 1994. *The Mild Voice of Reason: Deliberative Democracy and American National Government.* Chicago: University of Chicago Press.

Bohman, J. 1996. *Public Deliberation.* Cambridge, Mass.: MIT Press.

Cohen, J. 1989. "Deliberation and Democratic Legitimacy." In A. Hamlin and P. Pettit (eds.), *The Good Polity.* Oxford: Basil Blackwell, 17–34.

Crawford, V., and J. Sobel. (1982. "Strategic Information Transmission." *Econometrica* 50: 1431–51.

Dryzek, J. 1990. *Discursive Democracy.* Cambridge University Press.

Elster, J. 1986. "The Market and the Forum." In J. Elster and A. Hylland (eds.), *Foundations of Social Choice Theory.* Cambridge University Press, 103–32.

Ely, J. H. 1980. *Democracy and Distrust.* Cambridge, Mass.: Harvard University Press.

Guttman, A., and D. Thompson. 1996. *Democracy and Disagreement.* Cambridge, Mass.: Harvard University Press.

Habermas, J. 1984, 1987. *Theory of Communicative Action.* Boston: Beacon Press, vols. 1 and 2.

1996. *Between Facts and Norms.* Cambridge, Mass.: MIT Press.

Holmes, S. 1988. "Gag Rules." In J. Elster and R. Slagstad (eds.), *Constitutionalism and Democracy.* Cambridge University Press, 19–58.

1995. *Passions and Constraints.* Chicago: University of Chicago Press.

Hume, D. [1740] 1960. *A Treatise of Human Nature*, ed. Selby-Bigge. Oxford: Oxford University Press.

1963. *Essays: Moral, Political and Literary.* Oxford University Press.

Kurland, P., and R. Lerner (eds.). 1987. *The Founders' Constitution.* Chicago: University of Chicago Press, vols. 1–5.

Manin, B. 1987. "On Legitimacy and Political Deliberation." *Political Theory* 15: 338–68.

1997. *Principles of Representative Government.* Cambridge University Press.

Miller, W. L. 1996. *Arguing about Slavery.* New York: Knopf.

Nino, C. 1996. *The Constitution of Deliberative Democracy.* New Haven, Conn.: Yale University Press.

Ober, J. 1989. *Mass and Elite in Democratic Athens.* Princeton, N.J.: Princeton University Press.

Perelman, C., and L. Olbrecths-Tyteca. 1969. *The New Rhetoric*. Notre Dame, Ind.: University of Notre Dame Press.

Riker, W. 1986. *The Art of Political Manipulation*. New Haven, Conn.: Yale University Press.

1996. *The Strategy of Rhetoric*. New Haven, Conn.: Yale University Press.

Ross, L. 1995. "Reactive Devaluation in Negotiation and Conflict Resolution." In K. Arrow et al. (eds.), *Barriers to Conflict Resolution*. New York: Norton, 26–43.

Sunstein, C. 1985. "Interest Groups in American Public Law." *Stanford Law Review* 38: 29–87.

1993. *The Partial Constitution*. Cambridge, Mass: Harvard University Press.

White, M. 1987. *Philosophy, "The Federalist," and the Constitution*. Oxford: Oxford University Press.

Wood, G. 1969. *The Creation of the American Republic*. New York: Norton.

Chapter One

"Claro!": An Essay on Discursive Machismo

Among coachmen, as among us all, whoever starts shouting at others with the greatest self-assurance, and shouts first, is right.

Lev Tolstoy[1]

I delight in talking politics. I talk them all day long. But I can't bear listening to them.

Oscar Wilde[2]

Deliberation has been described, minimally, as "a conversation whereby individuals speak and listen sequentially" before making a collective decision.[3] Deliberative "conversations" fall somewhere between two extremes: *bargaining*, which involves exchanging threats and promises, and *arguing*, which concerns either matters of principle or matters of fact and causality. Discussions about the latter may occur even when ends are shared but views diverge as to the best means. The aim of arguing, unlike that of bargaining, is to persuade others of the value of one's views. Typically, both arguing and bargaining enter the deliberative process. Since arguments can also be put forward manipulatively for covert bargaining purposes, it is sometimes arduous to separate one form of deliberation from the other. However, the cynical reduction of arguing to a special case of strategic bargaining does not do: as Elster maintains, argument, even if hypocritical, has a powerful civilizing in-

For their comments and suggestions, I am grateful to the participants in the Workshop on Deliberative Democracy, held at the University of Chicago on April 28–30, 1995 – in particular Jon Elster, Stephen Holmes, and Gerry Mackie. I am also indebted to John Alcorn, Joshua Getzler, Valeria Pizzini, Adam Swift, Federico Varese, and Steven Warner for the many comments and suggestions I received from them.

fluence (1993; see also Chapter 4, this volume). If we accept this view, the extent to which a democracy can successfully deliberate by arguing rather than just by bargaining makes a great deal of difference. In this essay I consider some of the behavioral conditions required for successful deliberation.

To be fruitful, a conversation need not exclude the passions. As Stephen Holmes remarked in discussion, people who are too cool, analytical, and impartial may generate distrust or may fail to rally people around issues. A passionate style can lead to extremes, but this is not always a bad thing. It can generate the energy to sustain harder thinking about issues. Nor, for similar reasons, does a conversation have to be governed by meticulous procedural rules. Yet deliberative conversations, especially when concerning *reasons* rather than *interests,* rely on an elementary form of cooperation. If agents show up late at meetings, pay no attention to one another's speeches, jump the queue, speak all at once, or shout when they have no argument, the conditions for deliberation are simply not there. Deliberation, of course, relies on a grander factor, freedom of speech. Free speech, however, achieves functional significance only if somebody is prepared to listen.[4]

This cannot be taken for granted. There is no reason to expect the mix of dispositions that sustains fruitful deliberative conversations to exist everywhere. Attitudes toward conversation do not originate from democratic arrangements even though they can be shaped and controlled by them. They are likely to be by-products of a preexisting culture and may well be antithetical to deliberation. "It is a very dangerous thing to listen. If one listens one may be convinced; and a man who allows himself to be convinced by an argument is a thoroughly unreasonable person." I suspect many would still agree with Oscar Wilde (*An Ideal Husband*, act 1).

Albert Hirschman (1986) has identified a set of attitudes that can prove particularly disastrous for deliberative democracy:

> Many cultures – including most Latin American ones I know – place considerable value on having *strong opinions* on virtually *everything* from the *outset*, and on *winning an argument* rather than on listening and finding that something can occasionally be learnt from others. To that extent, they are basically predisposed to an authoritarian rather than a democratic politics. (42; emphasis added)

For the sake of brevity I dub this general attitude the culture of "Claro!" – Spanish for "Obvious!" "I knew it all along!" "Nothing *you* say surprises me" – a belittling snap response that greets those who express an argument, especially if not at all obvious, in countries of that culture.[5] (As I show later, under certain conditions this type of response is a dominant equilibrium of discursive competition.) In a culture of this kind, deliberative conversations of the arguing type succumb faster than those of the bargaining type: while agents are still likely to prick up their ears when threats and promises are voiced and make an effort to sort them out of the general noise, they are unlikely to listen to one another's arguments, let alone be persuaded by them. Even if democracy does not collapse into authoritarian politics, as Hirschman predicts, it drifts toward the bargaining extreme.

In this essay, I try to explain the apparently inane "Claro!" culture. Italy, rather than Latin America, will provide the background empirical case. I will identify a particular belief about the structure of knowledge that can make sense of why the "Claro!" culture is practiced even by rational individuals in countries in which that belief is common currency. I then explore the pernicious consequences of that culture on democracy and draw some normative conclusions. First, however, I review briefly the effects that deliberation of the arguing kind has on the quality of decisions. Most of them are discussed at greater length by the other authors in this volume.

1. Advantages of Deliberative Democracy

As with all human activities, deliberation does not invariably produce positive effects. Under certain conditions it does more harm than good. For instance, if the quality of outcomes declines rapidly with time, deliberation may simply waste precious time. In the ski–mountaineering club I used to belong to, the instructors always consulted about the best route, but in bad situations we had as a rule (on which we had previously deliberated) to defer the decision to the school director.

Less obvious drawbacks have also been identified. Benjamin Constant – as quoted by Stephen Holmes in discussion – pointed out two specific risks involved in public discussion: being duped by sheer eloquence and promoting conformism. Through discussion people find out about each other's preferences, and weaker people may sheepishly acquiesce to the stronger. A further risk involves the manipulation of information by lobbies that have much to lose (see, in this volume, Chapter 5 by Stokes and Chapter 6 by Przeworski). Finally, the subtlety that deliberation may bring to a discussion can have a paralyzing effect. Deliberation may subvert the preference ranking of deliberators, and this can be a good thing. But rather than going all the way and persuading them of a different ranking, it can simply make the choice indeterminate: it becomes impossible to rank options either because of incommensurability or, as in the case of Buridan's unfortunate ass, because of indifference.

However, several scholars maintain that, on balance, deliberation does more to benefit than to harm the quality of decisions or their legitimacy or both.[6] A possible term of comparison is a silent, merely "aggregative" democracy in which people vote with no prior discussion. This comparison, however, is largely artificial. In practice, a silent democracy hardly exists. Democracy tends to be a discursive enterprise *regardless* of whether deliberation makes for superior outcomes relative to the aggregative case. To be implemented, the aggregative model would require at least one successful deliberative exchange that persuaded all parties of its advantages. Thus, the question of what the effects of deliberation are should be cast against the imperfect deliberative models we have *anyway*.

The positive consequences of deliberation primarily concern the distribution of information. If information and reasoning skills are, for whatever reason, unevenly distributed among deliberators, deliberation improves their allocation and the awareness of the relative merits of different means. This may be useful even if we all agree on the desirability of an outcome. It improves the quality of our casual beliefs on the state of the world that can be brought about by each course of action in the feasible set. (Although some of the time some of us can be manipulated – as Stokes and Przeworski argue in Chapters 5 and 6 this volume – into believing as true or beneficial what is respectively false or against our interests, it is unlikely that all of us will be manipulated all the time by deliberation.)

Furthermore, since imagination is also unevenly distributed, deliberation may introduce into the discussion new solutions to shared problems. Deliberation, in addition, spurs the imagination indirectly if it reveals that, on all known options, no compromise is possible, for this provides an incentive to think of new ones. By the same process, it can instill the courage necessary to embrace solutions that were thought to be too daring before it became clear that no compromise was otherwise possible.

Moreover, public discussion – as Elster argues (1993; Chapter 4, this volume) – provides an incentive to dilute self-interested claims by injecting principled elements in order to persuade others of their merit, or at least legitimacy. Hypocritical as such claims may be, they may lead to making concessions to the general interest or to the interests of other groups. Thus, deliberation can facilitate compromise, improve consensus, and, through consistency, disseminate principles in public life. Principles, in turn, are likely to improve distributive justice and provide better outcomes for weaker groups, which would be penalized under a pure bargaining system.

The effects of deliberation tend to come in bundles that are sometimes hard to disentangle empirically, even in seemingly simple situations. I once heard two men discussing whether it was right to use "she" and "her" instead of "he" or "his" when referring to generic persons. A was for, B was against. B did not feel that arguments concerning equality or fairness had any force. Having exhausted all other (and better) justifications, A said that, if nothing else, B should use feminine pronouns because B was "a gentleman"! B was cornered and found it hard to disagree. What does this exchange accomplish? First, it appeals to an image of the self that may be generally agreeable to the obstinate B. It further points out an inconsistency in preferences by forcing into the discussion the notion that if B wants to stick to his male-gendered vocabulary, he must argue against a shared male norm: "be kind to women." It also provides a special kind of information on the cost of persevering in one's preferred course of action: a warning that others may think B is not a gentleman if he sticks to his "politically incorrect" practice, which contravenes a traditional norm, even if B does not agree with the norm or with other principles that may justify that linguistic practice. Deliberation channels old norms to new cases: it restates an unassailable principle and then shows that the opponent's argument violates that principle; thus, out of consistency or fear of sanctions, the recalcitrant party is induced to revise his preferences or else recant the principle. (This example also shows how a discussion initially meant to persuade may evolve to one in which warnings are issued and will thus more closely resemble the bargaining case.)

On the whole, effective deliberation can affect the quality of decisions in four ways. (a) It can render the outcomes of decisions Pareto-superior by fostering better solutions; (b) it can make the outcomes fairer in terms of distributive justice by providing better protection for weaker parties; (c) it can lead to a larger consensus on any one decision; (d) it can generate decisions that are more legitimate (including for the minority).

2. Analytical versus Indexical Knowledge

Why should people value strong opinions, on everything and from the outset of a discussion? Hirschman did not elaborate on the origins of what I call the "Claro!" culture. This is the question I address in this section.

A common, ad hoc understanding imputes this culture to the presence of stereotypical character traits; in essence, the argument is: "that's just the way some people are." A hot-tempered, volatile, argumentative disposition might be seen as the source of "Claro!" values in public life, and these traits are assumed to be inherently more widespread in certain ethnic groups than in others. A more promising line of research might focus on the sources of such cultural traits and seek in the specific history of countries which display the "Claro!" culture the social events that might have spread and legitimized those values. For instance, one could speculate that the cocky and bellicose chivalrous code of the Spanish aristocracy, once aped by the peoples it colonized, might have provided more than a fleeting inspiration for that culture – not just in Latin America but also in southern Italy and the Philippines.

Here I want to follow a different route. I suspect that cultural values are not the rock-bottom explanation of "Claro!" behavior but can themselves, at least in theory, be derived from beliefs concerning the structure of knowledge and from the mutual expectations that follow from them.

Imagine two ideal-typical societies that differ in one respect only: each is governed by one of two fundamental assumptions about knowledge. In one type of society, knowledge is deemed to be what, for want of a better term, I shall call *analytical* (AK). It is not necessarily seen as professionalized or even specialized, but it is thought to be the result of a combination of good reasoning, empirical verification, and generally hard work. Furthermore, it is believed to be tentative rather than definitive. This set of beliefs has a variety of consequences, one of which is particularly relevant here: if a person either knows or ignores something about a certain field of knowledge, no one automatically infers anything about her knowledge in other fields. If she happens to know nothing or to have no clear ideas about x, it will not be generally assumed that she knows nothing about y and z. No one infers that she is an ignorant person. Local ignorance is not thought to be dishonorable.

In the other type of society, by contrast, knowledge is assumed to be *holistic*: knowledge or ignorance about x is taken as a sign of knowledge or ignorance of the whole. It reveals more than a local failure; it stands for lack of *Kultur*. The notion of excellence in classical antiquity is a parallel case. Excellence, as Paul Veyne (quoted by Elster 1990: 40) argued, was seen as one and indivisible. Someone who does one thing well will do another equally well, even if the qualities required are quite different. Excellence is antithetical to specialization. "A perfection is not the same as a profession, such as philosopher, teacher of rhetoric, etc., which is a specialization, whereas a perfection is an example to everyone – the realization of what every man ought to become" (Veyne 1976: 150). Veyne calls this view of excellence *theorie de l'indice*, index theory. I shall call *indexical* (IK) the analogous beliefs regarding knowledge. (Indexical beliefs may, of course, be dominant *within* any one field of knowledge; in fact, they probably should, but I am not concerned with this special case here.)[7]

Note that beliefs about knowledge do not have a third modality: except in special instances, it does not make sense to have a *hydraulic*, or zero-sum, view of knowledge whereby if one knows nothing about x one must know a great deal about y. (If anything, the inverse hydraulic view may be more plausible: since resources are scarce, if someone knows a great deal about x, one is unlikely to know much about y, an inference that strengthens the analytical view.)

From the perspective of a developed society in which scientific thinking is a dominant model, it may seem ludicrous to entertain IK beliefs. The last man on earth to have read everything ever written is said to be Leibniz. Even if one could read everything, it does not follow that one would understand or remember everything. No one can possibly know everything – it has been a long time since this was a feasible feat. Renaissance men are dead and gone. Yet even a cursory appreciation of world cultures suggests that IK – often as a tacit assumption – is, if anything, more widespread than AK. Consider the following random selection:

1. From a religious perspective, knowledge is quintessentially holistic: everything worth knowing is in *one* book – the gospel, the Bible, the Koran. Truth is found in dogma rather than in doubt. Discovery comes, if at all, from reinterpretation rather than from research; knowledge is not a human construct but a gift bestowed upon us by revelation.
2. In the Muslim world (as described by Ibn Khaldun) a holistic view of honorable manhood is traditional. Artisans who work in cities and subject themselves to the limitations of the division of labor are held in contempt.
3. Much of nineteenth- and twentieth-century "Continental" philosophy – for instance, as espoused by Benedetto Croce or the Frankfurt school – is antiscientific and leans toward IK rather than AK.
4. If knowledge is unevenly distributed in a society, IK assumptions may be more cognitively natural in everyday life than AK ones. In the absence of a clear or readily available test of independent validation, or in the absence of clear boundaries between fields of knowledge, people may use as a signal of knowledge in general the simple ability to provide *a* reply and express *a* view: between two savants – one who replied to the first of our questions and one who could not (or not so promptly or eloquently) – we might feel more inclined to rely on the former for further questions.

If the indexical view is widespread, then the right approach might be to turn the starting question on its head. The puzzle is not so much why that culture exists at all as why it is not *more* widespread: the "Claro!" syndrome may be more popular in many folk cultures than its civilized counterpart. Discussions in Italian bars may not be very different from discussions in British pubs or U.S. diners as manifestations of a "Claro!" culture.

"Claro!" attitudes survive in the niches of countries in which the dominant culture is definitely not IK: "If you leaf through *Melody Maker* (a British music magazine) – as a young friend knowledgeable in these matters wrote to me – every week pop musicians are consulted on their opinions of politics, feminism, drug use, etc. There is no reluctance to engage in this sort of behavior which often sparks furious rows. In 1976 David Bowie was quoted as saying that 'Britain could benefit from a fascist leader' and apparently proposing himself as a feasible candidate for premier."[8]

Conversely, even in countries in which *clarismo* rules, niches in which an analytical approach is nurtured may survive if only in the minds of few enlightened individuals:

> Since it is difficult to distinguish the good from the bad prophet – wrote Primo Levi – we must be suspicious of all prophets; it is better to avoid revealed truths, even if we feel exalted by their simplicity and splendor, even if we find them comfortable because they come at no cost. It is better to be content with more modest and less inspiring truths that are laboriously conquered, step by step, with no shortcuts, by studying, discussion and reasoning, and that can be verified and demonstrated.[9]

The real question, therefore, might be the following: how is it that in some countries the political and intellectual elites managed to confine those attitude to *sub*cultures while adopting among themselves a restrained style of debate conducive to deliberative practices? I do not have an answer to this question. Maybe there is not just one answer. One could speculate about a variety of explanations: the influence of science percolating in the political sphere; the spread of literacy; the gentlemen's club style catching on; industrialization and the division of labor; Protestantism; or simply sound consequentialist reasoning bootstrapping wiser people out of their instinctive clarismo. Whatever the explanation, it is more likely to be solved by historical research than by sociological conjectures.

However, there is one conjecture – for which I am indebted to Gerry Mackie – that may be of use in ascertaining what we should be looking for. As much as there is evidence to suggest that the indexical view is not automatically discarded in advanced industrial societies such as Italy, there is anthropological evidence that the analytical view of knowledge is not necessarily an indication of "progress." In an essay on group decision making in an egalitarian hunter-gatherer band, George Silberbauer (1982: 29) writes that "success in promoting a particular argument confers further prestige but never sufficient to occasion an 'overflow' into habitual success. Expertise in one field of activity may be seen as not at all relevant to another field." According to James Howe (1986: 177–8), there is a

> strong tendency among the Kuna influentials to speak on the whole spectrum of village concerns. In this respect the Kuna contrast strongly both with the pattern of task-specific and nontransferable leadership Fried finds in simple egalitarian band societies and with

one of the principal conclusions of the pluralist school in political science, namely, that in modern communities in the United States, different groups and individuals have different scopes of influence. According to both Fried and the pluralists, influence in one area (tracking game, setting teachers' salaries) cannot be easily shifted to another (moving camp, urban renewal).

In traditional societies we find the same polarization between the two views of knowledge. On this evidence, it would seem that *equality of resources*, especially equal access to information and relevant experience, may be a key variable for explaining the predominance of AK. (It does not follow, however, that if *political* equality descends on a previously nonegalitarian IK society, AK beliefs will automatically spread, as I will argue in Section 4, point 13.)

3. The Behavioral Consequences of Indexical Beliefs

In this section I consider the features that conversations among people with indexical beliefs are likely to have. I make a general contention: if IK is widespread, the values of the *claristas* can be deduced by applying the principles of simple individual rationality. Relative to a society in which AK is the convention, IK beliefs establish an *incentive structure* that encourages this type of behavior.

Note that this is not a descriptive or historical contention. The "Claro!" culture may emerge in other ways, either independently or in conjunction with IK. Stendhal (1957: 138), for instance, points his finger at provincialism: "An extreme and vulgar dread of exhibiting an inferior self is the active principle in the conversation of provincials. Look at the fellow recently, who, on being told that Monseigneur de Duc de Berry had been murdered, replied: 'I know.' "[10] Rabbi Joseph Telushkin (1992: 60–1) invokes a special set of cultural values that would explain much the same attitude among Jews: "Two thousand year ago the Talmud admonished: 'Teach your tongue to say, "I do not know." ' Yet, because Jewish culture places so much stress on intellectual achievement, such confessions, even in minor matters, do not come easily to Jews." So what I present here is a hypothetical construct of the following form: if IK beliefs are widespread, they suffice to bring about "Claro!" attitudes, regardless of other factors.

Let us consider in detail how the features of clarismo identified by Hirschman can be derived from IK beliefs. Three main components, logically independent, must be considered: strong opinions, on everything, from the outset of the discussion. (Each attitude could conceivably be derived from alternative mechanisms, but IK can bring about all three of them.)

Strong Opinions. An opinion is strong if expressed in a definitive form that admits neither doubts nor nuances. The opinion is packaged in such a way as to silence the audience rather than to invite further argument. Under IK beliefs, the expression of genuine doubts, rather than mere rhetorical ones, signals a general and thereby dishonorable fragility of knowledge. Doubts are discouraged. Aldo Rico, an Argentinian general and clarista of the first order, said, "Yo tengo sangre asturiana y los asturianos no dudamos; la duda es una jactantia de los intelectuales" ("I have Asturian blood, and Asturians never doubt; doubt is the curse of the intellectuals").[11]

Under IK, the alternative to voicing strong opinions is not to express weak ones, but to offer no opinion at all. By keeping silent, one avoids creating an opportunity for a dispute that one may end up losing.

On Everything. Failure to deliver on one problem is a global failure. Whenever one asks even a simple question in the south of Italy, there is no way in which the person asked will let one go without an answer: even if he does not know the correct answer, an answer must be given, be it speculative or vague. (Southern Italians are not alone in this. "Israelis," writes Rabbi Telushkin [1992: 61] "are notorious for offering directions to questioning tourists even to places with which they are unfamiliar.") As a last resort one consults a third person: if one does not know the answer, better than remaining silent is to recommend someone else who does know. A question amounts to a challenge and replying "I do not know" amounts to defeat. I am not implying that if one asks a practical question one receives a fabricated answer; so if someone asks, "Can you fix this car for me?" people feel no compunction in replying negatively if they cannot. The IK beliefs apply not so much to those practicalities that are amenable to prompt empirical testing as to moral, political, historical, and philosophical questions, and to knowledge for its own sake.

At the Outset. This is a corollary of the greater value of certainty over that of doubt. No benefit is accrued from waiting. Waiting signals doubt. If one decides to express an opinion one might just as well put it forward without hesitation. By contrast, in AK societies there is an incentive to wait before expressing one's views; in committees in England there is a tacit ethos whereby coming up with a strong view too soon is generally inappropriate; it is important to take one's time in order to consider all angles of a difficult issue, or else one's impartiality and gravitas are jeopardized. In IK societies, impartiality is a property no one needs to prove, everyone has claim to it by right – "Somos todos caballeros!" – whereas under AK, claims to impartiality come from adherence to the proper procedure in pondering an issue and debating it. Sometimes, it may be objected, even in AK societies taking one's time before expressing one's views simply amounts to strategic posturing, since the important thing is to be *seen* to be taking one's time even if one has a perfectly clear idea of what one wants to achieve. However, even if only a portion of those who take their time before offering their views do in fact spend it usefully trying to shape their opinions, some positive effect will be felt. Under IK, by contrast, *no one* by definition – even those with poorly shaped ideas – will spend any time reflecting on them.

4. Discursive Competition under Indexical Beliefs

Hirschman further claims that part of the "Claro!" culture consists of putting considerable value on "winning an argument rather than on listening and finding that something can occasionally be learned from others." To work out whether this value can be derived from IK beliefs we need to consider how competition works under these assumptions. If anyone manifests a strong opinion to an audience that shares the same culture, the latter has three broad options:

1. To agree, acknowledging the validity and interest of the claim. In this case the claimant wins the match, which ends there; the party who agrees admits implicitly that she did not know or did not think of it first and thereby admits the superiority of the claimant. Under IK beliefs, she implicitly admits a more general kind of inferiority not limited to the issues in question. The immediate social effects do not change, even if the agreement is hypocritical.

Under AK, by contrast, she does not need to worry about the more general signals implied by agreement and can more readily show that she is learning from other people's opinions. Agreement, of course, can be ironic or condescending, but in the IK case this works only if there is a well-established superiority on the part of the agreeing party. Unless there exist asymmetries between the parties that are not alterable by the discursive exchange, the exchange in the IK society is unlikely to end, among peers, with agreement, pure and simple.

2. To agree with the strong opinion while at the same time undermining its claim to novelty or relevance. The "Claro!" put-down falls in this category. The exchange ends in something like a draw, in which the claimant may gain marginally by getting some sort of agreement and the counterclaimant is not seen as admitting inferiority; if anything, the "Claro!" response gives a slight edge to the counterclaimant, for not only did he know it all along, but he also did not waste other people's time voicing such triviality. A variant of "Claro!" – much in vogue among intellectual claristas – is to claim that whatever one says was said a long time ago by somebody else, better if a grand master.

3. To choose a frontal attack voicing an equally strong critical or alternative opinion. In this case the match is unresolved and can be repeated. The party who spoke first can move again and choose among the same three options; if he chooses 3 and restates his original claim, the exchange can in theory continue ad infinitum. Since this cannot happen in real life, the competition is likely to escalate, at first acoustically. The shouting match will then continue either until one party declares defeat or the match degenerates into a violent confrontation. In IK, whenever ideas are at odds the battle of arguments evolves into a battle of persons. In a world dominated by IK beliefs, the audience cannot just express a partial and qualified disagreement, for this amounts to expressing doubts on the wholesomeness of the knowledge of the other party. Effectively, this line of response collapses into 3. Nor, for the same reasons, can one admit mistakes without admitting a larger loss.

5. Predictions

The structure of incentives and the type of competition that develops allow a number of hypotheses to be made as to the shape political life will take in a society in which IK beliefs are dominant. The picture that emerges is more than vaguely reminiscent of Italy and many Latin American countries.

1. The accumulation of knowledge is harder to achieve in IK than in AK societies, partly because conversations are not as constructive, partly for a different reason. Even claristas can learn. They can object vehemently to all you say and then repeat exactly the same thing to someone else later on. But they will feel a temptation to say that it was they who thought of the proposition in the first place. The ownership of ideas is likely to be a source of dispute, and fear may keep people from sharing their ideas with others (or, to save time, from having ideas at all).

2. The number of people refraining from publicly voicing their views is likely to be higher in IK than in AK societies. People will be much more talkative in private, for they know their family has no interest in competing. (In Italy it is often difficult to listen to the news on radio or television, because everyone around has a view to express on whatever is going on. This is not so bad, only because television is of such poor quality there.) But publicly, we can expect larger masses of *neghittosi*, people who show no interest in or commitments to public affairs, a notoriously unhealthy bunch for democracy.

3. Among those who feel up to articulating their views publicly despite the greater challenge, the proportion of aggressive, impulsive, opinionated, and bullying people is likely to be higher in IK than in AK societies.

4. Ordinary people, by contrast, will make their views known only if they are so taxed by some issue or contrary opinion that they build up enough aggressiveness to speak up. It follows that, even assuming the *same* distribution of volatile characters as in an AK society, opinions in the IK case will come to the fore in outbursts mixed with destructive emotions, such as rage or indignation. The cocktail combining quiescence and outburst will make for greater political volatility.

5. There will be greater pressure on those who are professional holders of knowledge – academics and politicians – to always be ready to show that they do have strong views on anything that happens to be relevant. It is likely, therefore, that these professions will both attract and select individuals with particularly marked dispositions of type 3 above.

6. Norms against behaving in an aggressive and opinionated

manner will be weaker. There are two reasons for this: the political and intellectual elites will both set a bad example to others and will have no *individual* incentive to introduce norms against their own typical behavior. In IK societies, the distinction between arguments based on pride and arguments based on reason may be blurred. Acts that under AK assumptions would be seen as acts of pride are deemed normal. Quine, in his autobiography,[12] distinguishes between students who want to be right from students who want to *have been* right. The latter can be seen as claristas by character, people for whom in discussion pride takes precedence over reason. While this type will be under some normative control under AK, they will flourish under IK beliefs.

7. The preceding point can be generalized to those groups in IK societies who are more exposed to public life and have more opportunities or pressures to voice their opinions than others. We can expect a larger number of claristas:

- Among members of the middle class than among laborers. Susan Stokes reported in discussion that in Peru it is the middle class and not the Indios who think foreigners naive when they ask questions or admit their ignorance.
- Among men than among women. In a recently published letter, the late Natalia Ginzburg, an Italian writer, admits her sense of inferiority to men with regard to knowledge. Her anguish comes strikingly across as directly dependent on her *indexical* assumptions about what real knowledge should be about: "I never succeeded in learning either geography or history. So I have a fog in my head on many things. It seems to me that until I have understood everything clearly, until I know how a car is built and how a country is made, what the railway companies are, I will not be able to write anything serious. . . . Leone [her husband] was the opposite of me. He knew everything, everything about a country, everything about everything, how things are in reality" (*La Stampa,* March 26, 1996; my translation).
- Among younger men than among older ones. Robert Nozick, in *The Examined Life* (1990), says that when he was young he thought he should have an opinion about everything.[13] Albert Hirschman, in an autobiographical essay (1996), tells the story of when he was an adolescent and failed to get an answer from his father on some deep question. Young Albert was bitterly disappointed and confided to his sister: "You know what? Daddy has no world view." Later he

realized that his father was right and has become a champion of the view that we should not trust a strongly defined *Weltang-schauung*. Perhaps some degree of youthful clarismo, provided one eventually grows out of it, could have a positive effect and encourage greater participation in public life.

8. Even though media and politicians may make use of academic specialists, in AK societies "intellectuals" are likely to be regarded with suspicion. The conservative William F. Buckley once said he would rather be governed by a random drawing of names from the Cambridge, Massachusetts, phone book than by the faculty of Harvard University.[14] His view is likely to be shared by individuals on both the right and left of the political spectrum. In IK societies, by contrast, intellectuals are highly respected. In both the United States and Great Britain it would be inconceivable for academics and intellectuals to fill the television screen or the front pages of newspapers with their comments on every single political and international affair; harder still would it be for them to occupy ministerial positions. In Italy all this seems perfectly acceptable. In Italy, as well as in other "Latin" countries, writers of fiction are constantly interviewed on current affairs, and their opinions – often as silly as anyone's – spark furious rows in the main media. Countries such as these breed and promote a species of intellectuals aptly dubbed in Italian *tuttologi*, people ready to give us their view on just about anything.

9. There will be a greater probability of expressing hasty and mistaken views in IK than in AK societies due to the pressure to speak up at the onset of a conversation. More energy will consequently be spent battling with and dispelling inept and confused opinions. Rather than on individual proponents' thoughtful restraint the cost of discarding mistaken views will be dumped on the rest of society.

10. It will be harder to change an opinion once expressed. Taking a strong position binds agents' reputation accordingly. If point 9 is correct, people will also be more likely to be bound to mistaken views. Even if people in AK societies were equally worried about a loss of face (or even more so perhaps, since they voice their opinions as experts) than people in IK societies, IK would still create more opportunities for the loss of faces. Under IK assumptions, *amour propre*, a potential motive for action in most humans, will find an

incentive to manifest itself more often, even assuming the same distribution as in AK societies.

11. In IK societies, the more obvious the mistake, the more the mistaken party wants to be seen as changing her mind, if at all, without prompting by the other party. Persuasion by argument is arduous in argumentative societies. It must be carried out on grounds that are external to the matter at hand; an extraordinary amount of social emollient is required to soothe people who risk making fools of themselves. Rhetoric is more likely to succeed than argument.

12. Lofty rhetoric will happily coexist with mean bargaining, and jointly they will drive serious discussion on principles out of public life. Where arguing rapidly becomes confrontational and murky, bargaining becomes the dominant option and society will be more cynical, less fair in terms of distributive justice, and more conflictual. Shrewd politicians all over the world know how to bargain in order to strike compromises, but in IK societies they will need to be more so disposed and will more likely do away with discussions over principles altogether. Giulio Andreotti brought this strategy to perfection. He studiously never expressed a strong or principled opinion in his entire political career; he kept secret files on and contacts with everyone, and became the archmaster of political compromise. No one, not even the communists, could do without him. I cannot recall a political fight that was ever fought by the Italian political class on principled grounds. The automatic response to any claim, no matter how unreasonable or unsavory, be it from the Mafia or the Red Brigade, has been "bargain." (The typically Italian political phenomenon known as *trasformismo*, politicians changing party or side with great ease, is just one major consequence of this pervasive lack of principles.)

13. A dominant belief in political equality interacts with the predominant view of knowledge, whether indexical or analytical. The interaction, however, is far from simple. In conditions of political equality people give each other equal rights to voice an opinion and perceive themselves to be potentially as good (or bad) at forming one as anyone else. At first sight one would think that equality of this sort is required for AK to have a positive effect on deliberative processes. This is probably true in societies, such as the United States, in which political equality lies at the foundation. However, in IK countries in which there is a long tradition of po-

litical inequality, the effects of IK on the style of debate, rather than suppressed, may be multiplied as a result of greater political equality. In typical Tocquevillian fashion, we can expect that the emergence of equality will make everyone both less inclined to take other people's views as better than their own and more entitled to be opinionated.

By contrast, inequality, rather than weakening AK, can in fact strengthen it. In this respect Britain is an interesting case. In this country the analytical culture is generally dominant, and its effects are reinforced by a strong and widespread perception of the importance of class differences. Political and intellectual elites debate among themselves on AK principles, and *individually* they do not believe any one of them knows everything there is to know. *Collectively,* however, they display a peculiar form of "Oxbridge clarismo" toward everyone else: what *they* do not know is, quite simply, not knowledge.[15] There are therefore two mechanisms, rather than one, that make British people more tentative, averse to generalization, and accurate than most other cultures: AK and, as Tocqueville ([1837] 1988: 438–42) predicted, class. The style of British discussions is tamed by the sense of awe for those who know what is worth knowing, a sense that is not as widespread in either the United States or Italy. Combining the presence or absence of political equality with that of AK and IK yields four rather than two ideal types:

	Equality	Inequality
AK	United States, hunter-gatherer egalitarian bands	Britain
IK	Italy	Traditional authoritarian societies

Italy, in terms of the conditions conducive to good public discussion, is in the worst position of all: it has a belief in both IK and equality. (Note, however, that the fact that people in an IK culture are more inclined to be opinionated could – as suggested by an anonymous referee for the publisher – make them more resilient to the kind of manipulation discussed by Stokes and Przeworski in Chapters 5 and 6, this volume: if they do not listen to anyone, at least they will not listen to those who are trying to fool them.)

14. Hirschman claims that people of the "Claro!" culture will be more predisposed to authoritarian than to democratic politics. This may be partly a direct effect of the greater incentive to bully

people into agreeing with whatever opinion one voices. But mostly this predisposition will be generated indirectly as a response to the consequences listed earlier: partly thanks to more widespread preferences for a strong authority that can impose some order on the turbulent political system and partly because of greater opportunities for a *uomo forte*, a strong man, to exploit the political instability and take over. Even after the collapse of the regime that governed Italy for forty-five years after the war, politicians seem unable to grow out of the unprincipled but effective style of Andreotti – ceaseless bargaining, that is. Cries for a *uomo forte* have grown shriller in Italy in the past few years. Andreotti's characteristic comment was: "Uomo forte? Basterebbe un uomo" (A strong man? Just a man would do).

When I finished listing by deduction all the bad consequences that follow from the "Claro!" culture, I was astonished to find there were so many of them. This "model" seems much more powerful than I had anticipated, and as a scientist, albeit of the "social" breed, I was naturally suspicious of this. I found some comfort in discovering, thanks to Jon Elster, that my predictions were still quite modest compared with Montaigne's: "Many of this world's abuses are engendered – or to put it more rashly, all of this world's abuses are engendered – by our being schooled to fear to admit our ignorance and because we are required to accept anything which we cannot refute" (quoted in Elster 1996: 114–15).

6. Normative Questions

Some recommendations follow from the preceding observations. The first and foremost is that in countries of "Claro!" culture, democracy requires specially designed institutions to assist in countering its specific vices. This has an important practical implication. Many countries look at Anglo-Saxon democracy as *the* model to emulate. Among the arguments put forward for reform – be it constitutional, judicial, or electoral – *imitation,* or rather *pseudo-imitation* as Hirschman called it, of those democracies often plays a part. Democracy and justice are seen as successful in a certain country, and it is inferred that by adopting the same institutional arrangements, success will follow suit. This is not so.

The case of Latin American countries that adopted the U.S. Constitution is only the most famous illustration of the failure of simple imitation. An interesting case is that of the 1993 Italian electoral reform, which introduced a mildly diluted variant of the majority system. (The old and almost pure proportional representation system has been abandoned and blamed for much more than it was guilty of [Warner and Gambetta 1994].) Under "Claro!" values, such as those that inhabit the minds of many Italians, the adversarial system, which is to some extent promoted by the new electoral system, may be dangerously unsuitable, for it encourages radicalization and destructive competition rather than compromise. A host of other reasons must of course be considered, but the degeneration of Italian political life after the 1994 elections may be a manifestation of precisely that danger.

In designing their institutions, democracies that exist in a "Claro!" culture should worry not only about the excesses of self-interest – as Elster (1993) showed that the U.S. constitutionalists worried about – but also about the collective failures that may be engendered by their specific culture. To the extent to which the larger the audience the more extreme clarista-type attitudes will become, one could hope that by keeping the number of listeners small the discursive style might improve. As Elster argues (Chapter 4, this volume) secrecy – albeit at the cost of making partisan interests and logrolling more likely to come to the fore – may discourage "grandstanding and rhetorical overbidding." My guess, however, is that staunch claristas are unleashed by as small an audience as their own image in the mirror.

Beliefs in IK are very resilient. They need not even be truly believed to shape people's actions. They can be sustained by second-order reasoning: "I believe that everyone believes that IK is the case" suffices to motivate the same actions as much as the first-order belief. Even if people for some reason were to stop believing that other people truly believed in IK, they might continue to act on IK nonetheless. This state of affairs takes the form of an inferior convention: a practice that no one wants but no one can afford to be the first to stop. The practices that may originally emerge from IK beliefs take on a life of their own.

A social psychological process, suggested by Susan Stokes in discussion, could further strengthen the independence of practices from beliefs by the formation of suitable values. People are unlikely to be able to sustain "Claro!" attitudes for purely strategic reasons. Whenever there is strong pressure to adopt costly behaviors for instrumental reasons, people end up effectively attaching value, via cognitive dissonance reduction, to those behaviors. By expressing "strong opinions on everything from the outset," people end up rationalizing them and believing in their value and the desirability of the way they are expressed. The values are perhaps an excrescence of the beliefs. Yet they develop a separate nature, much like truffles are an excrescence of the roots of certain trees but acquire a strong taste of their own.

An interesting question concerns what happens when IK agents meet with AK agents. Can one type "invade" the other? Here I have only my experience to go by. Homo analyticus finds meeting a clarista both upsetting and useless, and is most likely to switch partners rather than engage in a confrontation. The clarista is somewhat attracted but ultimately irritated by conversations with homo analyticus. He is easily provoked because he senses an easy ride. The clarista's prejudices concerning the superiority of an argument – sweeping, complex, dynamic, realistic, holistic, contextually aware, and what not – find a fertile terrain on which to be discharged. His optimistic perception is that just one blow will knock the opponent out, and this tempts him to pick a fight. Our analytic David can fight back, however: he can sling piercing pebbles against the numbed organ of doubt of this Goliath, causing much unease. He will never concede victory, will at most retreat diplomatically to avoid a confrontation. The clarista, in turn, will never admit that any doubt can cause even a ripple in his mind, and if you ask whether he won the match he will reply: "Claro!" But he will never feel quite so sure and thus will hold his opponent in even greater contempt. In conclusion, except for brief friction-ridden encounters, the two types are likely to crowd each other out and remain in segregated groups.

All the points I have outlined suggest a tenacity of IK beliefs and their associated attitudes, which makes the question of how a group can switch from IK to AK at once pressing and difficult.

Deliberative democracy benefits from a style of debate typical of scientific discussion. Science and democracy, as Merton, Popper, and many others have pointed out, share, or rather gain from, a number of similar virtues, including tentativeness, which is of key relevance to this essay. Both science and democracy acquire legitimacy by public justification.[16] Yet they differ not only in terms of the procedure by which their respective justification is publicly achieved, but also, and particularly, in their objective. Deliberation concerns eminently unscientific matters for which there is no ready test available: it matters most when we have only partial information, or when we face long-term decisions whose effects are hard to establish, or when we are divided on principles. We cannot rely on the development of science to shape political discussions automatically.

Can we place our hopes on technology and its by-products? As usual, technology cuts both ways. Television seems generally conducive to clarismo. For one thing, it has large audiences – in fact the largest audiences ever available to individuals – which may be a tantalizing incentive to carry one's iconoclastic clarismo to unprecedented extremes. Furthermore, claristas are entertaining, make exalted statements, avoid subtle distinctions, and squabble with one another theatrically. Television thrives on strong views and definitive remarks. It competes for viewers by making programs less instructive and more fun to watch. Suppose, however, that our conversations took place by electronic mail. Unlike letter writing, which is slow and cumbersome, e-mail has an immediacy that makes communicative exchanges comparable with oral exchanges. Would this technology put some constraint on claristas? Having to write increases the cost of rhetoric and eloquence. It makes shouting at and interrupting each other difficult. The e-mail receiver, moreover, can wait longer to reply, without this being seen as a sign of weakness. "Speaking and listening" sequentially is unavoidable on e-mail. Or rather, the clarista would have to work harder to be true to his type when using this medium. He would have to use capital letters to "shout"; paste his opponent's text within his own reply and "interrupt" the latter's sentences in the middle with his own strong remarks; and so on. Committed claristas would be better off sticking to oral communication.

Is then passively hoping that the spread of electronic means of communication will miraculously turn us into better deliberators all we can do? An explanation in terms of beliefs of the "Claro!" culture gives us some normative advantage over one in terms of values: beliefs lend themselves to rational discussion and thus change. One can dispute beliefs in a way in which one cannot dispute values. If one could demolish IK beliefs and related conventions, the values associated with the "Claro!" culture would most likely evaporate more quickly than one would expect. The convention of binding women's feet was abandoned at the turn of the century in China. It collapsed more rapidly than any one would have predicted. The net of multiple values that entrapped this cruel practice by providing justifications went quickly with it, as Gerry Mackie (1996) has shown.

Perhaps the way in which that convention was finally demolished will teach us something in this albeit extremely different domain. One of the conditions that ended it was a particular form of bootstrapping. Circles of families formed and pledged to abandon inflicting the practice on their daughters and to marry their sons only to girls whose feet were not bound. This broke the vicious circle that prevented individual families from acting alone because that would have destroyed their daughters' chances of finding a husband. Whether a similar strategy – circles of intellectual and political elites mutually pledging to switch to an analytical frame of inference – would achieve the desired effect is open to question. Even if this were so, where would the necessary political energy and clarity of mind come from? This is anyone's guess. The way elites are selected suggests pessimism. They are more likely to be claristas or more unprincipled than average or both at the same time.

After all I have said, moreover, how could I possibly end with a strong opinion?

Notes

1. Lev Tolstoy, "Storia della giornata di ieri," *Tutti i racconti* (Mondadori, 1991) 14; my translation.
2. Oscar Wilde, *An Ideal Husband,* act 1.
3. Austen-Smith, in the paper presented at the Workshop on Deliberative Democracy, University of Chicago, April 28–30, 1995. Note that unless universal consensus is both reached and immediately observable, the final decision must be arrived at by some other arrangement, the most common of which in contemporary democracies is, of course, voting under some majority rule.
4. Even if nobody listens there must be an expressive value attached to free speech: witness the improvised orators at Speakers' Corners in London's Hyde Park.
5. I conform to the Italian political jargon in which a few Spanish or Spanish-sounding expressions are used in a derogatory way: *boatos* are loud cries and protestations that either are uttered in response to bogus dangers or achieve nothing or both; *somos todos caballeros* are dubious claims to innocence based on status rather than evidence; and *peones* are vociferous and ineffectual backbenchers. The latest in this family

are the *berluscones*, peones working in Silvio Berlusconi's party. By contrast, Latin appears in the political jargon when serious matters are at hand. A recent example is *par condicio*, which refers to fairness applied by media in giving all political parties a chance to express their views.

6. For example, Habermas (1984); Manin (1987); Elster (1993), and most contributors to this volume.

7. "Indexical" here is not used in the same sense as in the philosophy of language, that is, words whose meaning depends on context, such as "here," "today," "I."

8. Steven Warner (private communication).

9. Appendix of 1976 to "If This Is a Man," in Primo Levi, *Le opere* (Einaudi, 1987), 209–10; my translation.

10. I am indebted to Gerry Mackie for this quote.

11. I am indebted to Roberto Gargarella for this quote.

12. Quine (1985: 478) writes: "A vast gulf, insufficiently remarked, separates those who are primarily concerned to have been right from those who are primarily concerned to be right. The latter, I like to think, will inherit the world." I am indebted to Joshua Cohen for bringing this to my attention.

13. I am indebted to John Alcorn for pointing this out to me.

14. I am indebted to Gerry Mackie for telling me about this.

15. I am indebted to Steven Warner and Joshua Getzler for this point. The latter supplied the quote paraphrased in the text:

> First come I; my name is Jowett.
> There is no knowledge but I know it.
> I am the Master of this college:
> what I do not know isn't knowledge.

From "The Masque of Balliol" (composed by and current among members of Balliol College in the late 1870s), in W. G. Hiscock (ed.), *The Balliol Rhymes* (1939), in *The Oxford Dictionary of Quotations* (Oxford, 1992), 59:7.

16. For a discussion of these issues see D'Agostino (1996).

References

D'Agostino, F. 1996. *Free Public Reason*. Oxford: Oxford University Press.

Elster, J. 1990. *Psychologie politique*. Paris: Editions de Minuit.

 1993. *Argomentare e negoziare*. Milan: Anabasi.

 1996. "Montaigne's Psychology." In *Great Ideas Today, 1996*. London: Encyclopaedia Britannica.

Habermas, J. 1984. *The Theory of Communicative Action*. Boston: Beacon Press.

Hirschman, A. O. 1986. "On Democracy in Latin America." *New York Review of Books,* April 10.

1996. *A Propensity to Self-subversion.* Cambridge, Mass.: Harvard University Press.

Howe, J. 1986. *The Kuna Gathering: Contemporary Village Politics in Panama.* Austin: University of Texas Press.

Mackie, G. 1996. "Ending Footbinding and Infibulation: A Convention Account." *American Sociological Review* 61: 999–1017.

Manin, B. 1987. "On Legitimacy and Political Deliberation." *Political Theory* 15(3): 338–68.

Nozick, R. 1990. *The Examined Life: Philosophical Meditations.* New York: Touchstone/Simon & Schuster.

Quine, W. V. 1985. *The Time of My Life: An Autobiography.* Cambridge, Mass.: MIT Press.

Silberbauer, G. 1982. "Political Process in G/wi Bands." In E. Leacock and R. Lee (eds.), *Politics and History in Band Societies.* Cambridge University Press, 23–35.

Stendhal. 1957. *Love.* Harmondsworth: Penguin.

Telushkin, J. 1992. *Jewish Humor: What the Best Jewish Jokes Say about the Jews.* New York: Morrow.

Tocqueville, A. de. [1837] 1988. *Democracy in America.* New York: Perennial Library.

Veyne, P. 1976. *Le pain et le cirque.* Paris: Seuil.

Warner, S., and D. Gambetta. 1994. *La retorica della riforma. La fine del sistema proporzionale in Italia.* Turin: Einaudi.

Chapter Two

Deliberation as
Discussion

If one begins with "deliberative democracy," one is immediately drawn toward trying to define the term, and hence into arguments about how precisely it should be understood. While such arguments can be enlightening and are surely unavoidable for anyone interested in the subject, I will try a different approach here, one that bypasses the problem of deciding what should count as deliberation and deliberative democracy. Instead, I will consider the following question. What good reasons might a group of people have for discussing matters before making some collective decision, rather than simply voting on the issue or using some other decision rule that does not involve discussion? In other words, what is the point or value of *discussing things* before making political decisions?

Put in these terms, the question may seem trivial, but I will suggest that spelling out answers is a valuable exercise for anyone interested in the more academic idea of deliberative democracy. This is especially so if we keep in mind the contrast between discussing a decision before voting on it or otherwise deciding, and simply voting without benefit of discussion.

I see six major reasons or arguments for discussing a matter before reaching a decision on what to do. There are surely more, but I think these six constitute the most important ones and they certainly provide an interesting set of issues to examine.

A group of people might want to discuss matters before making a collective decision in order to:

For very helpful comments and efforts to acquaint me with an unfamiliar literature, I wish to thank Bernard Manin, Uday Mehta, Michael Neblo, and Frank Sposito. They are in no way responsible for errors of omission or commission that remain.

1. Reveal private information
2. Lessen or overcome the impact of bounded rationality
3. Force or encourage a particular mode of justifying demands or claims
4. Help render the ultimate choice legitimate in the eyes of the group, so as to contribute to group solidarity or to improve the likely implementation of the decision
5. Improve the moral or intellectual qualities of the participants
6. Do the "right thing," independent of the consequences of discussion

1. Revealing Private Information

Consider a group of five people who need to choose a restaurant for dinner. One obvious reason for discussing the matter would be to allow these people to express their preferences about where to eat. Note, however, that voting can also be a means of revealing (private) information about preferences, so we should ask why discussing the matter might be better than simply having a vote.

In the first place, simply to hold a vote it might be necessary first to have a discussion to settle on a procedure. But this is not really the sort of discussion we are interested in, and in all legislatures (for which the restaurant seekers are a metaphor) procedures exist. Provisionally, then, I will just assume a procedure – for example, suppose everyone writes down his or her first choice on a piece of paper and the plurality winner is chosen. In the case of a tie, the winning restaurant will be chosen randomly.[1] Why might a group of people prefer to discuss the choice rather than simply vote on it in this or some similar way?

One reason is that discussion allows people to express diverse *intensities* of preference – that is, whether they have strong or indifferent feelings about particular choices. Of course, a voting system could be devised to allow for the expression of more finely grained preferences than "I vote for Siam Garden." For instance, after the individuals were polled for their suggestions, they could write a number between 0 and 10 next to each suggestion and then use some rule to aggregate the votes and choose a winner. But here we encounter a general problem with the voting approach: the group could know what sort of voting scheme would be appropriate to the particular issue at hand only if they discussed the matter first. It may be that there always exists a voting system that can simulate discussion by allowing for as many possible "messages" as ordinary language allows, but the particular voting system needed to allow for appropriate degrees or types of expression on any particular issue would have to be settled case by case by discussion. So why bother? Why not simply use the richness of ordinary language to suggest alternatives and to express intensities of preference?[2]

Thus, one reason for discussion is that it can facilitate relatively nuanced revelation of private information (here, preferences) when it would be cumbersome to try to devise a voting mechanism that would allow for the same range and manner of expression. Put slightly differently, for any *given* voting procedure that a legislature is committed in advance to employing (e.g., majority rule with a sequential agenda), the voting procedure will rarely if ever allow individuals to send as many "messages" characterizing their preferences or private information as free discussion would. For example, if you are a legislator deciding whether to vote yes or no on a bill (two possible messages), you may wish to be able to express a strong or weak preference, and also to know whether some other legislators feel strongly about the outcome. If in discussion another legislator says that she and her constituents are very strongly opposed to passing the measure, you might change your vote to no, whether out of altruism and the fact that you don't care much about this issue, or because of an implicit reciprocity ("You support me on the measures I care a lot about and I'll support you on yours"), or because you think it is normatively right that the social choice maximize some notion of aggregate satisfaction or welfare.

The foregoing examples suggest why discussion might be justified as a means of revealing private information about individuals' preferences over the outcome of the decision making. But the argument applies just as well to private information about other sorts of things. For example, individual members of the group might have private information about factors bearing on the *probability of different outcomes* of the different choices, or on the nature of these outcomes, and making a good decision for the group might require the revelation of such private information. In the restaurant example, one person might happen to know that one of the favored restaurants is closed or is likely to be extremely busy, and so on. In the U.S. Congress, committee members typically know more about the likely consequences of bills in their domain than do floor members, and floor members realize this.[3] As in the case of private information about preferences, information about likely outcomes could in principle be aggregated through an appropriately designed voting mechanism, but it would take discussion to design the mechanism and this discussion could be used to elicit the relevant information anyway. Or if the group is committed in advance to a voting procedure, the procedure might not be fine-grained enough to allow for full or efficient revelation of the private information, so that prior free discussion would be a good idea.

The principal dilemma for discussion as a means of revealing private information relevant to a political choice is that people can have strategic incentives to misrepresent their preferences or special knowledge. This problem takes center stage in game-theoretic work on debate and other sorts of "cheap-talk" signaling in legislatures.[4] In these models an individual legislator has private information about the likely consequences of this or that bill, and may signal this information by making a speech or by proposing a particular bill. A typical result is that less information can be credibly transmitted by discussion the more the speech maker's preferences over the outcome of the decision differ from (i.e., conflict with) those of the listeners, relative to their common preference for reducing uncertainty.[5] Intuitively, if a member of the U.S. House claims that his research indicates that much more defense spending is needed, one will take this more seriously if the speaker is a political moderate than a hawk.

By this logic, discussion as a means of revealing private information can be effective only when the members of the group do not understand themselves to have widely divergent or conflicting interests. Otherwise, the perception of conflicting interests will undermine trust by making people (reasonably) doubt whether others are telling the truth about their private information.[6]

Now, these incentives to misrepresent apply to voting mechanisms just as well as to free discussion – rational behavior may entail casting votes that distort or do not reflect one's private information, leading to social outcomes that could have been improved had everyone voted "sincerely." So it is not clear whether voting has any edge over discussion with regard to this problem. Given preference diversity and thus incentives to misrepresent, is a group better off simply voting or discussing things before voting? Existing work suggests that there may be no general answer here. For example, Gilligan and Krehbiel's (1987) results suggest the following. Suppose it is known in advance that some member of the group has better information than others about the likely effects of a decision, although all members of the group have some private information. Then the group might rationally choose a restrictive amendment procedure that in effect does not allow the less well informed individuals to have their say and that gives extra power over the decision to the better-informed member. In this way, the better-informed member's incentive to misrepresent is reduced and information transmission improved. Austen-Smith and Banks's (1996) work, however, appears to provide a contrary example. In their study of Condorcet's Jury Problem, they find that rational individuals voting yes or no on some measure may systematically vote the opposite of what their own private information suggests is socially best, *even if* everyone shares exactly the same preferences over outcomes. Here voting without discussion may lead to dramatically suboptimal results. I am not certain, but I believe this pathological outcome would disappear if individuals were allowed to discuss matters first.

More generally, it is not hard to come up with reasons for why people might be either more *or* less inclined to misrepresent their preferences or knowledge in public speeches than they would in private votes. On the one hand, public discussion might allow people to cultivate reputations for being truthful, and in the case of private information about probable outcomes rather than preferences, truthfulness can to some extent be checked empirically after the fact (thus creating the possibility of tarnishing one's reputation and an incentive for truthful revelation). Or social conventions might just entail discomfort for people caught publicly lying, so that if there is some chance of being caught, discussion might be rendered somewhat informative while private voting would be less so. On the other hand, a principal justification for secret ballots and anonymous voting without open discussion is that individuals can then vote as their conscience dictates rather than give in to the pressure to misrepresent their real views for the sake of social conformity.[7] Of course, allowing for discussion first and then a secret ballot would enable both the revelation of information and voting according to one's conscience. This system, however, may require people to take public positions that they know are disingenuous and that they will vote against privately; some people might not be able to cope with the cognitive dissonance and will vote in accord with their public line.[8] Another possibility is that people might have much greater facility in misrepresenting their own views in ordinary language discussion than in figuring out how to strategize in a complicated voting system. So it simply isn't clear whether incentives to misrepresent private information in open discussion would tend to be greater or lesser than in voting by itself.

Regardless, we can say that a group wishing to make a collective decision might want to discuss the issue rather than simply vote if (a) the voting procedure would not allow the revelation of private information to be as fine-grained as free discussion would, and (b) individual preferences over possible outcomes would not be so divergent as to render "cheap-talk" discussion uninformative and useless.[9]

2. Lessening or Overcoming Bounded Rationality

For a great many collective decisions, a significant problem is not that people have private information about preferences or likely consequences, but rather that it is simply hard to figure out the best course of action because the problem is so complicated. For example, even if one could gather all kinds of relevant private information from doctors, insurance companies, Medicare patients, businesses, and so on, it would still be anything but obvious how best to reform the U.S. health care system. And this would not be simply because different parties would have different preferences concerning how to distribute benefits and costs of reform. Rather, even if one could appoint a health care czar with dictatorial powers and all the relevant private information, the czar would still face an enormously complex decision problem. The czar might wish to discuss what ought to be done with others, not in order to elicit private information, but in the hope that the process of discussion would clarify the likely consequences of different policies and suggest entirely new ideas through brainstorming. And note that voting would be of little alternative use here. Voting systems always require some prior statement of what the alternatives are, which is precisely what discussion might be intended to reveal, and voting would be an incredibly inefficient way to make complicated arguments about possible chains of events and consequences.

To use Herbert Simon's famous term, discussion might then be a means for lessening the impact of bounded rationality, the fact that our imaginations and calculating abilities are limited and fallible.[10] So, faced with a complex problem, individuals might wish to pool their limited capabilities through discussion and so increase the odds of making a good choice. Discussion might lessen the impact of bounded rationality for two reasons. First, it might be "additively" valuable in that you might think of some possibility that hadn't occurred to me, and vice versa. Second, it might be "multiplicatively" valuable in that in the course of discussion we might think of possibilities or problems that would not have occurred to either of us by ourselves (this is brainstorming, I suppose).

Simon's core illustration of bounded rationality was the game of chess, which would be easy – like tic-tac-toe – if we were unboundedly rational calculators. Note that in chess there is no private information in the normal sense; it is not like poker or bridge, where part of the interest is that players have private information about the cards they hold. Instead, the interest of chess derives almost entirely from the problem of thinking ahead into an explodingly complex thicket of possible moves.

To explore the role of discussion as a means of lessening bounded rationality, consider the following example, which I will call Team Chess. Imagine playing chess two against two, where each team deliberates privately over what to do each turn. Except in pathological cases, it seems likely that a team of two would always fare at least as well and usually better than either individual member. Adding more members would probably help even more, although this might slow things down. Note also that the scope for bullying or social pressures as obstacles to effective discussion might be fairly limited here, since in the case of chess, stronger, more farsighted arguments about what to do can be objectively shown to be better than weaker, less farsighted arguments. As a means of overcoming bounded rationality, then, open discussion might be quite conducive and responsive to intelligence.[11]

In the Team Chess example, the members of a team understand themselves to have completely coincident interests in winning the game and nothing else. In legislatures and other political forums, however, this is rarely the case. So suppose, instead, that the members of a team have a common interest in winning the game, but they also have interests in the fates of particular pieces – say, member A is partial to or "represents" the left-hand-side pieces, while member B represents the right-hand-side pieces (excluding the king). Now we have a case parallel to the case of discussion intended to reveal private information when there are conflicting preferences and so incentives to misrepresent. What would we expect in this instance? There are some interesting similarities and differences.

Regarding similarities, if my partner says, "Let's play . . . , because then . . . ," I may well be a bit suspicious. I may worry that while she is offering this argument on the grounds that it is the best move for the team, perhaps it will lead to a better outcome for "her" pieces than for "mine." I might worry about this for two reasons. First, my partner might be trying to deceive me by suggesting a move that she expects will have some bad consequences for my pieces and not elaborating the train of thought that reveals these possibilities. In this instance, the situation seems very similar to the private-information case discussed earlier. Under bounded rationality, once we have thought a while about a complex problem, we come to have private information about particular scenarios or possibilities (on the chessboard), and we may also have incentives to misrepresent this sort of private information. It is natural to expect as well that the greater the divergence of interests, the greater the incentive will be to offer specious or consciously incomplete arguments to try to persuade the other parties, and thus the more skeptical people will be about "objective" arguments.[12]

On the other hand, my partner might not be consciously trying to deceive me, but the fact that she favors her pieces leads her to explore mentally certain paths of play that I am less drawn to consider. Thus, she will have worked out different aspects of the complex decision problem facing us both, and this will make her arguments "partial" in a sense. This case is rather different from the conventional private-information problem, because there is no conscious intent to deceive. Instead, one consequence of bounded rationality may be a *natural partiality* that is more amenable to correction or amendment through discussion.

There is at least one other significant difference concerning the role of discussion in lessening bounded rationality versus revealing private information. In the case of private information, there is always some level of conflict of interest such that discussion will be pointless because the incentives to misrepresent are too great. This does not seem to be the case when the decision to be made is complex enough that bounded rationality comes into play. Even in the case of strictly opposed interests, it seems likely that discussion could have behavioral consequences and result in real information transmission. For example, consider discussion between the two *opponents* in a chess game. One might say to the other, "Be careful about your rook" in an effort to confuse or trick the other, but even so this suggestion could lead the other to a train of thought that affects the move chosen. More generally, even if I think that a speech maker in a legislature has strong reasons to try to trick me, insofar as we are considering a problem in which bounded rationality is a significant obstacle, then I still may be persuaded by the argument given because it is objectively compelling. If my partner in the Team Chess game says, "We shouldn't move the knight because then we will lose the queen," this can persuade me even if I know that my partner favors the queen – the argument is simply objectively or rationally demonstrable.

In sum, one reason a group might want to discuss something rather than simply vote on it is to lessen the effects of bounded rationality, and discussion may serve this purpose, even when there are known conflicting interests in the group. While voting systems may in some instances be good means of eliciting private information, they are *very* unlikely to be good means of overcoming bounded rationality.

Deliberative democracy is sometimes advocated on the grounds that deliberation allows one person or group to represent to others "how things look" from perspectives, situations, and vantage points that the others had never considered or thought of. Such a justification is, in my terms, at least in part a bounded-rationality justification. The inability to see things from another's perspective may have some origins in private information – for example, if you know things about what it is like to be really poor that I do not. But in the Bayesian framework that undergirds the private-information story, even if you know specific things about what it is like to be poor that I do not, I must have already *conceived of* these things as being possible; they must have occurred to me as things that could be the case. But in general, learning to see from another person's or group's vantage point means learning things that you never even conceived of, which implies that the intended effect of discussion is to lessen bounded rationality, a failure of the imagination.

3. Forcing or Encouraging a Particular Mode of Justifying Demands or Claims

Voting by secret ballot is a private and to some extent anonymous act. Indeed, privacy and anonymity are the very points of using a secret ballot. However, the benefits gained from privacy and anonymity – freedom to vote according to one's conscience without social pressures or worse, and increased difficulties for those who

would buy votes – may come at a cost as well.[13] One consequence of privacy and secrecy is that the voter is under no obligation to offer any public justification or reason for her vote. So nothing stops the voter from voting on purely self-interested grounds, without any consideration for what would be a good decision for the collectivity. Suppose, for example, that the collective decision concerns the allocation of "pork" of some sort. In a secret ballot, a person (or group) does not have to justify her vote for pork for herself to anyone, even if, in a particular case, it is patently obvious that this is collectively suboptimal.

Why might this be a less difficult problem if people had to discuss the issue at hand before voting? Why couldn't a person (or group) say simply, "I think more pork for myself is a good thing, in fact the best thing, and that is how I am going to vote. I think this because I simply do not care what anyone else here gets." In fact, no person or group in an assembly or other sort of public discussion is physically prevented from offering reasons of this sort. However, one very rarely hears such claims put this baldly in public discussion, even when one suspects them to be the true rationale. Why aren't such reasons given?

One could argue that offering purely private or self-interested reasons in a public discussion is inherently contradictory, or at odds with the idea of having a public discussion before making a choice that affects all. The listeners to such a speech could say, in so many words:

(S) No, you have misunderstood what we are doing. There is no point in discussing matters if you are going to reason this way. Simply by participating in a public discussion of what to do, you have accepted the presumption that we are seeking an outcome that is good, in some sense, for everyone here. Consistency should compel you to act on this presumption.

Of course, only students of moral philosophy would either make or fear a response exactly in the terms of (S). If people have an urge to achieve consistency that prevents them from offering self-interested public justifications, they do not experience it in the first instance as a desire to be consistent or to avoid "performative contradictions."[14] Rather, considerations of strategy and the desire not to appear selfish probably explain to a large extent why participants in a public discussion rarely give manifestly self-interested justifications. The strategy considerations are clear enough, and

may apply either to an individual or to a group of legislators too small to pass a bill on their own: an argument that says, "Vote for our bill because it will make us better off (while making others worse off)" is unlikely to persuade anyone else.[15] But note that even *majorities* commonly justify their actions in terms of the general public good rather than the narrow interest of the voting majority. There may be other reasons for this as well (and some of them strategic), but I would conjecture that often what is most important is the desire not to appear selfish or self-interested. There is something embarrassing or even shameful about statements like "We don't care what anyone else gets; we just want more for ourselves."

Thus, one advantage of public discussion before a vote would be that the participants might be disinclined to make or support purely self-interested proposals for fear of appearing selfish.[16] Of course, nothing stops a person from offering high-minded, public-spirited arguments in discussion and then voting out of pure self-interest. However, if the discussion shapes the formulation of the alternatives for a vote (the nature of the bills and the agenda), then one may never get the option to vote for a baldly self-interested option. There is also the possibility that arguing publicly for a position would, by various psychological mechanisms, reshape one's private desires.[17] And perhaps most important, public discussions are in principle most feasible and common in bodies of *representatives* rather than citizens (who are too numerous), and representative assemblies rarely use the secret and anonymous ballot. Rather, whereas we want the secret ballot for citizens in order to prevent vote buying and vote extortion and to allow people to vote according to their consciences, in the case of representatives these advantages are outweighed by the desire to ensure accountability – are our representatives faithfully representing us? And if voting is public, it becomes harder to offer public-spirited rationales in the discussion and then turn around and publicly vote for narrow self-interest. This *would* be an embarrassing contradiction for most. Therefore, even if people want only to appear unselfish, consequent efforts to dress up narrowly private interest as the public good may positively affect the outcome.

Three additional points about this approach to justifying discussion merit brief development. First, the argument depends, ironically, not on people being unselfish, but rather on the presumption that they desire not to appear selfish though they actually are. For a group of purely unselfish types, the implicit constraints of public

discussion would not be necessary to induce public-spirited arguments and proposals. Thus, some more direct voting mechanism might be fine in this case (putting to the side other reasons for having a public discussion).

Second, a desire not to appear selfish or self-interested might be argued to imply a desire to be "consistent," as in the abstract speech (S). A desire not to appear selfish before others is possible only if one has some concern for the opinion of those others, and thus some desire to take into account their welfare (at least as far as this affects their opinions). Thus, a desire not to appear selfish presupposes a concern of sorts for a "public" of those whose opinions matter, even if their votes may not.

Third, at the very least it is not obvious that merely participating in a public discussion about what to do *logically* presupposes an orientation toward justifying proposals in terms of the common good.[18] For example, consider again the justification "We do not care if this hurts the minority; we individuals in the majority are made better off by this proposal." This might be offered as a short restatement of a social contract story in which one opts out of the state of nature and into a legislature in the hope that enough of the time one will find oneself in the majority – it is not obvious that individuals in this story need have any concern for a public interest beyond their individual well-being.

In sum, insofar as the people in question have the motivation, or can be motivated, not to appear selfish or self-interested, then a reason for having public discussion rather than following a more mechanical voting procedure would be to encourage public-spirited justifications and proposals, which might redound to the benefit of all.

4. Rendering the Ultimate Choice Legitimate in the Eyes of the Group

In some cases, once the deliberating or voting group reaches agreement on a collective choice, the choice will be implemented straightaway and in a manner that does not really depend on subsequent compliance, assistance, or other behavior by members of the group. For example, if a parliament decides to vote to censure one of its members, the mere act of doing so is the implementation of the decision. However, probably much more often the implementation of the collective choice depends in some degree on the behavior or compliance of those who are party to the decision. Thus, if a legislature enacts a 55-mile-per-hour speed limit, this does not mean that all citizens (or all legislators) will comply, and laws passed that affect the operations of a government agency (e.g., the U.S. Environmental Protection Agency) may be subverted or weakened by legislators or citizens who are opposed to the collective decision.

So another potential rationale for having a discussion rather than merely proposing and voting on bills would be to make sure that everyone has a chance to have their say, and thus will be more willing to abide by or support the result. We need to ask, however, why discussion would make people more inclined to support the result of the collective choice process than simply voting would. There would seem to be two main possibilities here.

First, if discussion tends to produce *greater consensus* due to any or all of the preceding three mechanisms – revealing private information, lessening bounded rationality, or encouraging more public-spirited proposals – then the participants to a discussion may be more inclined to support the implementation of the choice simply because more of them are in agreement that the choice is the right thing to do. Put differently, a group might want to discuss a problem rather than just vote not simply because discussion may improve the quality of the collective choice by itself, but also because as a *by-product* of improving the decision more members of the group will be brought to agreement and thus a greater number will work together to implement the decision properly or comply willingly with it. U.S. presidents and congressional leaders are sometimes criticized for not having prepared the public for a particular policy proposal by initiating a "national debate." One interpretation of such arguments is that they claim that through a national debate a larger number of people could be brought to see the reasons for the proposed policy change, and so would support its enactment or implementation.

Of course, this rationale depends on the claim that, on average or in the most important cases, discussion will increase social consensus on what should be done or what is right. One can easily imagine particular counterexamples, cases where consensus may decrease because of discussion rather than simply voting. For example, the O. J. Simpson trial sustained a broad and intense "national discussion" and revealed much private information about the case, but while consensus on what happened may have increased within black and white communities, views tended to polarize across communities in the course of the trial. More generally, if discussion can effectively reveal private information about people's preferences over policy outcomes, then there is no reason why in particular cases it might not reveal that the extent of conflict is greater than previously believed. One might still want to have the discussion in order to find the best policy, given preferences, but it could also be that revealing the extent of the conflict might make the implementation of whatever resulted more problematic. Likewise, even if discussion lessens the impact of bounded rationality, one can imagine cases where people begin with a common understanding of how to reach some public goal, and discussion has the effect of creating disagreements as they think more deeply about the problem. So it would seem that the "discussion increases consensus and thus improves implementation" argument also requires a claim about why discussion would on average promote rather than decrease consensus.

The second reason that discussion, versus simply having a vote, may improve implementation involves a possible psychological effect. Namely, the opportunity to have one's say may make one more inclined to support the outcome of the discussion, even if one ends up opposing the collective choice. Perhaps people feel that the decision process is fairer if they are allowed to have a discussion before voting, and this sense of procedural fairness then makes them more inclined to abide by or support the results. John Stuart Mill speaks of a parliament as a "Congress of Opinions" "where those whose opinion is overruled, feel satisfied that it is heard, and set aside not by a mere act of will, but for what are thought superior reasons" ([1861]1991: 282).

Once again, we need to ask why having a discussion would foster a greater sense of fair procedure than would simply making proposals and then voting on them. And once again, it is not difficult to imagine circumstances where the opposite would be the case. What people view as constituting a fair procedure for making a collective choice will obviously vary with culture and perhaps with traditions or norms that are specific to the political or social setting of the group deliberations. For example, imagine a culture in which people feel tremendous shame, displeasure, and anger if they publicly advocate a position that is not in the end collectively chosen. In such a culture, public discussions would be a prescription for intense conflict; it might be better to have alternatives submitted anonymously and then to hold a secret ballot, so that no one would be publicly identified with a losing alternative. Or it might be best in such a culture to have the legislature deliberate in private, so that representatives on the losing side of a proposition would not feel humiliated and vengeful because the rejection of their arguments was observed by the public at large.

More broadly, it is obvious that whether a group of people will want to have a discussion before making a collective choice will depend on their traditions and conventions concerning how collective choices should be made, and there is no reason why in any particular case these conventions would hold discussion to be most appropriate. This is surely true, but in a sense it begs the question I am trying to answer: What *good* reasons might people have for discussing matters before they make a political decision? Is the existence of a norm or tradition against discussion a good reason for not having a discussion? Arguably yes, on the grounds that breaking traditions or norms may have various bad consequences, such as making implementation of the collective choice less successful or reducing group solidarity or sense of community. But we should really ask, Would it be a good thing to have a norm or tradition opposed to public discussion before voting? And this brings us back to the problem of evaluating the likely consequences of discussion versus voting in the absence of any prior social norms concerning whether this is the right thing to do.

It seems unlikely that the psychological effect mentioned earlier is anything like a human universal – that being able to have one's say in a discussion implies, in all cultures and contexts, that one will feel more inclined to support the outcome of discussion regardless of what it is. If so, then all we can say is that (a) if discussion tends on average to promote consensus, it may be desirable beyond simply voting on the grounds that it will favor the implementation of decisions and perhaps social solidarity more broadly; and (b) in cultures or contexts where people associate fair procedure with having the opportunity to have their say, discussion may be desirable for similar reasons.

5. Improving the Moral or Intellectual Qualities of the Participants

One could argue for discussion rather than just voting on the grounds that discussion has good effects on the people who participate in it, independent of any effect it has on the quality of the decisions reached or their implementation. In this view, discussion or "deliberation" is seen as a sort of *exercise program* for developing human or civic virtues.

Although he is concerned with political participation in general rather than deliberation in particular, John Stuart Mill's ([1861]1991) argument for representative government takes this form. For my purposes, the argument may be summarized as follows. (a) The principal criterion of good government is the extent to which a government improves "the virtue and intelligence of the people themselves." Government should be "an agency of national education" that promotes the "general mental advancement of the community" (226, 230, 229). (b) With regard to the cultivation of intellectual, moral, and "practical" virtues, "active types" of character, who "struggle against evils," are better than "passive types," who are inclined to endure them (248–9). (c) "[T]here can be no kind of doubt that the passive type of character is favoured by the government of one or a few, and the active self-helping type by that of the Many" (252). Numerous reasons for (c) are advanced, but the core claim is: "Let a person have nothing to do for his country, and he will not care for it" (240). That is, if the mass of the people cannot participate in government, there will be no spur to the public engagement of their faculties, and they will langor in moral and intellectual indolence.[19]

Certainly, having discussions rather than just making proposals and voting would tend to result in the development of certain skills and perhaps virtues in the participants. The following come to mind as possibilities: eloquence, rhetorical skill, empathy, courtesy, imagination, and reasoning ability.[20] And it seems plausible, as Mill's argument implies, that if people expect to engage in public discussions about what to do, they will be encouraged to invest more time and energy preparing themselves – gathering information, thinking about the problem, and so on.[21]

But *by itself* this justification for discussion is rather backhanded. It would be strange to discuss matters purely for the sake of improving ourselves morally and intellectually if we had no expectation that discussion would have any positive effect on the quality of the collective choice. This would tend to make discussion or deliberation a peculiar sort of charade: either we are being tricked for our own good by some wise political philosopher who tells us to deliberate in order to make good decisions when the real end is moral improvement, or we engage in collective self-deception about the real aim of our deliberations, pretending that it is to produce better policy. So I would argue that this justification cannot stand alone, but requires arguments about why people would have good reasons for thinking that discussing matters before voting was desirable because this would produce better results.[22] As with 4 above, "moral improvement" rationales for deliberation are by-product arguments.[23]

Some work in political theory on deliberative democracy has stressed the related justifications that (a) active participation in deliberation makes people better citizens and perhaps better people (e.g., they gain "autonomy"), and (b) broader public deliberation will increase people's sense of shared community and shared fate. The analysis here suggests a weakness or incompleteness in both justifications taken by themselves. Regarding the first argument, if it is not supported by a developed case for why greater deliberation should generally improve policy outcomes, then it is proposing either that people be deceived about the purpose of deliberation or that they engage in a strange sort of collective self-deception. Regarding the second, it is not entirely obvious why discussion should always or on average increase social consensus or the sense of community – one can think of any number of counterexamples from everyday experience. And if "deliberation" is then *defined* to mean "public discussion of a sort that tends to increase social consensus or the sense of community," little has been said.

6. Doing the "Right Thing," Independent of Any Consequences of Discussion

All of the preceding arguments for discussing matters before making a collective decision are consequentialist. They justify discussion by arguing that it can have good consequences of various sorts – either a better decision, as in 1, 2, and 3, or by-product effects that are good, as I have argued for 4 and 5. A very different approach to justifying discussion would be to argue that this procedure is good or right in itself, independent of any anticipated consequences. Thus, even if we could anticipate that in general or in particular cases discussion would produce negative results – for example, outcomes that *everyone* disliked relative to some alternative (such as a civil war) – then we should still want to have discussions, because this would just be the morally right thing to do, or because no other process could produce a politically legitimate decision.

Manin (1987) suggests a deontological argument of this sort.[24] He argues that "the source of legitimacy [of political decisions] is not the predetermined will of individuals [as in a majority-rule vote without prior deliberation], but rather the process of its formation, that is, deliberation itself" (351–2). A mechanical aggregation of particular individual wills by means of a vote cannot confer legitimacy on a collective choice, since if this were so, then the only possible rule that could generate legitimate collective choices would be unanimity (anything else implying that some individuals' wills are being disrespected), and unanimity is unrealistic and inefficient.[25] Instead, since (a) "[a]n individual's liberty consists . . . in being able to arrive at a decision by a process of research and comparison among various solutions," and (b) "political decisions are characteristically imposed on *all*," "it seems reasonable to seek, as an essential condition for legitimacy, the deliberation of *all* or, more precisely, the right of all to participate in deliberation" (352; emphasis in original).

There are two key deductions in this argument. First, from the fact that political decisions are binding on all, it is concluded that all (as equal individuals) should have the right to participate, if the decision is to be legitimate. Note that this does not fix the nature of the participation – it might as well be voting without deliberation, for instance. Second, from a claim that a certain characteristic is essential to our political being – namely, that we do not arrive "at the forum" with predetermined wills but rather must weigh reasons and arguments in order to make up our minds – it is concluded that the nature of the participation must involve deliberation to render a decision legitimate.

For my purposes, the one remaining question is why this deliberation has to involve *discussion* rather than being a solitary affair – in Manin's (1987) terms, why deliberation has to be "collective" as well as "individual." Surely it is possible to deliberate privately, weighing reasons and arguments in a mental dialogue, even if this might not be as consequentially effective as deliberation via discussion. It is not completely clear why, when Manin (1987) says that "legitimate law is the *result of general deliberation*, and not the *expression of the general will*" (352), the general deliberation has to involve the social exchange of reasons and arguments to be legitimate rather than just private contemplation by each individual (followed, say, by a vote).

There would seem to be two major possibilities here.[26] The first, suggested by Manin's characterization of deliberation as a process of mutual persuasion, is that if we all deliberated privately, the losers in a vote would not know exactly what reasons and arguments the winners had judged to be stronger in deciding the merits of the case. Thus, it would not be clear why the decision would be legitimate *for them,* if they had no grounds for understanding why the majority thought this the most reasonable thing to do. Now, if people were assumed to be unboundedly rational calculators, then they could simply *infer* from losing a vote that a majority must have judged arguments x, y, and z to be stronger, and the effect would be the same as if they had held a discussion. But if people are boundedly rational, which Manin explicitly takes as a politically salient human attribute, then losing the vote may leave the losers perplexed as to exactly why and thus unclear as to why they should view the decision as legitimate. Further, without public discussion, the losers could not have complete confidence that members of the majority had thought of and carefully weighed the minority's arguments against the decision. Hence, discussion rather than private deliberation would be necessary to "put on the table" the various reasons and arguments that different individuals had in mind, and thus to ensure that no one could see the end result as arbitrary rather than reasonable and justifiable, even if not what he or she happened to see as *most* justifiable.

The second possible rationale for producing legitimate decisions from collective rather than individual deliberation concerns Manin's (1987) notion that what confers or grounds the legitimacy of a decision process is the engagement of human qualities assumed to be distinctive or essential in some way to our political being. These are summarized under the heading of "an individual's liberty," which in Manin's treatment consists of our capacity to weigh reasons in "a process of research and comparison among various solutions" (352). Thus, the more this faculty of being able to compare and assess different reasons is engaged by a decision process, the more legitimacy it will have. And thus, if we are boundedly rational so that discussion involves not simply the pooling of information but also the mutual discovery and exploration of arguments, then a collective discussion will engage the faculty of weighing reasons more than individual deliberation would, and so be more legitimate.[27]

7. Conclusion

What is gained and lost by considering discussion rather than deliberation? Arguably, not much is lost. The terms, of course, do not refer to exactly the same things. "Deliberation" refers either to a particular sort of discussion – one that involves the careful and serious weighing of reasons for and against some proposition – or to an interior process by which an individual weighs reasons for and against courses of action. By contrast, a discussion need not be careful, serious, and reasoned, and while it makes sense to say, "I deliberated on the matter," it does not to say, "I discussed the matter with myself." But little is lost here by examining reasons for discussion rather than reasons for deliberation. In the first place, theorists interested in deliberative democracy are interested in promoting *public* deliberation – a particular sort of *discussion* – rather than just private or "interior" deliberation. Second, if public deliberation is a subset of public discussion, then arguments as to why a group might want to discuss matters before making a political decision should also hold for why they would want to deliberate.[28]

What is gained? Discussion is a more concrete object of analysis than is deliberation. If a theorist begins with the sense that (say) U.S. democracy is insufficiently "deliberative" – meaning in brief that more people should be brought into a richer conversation about public policy and politics – then there will be a tendency to load all good things onto "deliberative democracy," and the term then becomes merely a site for fighting over what should be done and why. There is nothing wrong with arguing about what should be done, but we should keep distinct (a) arguments for why more deliberation would be a good thing and (b) arguments that in effect *define* deliberation or "deliberative democracy" so that these entail good things. Because "discussion" is more concrete than "deliberation" and thus less subject to implicit or explicit investment with theorist-specific meanings, it may be better for getting at (a), as I hope my analysis has suggested.

In two important ways, the statement here concerning the main reasons a group of people might have to discuss matters before making a political decision is preliminary and incomplete. In the spirit of "first things first," the arguments for discussion given here were developed with a relatively small group of people in mind, a group not performing in front of a massive audience. New issues and obstacles arise if the problem is to justify discussion for either a large number of people (e.g., millions of citizens) or a representative assembly that discusses matters before a mass of voters. In the first case, the main problem is to explain how it is even possible to have a "discussion" among thousands or millions of people. Any call for broader "deliberation" in U.S. politics is simply meaningless without specific recommendations about how the broader discussion would be institutionally structured and an analysis of how these institutions would condition the discussion that resulted. For the second case – discussion in a legislature of elected representatives – we would need to consider more carefully how the electoral connection conditions discussion and bears on the arguments advanced in this essay. For example, an important reason for representatives to discuss matters before voting would be to learn different ways of justifying their vote to their constituents in a compelling manner, which is not exactly the same thing as discussing matters to improve the quality of the decision.

Notes

1. Thus, if everyone happened to write down the name of a different restaurant, the procedure would amount to drawing the name from a hat.
2. And in fact *no* voting system – understood as a device whereby individuals submit simple "messages" that are mechanically aggregated – could possibly allow for the expression of the same range and types of private information that human speech can. No voting system could have the same effect or convey the same "information" that, at times, poetry, song, or eloquent speech can.
3. See Krehbiel (1991).
4. See Krehbiel (1991); Gilligan and Krehbiel (1987); Austen-Smith (1990). The problem was posed in a more general way in the economics literature on "mechanism design"; see, e.g., Myerson (1985).
5. See Crawford and Sobel (1982).
6. While I have not seen a formal model in which legislators use cheap-talk signals to report private information about their preferences rather than about likely consequences of actions, I would expect similar results to obtain. For a model of this sort in an international relations context, see Fearon (1995: app.).
7. Timur Kuran (1995) has argued that social pressures to misrepresent one's actual views are pervasive and often invidious.

8. Will Rogers is said to have remarked that "Oklahomans will vote for Prohibition for just as long as they can stagger to the polls." (Of course, there might also be a precommitment story to tell here.)

9. The preceding implicitly assumes that more private information is a good thing in making collective decisions, although if there are no constraints on relevance then at some point "information overload" might set in, possibly to the detriment of making a good choice. Indeed, a major rationale for devices like votes, tax forms, and rules of debate is that without some such structure put on the information revealed, collective choices involving a large number of people would be impossible. I am grateful to Uday Mehta for stressing this point.

10. See Simon (1983). Manin (1987) also employs bounded rationality as a justification for deliberation.

11. Perhaps this might not be the case when there are major uncertainties about the likely consequences of various actions, so that "group think" pathologies can develop around them; see Janis and Mann (1972).

12. There is one crucial difference from the private-information case, however. In the standard Bayesian framework applied to situations where parties have private information, each player knows what the other player *might* know, but not necessarily what she *does* know. In the chess example, by contrast, players presumably cannot imagine exactly what other team members *might* know.

13. A Chicago-school economist might ask, What would be wrong with having a public market for individuals' votes? One reason is that it may be difficult to make vote buying possible without also making vote extortion possible. Vote buying requires that the buyer be able to ascertain how the seller voted, but then threats and coercion will also be possible. The economist might reply, "But threats and coercion are already possible for other private goods (like property); why can't the police and the judicial system serve to enforce property rights in votes just as easily as other markets?" Perhaps they can, but since the police and judicial system are controlled by politicians, who are the ones with incentives to engage in vote extortion, this might not work so well.

14. On performative contradictions and the justification of moral norms through discussion, see Apel (1980) and Habermas (1990). It should be noted that at least in "Discourse Ethics" (1990), Habermas is concerned not with the empirical question of whether public discussion would encourage a particular mode of justification of claims and thus influence outcomes positively, but rather with the deontological question of what makes a moral norm (or public choice) morally justifiable.

15. See Elster (1995) for a broader discussion of strategic reasons for offering impartial arguments.

16. For the case of strategic reasons, it is not immediately obvious why the

same considerations would not induce relatively public-spirited proposals in aggregative procedures that do not involve open discussion.

17. Along these lines, Elster (1995) argues that there may be a "civilizing force to [the] hypocrisy" involved in trying to dress private interest in the clothes of the public good.

18. This seems to be the suggestion in Habermas (1990).

19. Mill also makes the point that governments of the few have an incentive to encourage their subjects to be passive, fatalistic types.

20. Of course, holding regular public discussions could in some circumstances also foster mean-spiritedness, one-upmanship, grandstanding, incivility, and so on.

21. In academic departments, the norm of holding discussions before voting on candidates probably encourages more investment in reading the files than would a system where department members just voted.

22. Or, as discussed later, because deliberation is justified independent of consequences. In principle, one could argue that deliberation improves people's moral and intellectual qualities, which in turn improves the quality of the decisions they reach. I do not know whether anyone has explored this avenue of justification.

23. Mill ([1861]1991) thought that public participation and deliberation on collective choices *could* be justified in terms of improved results, but he was very cautious about giving the public or even legislatures much of a role in actually governing. He says that "numerous representative bodies ought not to administer" and that "a numerous assembly is as little fitted for the direct business of legislation as for that of administration." What remains? Representative assemblies are competent to delegate work to committees or individuals, and to give or withhold "the national sanction" regarding their performance (279). Further, "What can be done better by a body rather than by any individual, is deliberation" (272). A parliament – and, by extension, the informed citizenry – is to be a "Congress of Opinions," a talking shop, which can challenge the government, reveal information about public opinion, test arguments "by adverse controversy," and so on (282–3). It seems to me there is tension between Mill's argument that the opportunity to participate in and influence government promotes active types and the very limited role he assigns to assemblies (and, presumably even more, the mass public) in actual governing. There is a sense in which the representative assembly pursues its business as a moral tonic not tightly connected to the aim of governing well.

24. Habermas (1990) develops a different deontological justification for deliberation, which I feel even less competent to consider in light of the question of the essay (why discuss rather than just vote?).

25. I take "legitimacy" here to refer to two things: collective authorship, so that it is correct to say of legitimate political decisions that "the

group decided to do such and such"; and moral obligation, so that all members of the group are morally bound to uphold and support the implementation of legitimate decisions.

26. That is, if we stay within the framework of Manin's (1987) analysis. Habermas (1990: 66–8) deals with the same issue in his deontological argument for deliberation, where he speaks briefly against "monological" efforts to justify moral norms. (Monological theories envision a "hypothetical process of argumentation occurring in an individual's mind," as in Rawls's original position.)

27. This paragraph develops a helpful suggestion by Manin himself (personal communication).

28. It might also be argued, as Lynn Sanders (1995) does, that theorists' association of "deliberation" with a particular sort of careful, serious, and reasoned discussion is actually politically loaded and would tend in practice to reinforce existing hierarchies and inequalities. If so, this may be another reason to employ the broader, perhaps less loaded term "discussion." Similarly, James Johnson's argument (Chapter 7, this volume) that advocates of deliberative democracy make their case easier by stipulating that deliberators hold a "reasonable pluralism" of views may have less force when applied to arguments for why discussion might be desirable. While fundamental differences in "world-views" or "basic visions" might make discussions less productive for a number of reasons, for none of the rationales I have considered (partially excepting 1 and 6) was an assumption that participants share a basic vision or worldview crucial for its operation.

References

Apel, Karl-Otto. 1980. *Towards a Transformation of Philosophy*. London: Routledge & Kegan Paul.

Austen-Smith, David. 1990. "Information Transmission in Debate." *American Journal of Political Science* 34: 124–52.

Austen-Smith, David, and Jeffrey S. Banks. 1996. "Information Aggregation, Rationality, and the Condorcet Jury Theorem." *American Political Science Review* 90(1): 34–45.

Crawford, Vincent, and Joel Sobel. 1982. "Strategic Information Transmission." *Econometrica* 50: 1431–51.

Elster, Jon. 1995. "Strategic Uses of Argument." In Kenneth Arrow et al. (eds.), *Barriers to Conflict Resolution*. New York: Norton, 236–57.

Fearon, James D. 1995. "Rationalist Explanations for War." *International Organization* 49 (3): 379–414.

Gilligan, Thomas, and Keith Krehbiel. 1987. "Collective Decision Making and Standing Committees." *Journal of Law, Economics, and Organization* 3: 287–335.

Habermas, Jürgen. 1990. "Discourse Ethics: Notes on a Program of Philosophical Justification." In *Moral Consciousness and Communicative Action*. Cambridge, Mass.: MIT Press.

Janis, Irving, and L. Mann. 1972. *Victims of Groupthink: A Psychological Study of Foreign Policy Decision Making and Fiascos*. Boston: Houghton Mifflin.

Krehbiel, Keith. 1991. *Information and Legislative Organization*. Ann Arbor: University of Michigan Press, 1991.

Kuran, Timur. 1995. *Private Truths, Public Lies*. Cambridge, Mass.: Harvard University Press.

Manin, Bernard. 1987. "On Legitimacy and Political Deliberation." *Political Theory* 15 (3): 338–68.

Mill, John Stuart. [1861] 1991. *Considerations on Representative Government*. In *On Liberty and Other Essays*. Oxford: Oxford University Press.

Myerson, Roger. 1985. "Bayesian Equilibrium and Incentive Compatibility: An Introduction." In Leonid Hurwicz et al. (eds.), *Social Goals and Social Organization*. Cambridge University Press.

Sanders, Lynn. In Press. "Against Deliberation." *Political Theory*.

Simon, Herbert. 1983. *Models of Bounded Rationality*, 2 vols. Cambridge, Mass.: MIT Press.

Chapter Three

All Men Are Liars: Is Democracy Meaningless?

1. Introduction

One current of thought within the rational choice approach to the study of politics asserts that democratic voting and democratic discussion are each, generally, inaccurate and meaningless.[1] I will call an emphasis on these descriptive assertions against democracy "the Rochester current," because its exemplar, the late William Riker, was long a professor of political science at the University of Rochester, and his work on social choice and democracy influenced many of his students and colleagues there.[2] The Rochester current is heir to a tradition of skepticism about the possibility of democratic politics, most respectably expressed earlier in this century by the economists Pareto and Schumpeter.

In the United States the skeptical view of democracy is often accompanied by a family of arguments to the effect that "most public sector programs . . . are inappropriate, or are carried on at an inappropriate level, or are executed in an inappropriate manner."[3] The normative recommendation that is supposed to follow from these descriptive assertions is that we are best protected from the absurdities of democracy by liberal institutions that, to the maximum extent feasible, shunt decisions from the incoherent democratic forum to the coherent economic market and that fragment

The title of this essay is taken from the verse "I said in my haste, All men are liars," 116th Psalm, Prayer Book, in Blunt ([1662]1866: 483). Adam Przeworski demanded that credibility be explained, not assumed; this essay is a response. I thank the participants in the Workshop on Deliberative Democracy, University of Chicago, April 28–30, 1995. I also thank Jon Elster, Diego Gambetta, Desmond King, Stuart Romm, and Steven Warner for specific criticisms; as always, I am responsible for the contents.

political power so that ambitious elites circulate and contest in perpetual futility – in other words, that the U.S. Constitution, especially as it was interpreted before the New Deal to prevent political interference in the economy, is one of the best of all possible political arrangements.[4] The descriptive assertions against democracy and that normative recommendation are not necessarily linked, however. There are those who grant some credence to the descriptive assertions, yet would presumably recommend institutions more social democratic than conservative in content.[5] Others could plausibly argue that if voting and discussion are inaccurate and meaningless, then coercive paternalism is necessarily better than any liberalism for coherently shaping and satisfying people's needs.[6]

In his *Liberalism against Populism*, an interpretation of the results of social choice theory, Riker makes an apparently powerful case against the very intelligibility of majoritarian democracy.[7] Because different voting systems yield different outcomes from the same profile of individual voters' preferences, he argues, democracy is *inaccurate*. For a simple example, consider that if a group of people were voting for one among three or more candidates for an office, then a voting system that on one ballot selected the candidate with a plurality (the most votes, but not necessarily a majority) might select a different candidate than a system that held a second ballot for a majority runoff between the two top vote getters from a first ballot. Different methods of aggregating individuals' fixed choices may yield different group choices.

Next, Riker continues, given a fixed voting system, then democracy is *meaningless:* the outcome of voting is manipulable, and it is not possible to distinguish manipulated from unmanipulated outcomes because of the unknowability of private intentions underlying public actions. The spirit of the argument is best conveyed by presenting Condorcet's paradox of voting. Suppose that there are three persons, named 1, 2, and 3, deciding by majority vote among three alternatives, *a, b,* and *c,* and that individual preference orders are as shown in Table 3.1. As most political scientists know, with that particular profile of individuals' preferences, alternative *a* has a majority of votes against *b, b* a majority against *c,* and *c* a majority against *a,* so that no alternative beats all others, and "collective preference" cycles meaninglessly from one alternative to the next. The Condorcet paradox of voting is a special case of the Arrow possibility theorem; the Arrow theorem shows more generally that, assuming all logically possible individual orderings over alternative

Table 3.1. Cycling Preference Profile

Voters	Preferences (Left > Right)		
1	*a*	*b*	*c*
2	*c*	*a*	*b*
3	*b*	*c*	*a*

social states, no method of aggregating individuals' transitive preference orderings guarantees a collective preference ordering that
is transitive. Therefore, even the same method of aggregating individuals' fixed choices may yield different group choices, permit-
ting undetected manipulation of outcomes. I will return to Riker's
arguments in Section 2.

As Arrow's possibility theorem and similar results of social
choice theory came to be more broadly known and understood, political thinkers began to ask why these results were so at odds with
our commonsense notions of democratic life. Riker declared that
"[v]oting . . . is the central act of democracy,"[8] and that is a clue as
to what might have gone amiss. Democracy involves both voting
and discussion, and discussion is obviously at least as important to
democracy, descriptively and normatively, as voting. Also, the more
individuals' preference orders are similar to one another's, the less
likely is cycling of aggregate outcomes and the related problems of
democratic voting; and discussion does seem to be the only means
at hand to reduce differences between people, bringing them closer
together on issues or getting them to agree on a single dimension
of consideration (although there is no guarantee that discussion will
succeed in reducing differences on any particular issue). Because
processes of discussion and associated individual and collective deliberation and attitude change are not captured well by social
choice theory, perhaps some thinkers were tempted to dismiss
these processes as inessential as well.

Around the same time as Riker's vivid salvo against democracy,
the German social theorist Habermas propounded his theory of
communicative action.[9] Habermas distinguishes two mechanisms
for coordinating social actions: in strategic interaction, one person
seeks to influence another by means of threatened punishment or

71

promised reward (the typical representation in economic models); in communicative interaction, one person seeks to convince another by means of rational argument. This distinction is worthy of attention, since the difference is quite striking between saying something because one believes it to be true or right and saying something merely because someone else is making one say it. Habermas's work seems to be as murky in its substance as it is in its style,[10] but his emphasis on rational agreement as a theoretically neglected basis of social action inspired more precise thinkers to pursue the issue in democratic theory. Elster argued that social choice theory fails to capture the distinction between the isolated and private expression of preferences on the market and the open and public activity of politics in the democratic forum.[11] Manin proposed deliberation in place of idealized unanimity (as found in Habermas and, incidentally, in some economic models as the Pareto frontier) as the basis of democratic legitimacy; public preferences over public ends are not merely reported but formed in the process of public deliberation.[12] For Cohen, building on Rawls, properly conducted "democratic politics involves *public deliberation on the common good*, requires some form of *manifest equality* among citizens, and *shapes the identity and interests* of citizens."[13] The work in the Rochester current came to be known as the aggregative conception of democracy, as contrasted to an emerging deliberative conception of democracy. The deliberative conception presumes that it is possible for properly designed democratic institutions to provide for generally accurate and meaningful discussion of public issues.

Austen-Smith and Riker constructed a game-theoretic model of legislative committee discussion and decision intended to show that in equilibrium at least some legislators have incentives to conceal private information so that the final committee decision can be "incoherent" by failing to reflect fully the preferences of all committee members. The details of the model as it evolved can be found in the source documents.[14] What I want to emphasize here is Austen-Smith and Riker's *interpretation* of the results. Because of the authors' "pessimism about the rationality of social life," they apologize for demonstrating the "obvious" main result on incoherence. They go on to say:

> Admittedly these results come from a sparse model. However. . . .
> [o]ur model . . . is biased toward full revelation [of information]. As

such, the results have substantive implications both descriptively and normatively . . . generally, our result calls into question some extreme claims of liberalism, for instance that truth triumphs in the marketplace of ideas. . . . [I]t is reasonable to inquire whether our main result – that coherence cannot be guaranteed – carries over into more complicated models and even into the real world. We conjecture that our result holds up.[15]

Thus, it seems that political science proves that democratic discussion is inaccurate and meaningless.

Austen-Smith refined a costless signaling model of legislative debate, and concluded that there is "little opportunity for credible transmission of information in debate" and that the conclusion "can be expected to hold in more general environments of which the present model is a particular case."[16] In unpublished notes, Austen-Smith seems to endorse the skeptical view of democracy. With respect to the minimal conception of deliberation as an informational activity, he asks whether public discussion would

insure that all individuals share common beliefs about the consequences of any collective decision. . . . There is a sizable and growing game-theoretic literature on signaling, especially costless signaling (natural language), that suggest the answer is in general No. There are essentially two reasons for this when communication is with natural language.[17]

First, unless individuals have sufficiently similar interests, no credible communication occurs, according to Austen-Smith. Second, variations in the mere sequence in which people speak in deliberation may change what private information is revealed for public consideration (reminiscent of Riker's argument for the inaccuracy of voting).

In Section 2, I identify Riker's basic pattern of argument against the intelligibility of democratic *voting* and show why it is wrong. In Section 3, I summarize the costless signaling models of political talk that are interpreted so as to conclude that democratic *discussion* is inaccurate and meaningless; I show that such an interpretation would just be a repetition of Riker's mistaken pattern of argument against democratic voting, and show also that more realistic rational choice models of the democratic forum support the intuition that public discussion is *generally* credible. In Section 4, I explain that credibility is largely a matter of costly consistency, that deception is coercive and likely to be interpreted as malevolence, and that democracy is the best way to subdue deception.

2. Is Democratic Voting Meaningless?

Riker acknowledges that there are similarities in judgment among individuals, and thus that uncontrived cyclical outcomes are quite rare. His objection is rather that cycles can be contrived, and thus outcomes can be manipulated. He interprets various formal results to show that every democratic method of voting can be manipulated, by means of strategic voting, by agenda control, or by introducing new issues or dimensions to the decision. In strategic voting a person votes against her true taste in order to bring about a more desirable outcome. For example, in a plurality runoff system, one might vote against one's first choice and for one's second choice in the primary election as the best candidate to defeat one's third and least-favored choice in the general election. *"Since we can never be certain what 'true tastes' are – all we ever know are revealed tastes – we can never be certain when voting is strategic."*[18] Strategic voters manipulate the outcome, their manipulation can not be certainly detected, strategic voting is possibly, even probably, commonplace; thus,

> *all* voting is rendered uninterpretable and meaningless. Manipulated outcomes are meaningless because they are manipulated, and unmanipulated outcomes are meaningless because they cannot be distinguished from manipulated ones.[19]

If one person is able to decide the content and order of propositions to be voted on, his control of the agenda may allow him to influence or determine the outcome of voting; it can be shown, in the abstract, that simple majority voting can lead to any outcome in a space of issues if the agenda of voting is appropriately manipulated. Since we know from observation that much political dispute concerns agenda control, we may infer that manipulation by agenda control is commonplace, according to Riker. And "we never know precisely when and how such manipulation occurs or succeeds . . . this manipulation is frequent but unidentified . . . *all* outcomes of voting are rendered meaningless and uninterpretable."[20] Another method for manipulating outcomes is the introduction of new issues or dimensions. For example, from 1800 to 1860 a majority agrarian faction dominated a minority commercial faction in American politics, and, Riker claims, by 1860 the commercial faction had found through trial and error an arbitrary third issue, slavery, that divided the agrarian faction and thus created a new commercial – antislavery majority faction, which consolidated its dominance in civil war. "Again the meaning of outcomes is hard to interpret."[21]

I examine Riker's *Liberalism against Populism* at length in another document.[22] There I am able to show, first, that his conjecture, that democratic voting is inaccurate because different voting systems give different outcomes from the same profile of preferences, fails, if, as is the case, there is a slight similarity of preference orders among voters. Second, I claim that majority cycling, or the Condorcet paradox, has no empirical relevance because it is *most* improbable with a *slight* similarity of preferences; moreover, with respect to distributional contests, if individuals' preference orders over public states of affairs are mostly impartial, then the profile of individuals' preferences that produce a cycle will most likely not occur; and if preferences are mostly partial, then any impartial preference orders will most likely prevail over the partial preference orders. Third, I maintain that strategic voting and agenda control are not empirically relevant and that manipulation of issues and dimensions is rationally constrained by consistency requirements.[23] It is not appropriate to repeat here the arguments that support those conclusions; but it is relevant to examine here Riker's basic pattern of argument about voting, and to show why it is mistaken, because a similarly mistaken pattern of argument is central to the skeptical interpretations of democratic discussion that I criticize at length in Section 3.

The basic pattern of the argument goes like this:

1. Revealed tastes, actual choices such as votes, are directly observed, but true tastes, the underlying preferences, must be indirectly inferred.
2. Undetected manipulation is possible in any one instance of voting (and probably frequent, although frequency does not bear on the argument).
3. Therefore, in all instances taken together, underlying preferences cannot be inferred from votes.

The next step is that if underlying preferences cannot be known, then any claim to aggregate the preferences of different individuals is meaningless. Notice that by substituting "communication" for references to voting, the amended argument would prove the

75

"meaninglessness" of all communication, including political discussion. Statement 2 I grant as true (however, if true preferences cannot be inferred, then it is awkward for Riker to make any claim about the frequency of manipulation in voting). Statement 1 is confused in the context of this argument, but to go into that here would take us too far astray.[24] Granting the first statement, the conclusion still does not follow.

If all we know are public votes over alternatives, without discussion, in a single, static instance, then what do we know about the underlying preferences behind the actual choices? Strictly speaking, we do not even know what kind of entities emit the vote; all we know are some bare rankings, an aggregation rule, and an outcome. With so little information, we could not say that choices might strategically misrepresent preferences. The best we could say is either that choices *are* preferences or that "underlying preference" is a meaningless concept. We could not discover that choices may strategically misrepresent preferences unless we had information from beyond the single instance. It is obvious to us that choices may misrepresent preferences because we do not live in the single instance. In the richer information environment, we know that choices sometimes misrepresent preferences only because we know that choices sometimes do represent preferences.

Much of one's knowledge, and almost all of one's discursive knowledge, political or not, depends on the testimony of others.[25] Could that testimony be "generally" wrong? The skeptic denies the possibility of knowing an outside world, or denies the possibility of knowing other minds, on the argument that since *each* of our beliefs (about an outside world or about other minds) taken alone may be false, they might *all* be false. The philosopher Donald Davidson replies that it does not follow from the fact that any one of the bills in my pocket may have the highest serial number that all the bills in my pocket have the highest serial number, nor that since anyone may be elected president, everyone may be elected president. Nor could it happen that all our beliefs might be false.[26] "[E]nough in the framework and the fabric of our beliefs must be true to give content to the rest."[27]

There is no assigning beliefs to a person one by one on the basis of his verbal behavior, his choices, or other local signs no matter how plain and evident, for we make sense of particular beliefs only as they cohere with other beliefs, with preferences, with intentions,

hopes, fears, expectations, and the rest. . . . Crediting people with
a large degree of consistency cannot be counted mere charity: it is
unavoidable if we are to be in a position to accuse them meaning-
fully of error and some degree of irrationality. Global confusion, like
universal mistake, is unthinkable, not because imagination boggles,
but because too much confusion leaves nothing to be confused about
and massive error erodes the background of true belief against
which alone failure can be construed.[28]

In interpreting the beliefs of another as intelligible, I must assume
that the objects of her beliefs correspond well enough to the objects
of my own to permit contrast on points where we plainly disagree;
much the same is true in interpreting another's desires. In interpreting the beliefs of another, we must, to make sense of exceptions, assume a pressure in the direction of logical consistency and
a pressure in the direction of truth. In interpreting desires, to make
sense of exceptions, we must assume a pressure in the direction of
transitive consistency and, although less so than in the case of belief, a pressure in the direction of similarity, a prior assumption of
homology in desires: "[W]ith desire as with belief, there is a presumption (often overridden by other considerations) that similar
causes beget similar evaluations in interpreter and interpreted."[29]
The Rochester current resuscitates Descartes's evil demon as a
democratic legislator, but fails in the same way that skepticism
about an outside world or other minds fails.

The Rochester current may object that I misrepresent Riker. He
did not say that it is impossible to know other minds, only that there
are insufficient data from voting choices to infer underlying preferences. He could say that we know others' beliefs and desires well
enough in private life and on the market, but not when we enter
public life and the government. Incentives to misrepresent are at
least as ubiquitous in private life as in public life, but leave that
problem aside. Riker's claim is that if communication is limited to
voting choice, then it is impossible to know underlying preferences.
This may be so for *each* of our votes taken alone, but from that it
does not follow that it is so for *all* of our votes considered together.
A series of votes on similar issues would begin to generate enough
data to allow inference of underlying preferences, presuming at the
individual level logically consistent beliefs, their correspondence to
objects, and transitively consistent desires that are sufficiently similar. If communication includes not just voting choices, but the public discussion surrounding the issue, then even more data become

77

available to "triangulate" on a reading of others' underlying preferences. In discussion, individuals may sometimes misrepresent their desires and beliefs, but enough must be true to give content to the rest. Finally, the whole of one's life experience provides additional data and principles for the inference of others' preferences. The sum of evidence permits one to form judgments about what other people want and know, judgments that are fallible but reliable enough for human affairs.

It is the peculiar misfortune of the skeptic that he is always forced to act as if his conclusions were false. The skeptical philosopher dresses warmly for cold weather and worries about what's for dinner, even if all his experiences are just delusions. The skeptical political theorist infers preferences behind choices in every human situation, even, as it turns out, in making his case against the possibility of doing so. In analyzing the Wilmot Proviso, Riker confidently identifies eight factions and infers the preferences of each over three alternatives: "There were not enough votes to ascertain preference orders, but it is easy to guess what they were."[30] In analyzing the Powell amendment, from two recorded votes and an implicit auxiliary assumption that elected representatives represent the interests of their districts, Riker confidently identifies five "natural political groups" (!), almost the exact number of representatives in each group, and the preferences of each *group* over three alternatives.[31] He seems to have forgotten, among other things, that on his account there is no such thing as a district interest that could be discovered by electing a representative. Finally, from minuscule data in an obscure letter written 1900 years ago by Pliny the Younger, Riker is able to identify and estimate the strength of three factions in the Roman Senate on an issue, involved in a process of voting that resulted in the socially better outcome, despite rampant manipulation:

> In general, parliamentary situations are like this. Leaders have the kind of [agenda-setting] power that Pliny exercised, but backbenchers can counter with strategic voting. So the fox can be outfoxed. And thus a balance can be maintained, often resulting, as here, in the selection of the . . . socially better outcome.[32]

There is one unfortunate difference between the skeptical philosopher and the skeptical political theorist. The philosopher would be ignored if he recommended that human institutions be designed as if his conclusions were true, but the political theorist might mistakenly be heeded.

3. Is Democratic Discussion Meaningless?

The economic approach to communication emphasizes the problem of credibility: a speaker will make true or false statements about her desires or beliefs only if it is somehow in her interest to do so, only if it furthers her goals. The prototype economic model of communication is Spence's costly signaling game, a two-player, two-stage game of incomplete information.[33] In the costly signaling game there is a sender and a receiver. The sender has private access to some information that the receiver does not have – for simplicity, say, some number between 0 and 1. The sender sends a message about that information to the receiver, and the receiver then takes an action that affects the payoffs of both players. Each player's payoff depends on private information, message, and action. For example, imagine a labor market. The bosses want greater ability in a worker but cannot observe ability directly, more able workers are able to obtain costly education at less cost than less able workers (assume for the sake of the model that education does not increase ability), and a worker knows whether he has high ability or low ability (private information) and then chooses what level of education to attain (message). In equilibrium, the level of education attained acts as a costly signal to bosses such that a high level of education means high ability and a low level of education means low ability, and bosses pay high wages to high-ability workers and low wages to low-ability workers (action). What if the situation were different, what if "education" were something more costly for the high-ability worker than for the low-ability worker? Then, the high-ability worker would not be able to distinguish herself with education, and bosses unable to distinguish ability would pay an average wage to all workers; education would not work as a signal.

Both the high-ability and low-ability workers (senders) in the Spence costly communication model had the same order of preferences over the bosses (receivers') actions – that is, both would like higher wages, and the high-ability worker was able to distinguish herself with a costly signal. In a different sort of situation, a sender may want the receiver to take one action if private information is of one type and to take another action if private information is of another type. Here *costless* communication can be credible roughly to the extent that the sender's and the receiver's interests coincide; each player's payoff depends on private information and action, but the message is "cheap talk" that does not affect the payoffs. Suppose that sender and receiver have a purely common interest. Sender arrives first at the new vacation spot and telephones receiver to tell him whether the climate is warm (receiver to bring summer clothes for both) or the climate is cold (receiver to bring winter clothes for both). Obviously, sender may confidently send a *costless* signal to receiver; receiver knows that sender will report truly and sender knows that receiver will believe the report and act accordingly. Suppose that sender and receiver have a purely conflicting interest: each wants to eat all the cookies by himself. Sender is in the kitchen, and observes whether or not there are cookies left in the cupboard. Sender could yell out a message to receiver in the front room, either "There are cookies left," or "There aren't cookies left"; receiver knows that sender will not report truly and sender, knowing that, says nothing meaningful (perhaps, "I can't hear you!"). Suppose that sender and receiver have some common interest and some conflicting interest. Sender (suitor) wants receiver (prospective mate) to believe that he is wealthy enough to provide good family security but not so wealthy that receiver thinks she need not contribute outside income to the marriage. One equilibrium is for sender to be somewhat vague but not inaccurate about his wealth.[34]

Austen-Smith elaborately extends the costless communication model to the topic of talk in political decision making.[35] He summarizes the framework in a review essay that I will follow for a while, for the convenience of using the article's informal illustrations for understanding, and then critique. Political talk can be a matter of costly signaling, as in the Spence model: "Insofar as talk is costly – for instance, because statements are easily verifiable by listeners, and liars can be punished – speech can be treated in a similar way to the educational signal."[36] But "frequently" political talk is costless and the content of speeches too costly to verify; then the cheap-talk model applies, according to Austen-Smith.

Imagine that there is an uninformed legislator who has to decide among voting for a bill, voting against the bill, or abstaining on the bill. The legislator does not know whether the complicated bill is good or bad for most of her constituents; assume that she assigns a 50 percent chance to each possibility. There is an informed lobbyist who does know for sure whether the bill is good or bad for

Table 3.2. No Communication

		Legislator's Decision		
		For	*Against*	*Abstain*
Truth	*Bill Good*	3,3	−1,0	0,2
	Bill Bad	3,0	−1,3	0,2

most of the legislator's constituents. (We can imagine the game as being between one informed legislator and another uninformed legislator as well, but calling the sender the lobbyist and the receiver the legislator makes for easier exposition.) Suppose that incentives are as shown in Table 3.2. The cells describe payoffs to each player given a true statement by the lobbyist and a decision by the legislator. The first number in each cell is the lobbyist's payoff; the second number is the legislator's. What would happen? If the lobbyist made no speech, then the legislator would abstain, because by abstaining the legislator would obtain a payoff of 2 > $(1/2)(3) + (1/2)(0) = 3/2$. The legislator would vote for the bill if she knew it were good for constituents and would vote against the bill if she knew it were bad for constituents. Notice that the lobbyist wants the legislator to vote for the bill, no matter whether the bill is good or bad for the legislator's constituents. Suppose the bill actually is good for constituents; then for the lobbyist to tell the truth coincides with his interest in the bill's passage; but it is in the lobbyist's interest to say the bill is good whether it is good or bad; thus, the legislator cannot believe the lobbyist's statement that the bill is good even when it is true, so the lobbyist might as well say nothing. What if the lobbyist says the bill is bad for constituents? The legislator should believe that and vote against the bill, because she would be better off than she would be by abstaining; but the lobbyist would never say that the bill is bad because he wants the legislator to abstain rather than vote against the bill, whether the bill is good or bad. The legislator cannot believe the lobbyist even when there is a common interest between them to vote for the bill when it is good for constituents.

In the preceding illustration (Table 3.2), sender's and receiver's interests are too conflicting for credible communication. Given the

Table 3.3. Honest Communication

		Legislator's Decision		
		For	*Against*	*Abstain*
Truth	*Bill Good*	3,3	−1,0	0,2
	Bill Bad	−1,0	3,3	0,2

Table 3.4. Deceptive Communication

		Legislator's Decision		
		For	*Against*	*Abstain*
Truth	*Bill Good*	3,3	1,0	0,2
	Bill Bad	3,0	1,3	0,2

incentives in the following illustration (Table 3.3) their interests are sufficiently common for fully credible communication. The lobbyist always tells the truth, and the legislator always believes him. In the first illustration, shown in Table 3.2, the lobbyist's lie would not be worth the smallest effort, because it would never be believed. Real lying emerges in the third and most interesting illustration, shown in Table 3.4. The legislator's preferences are the same as in the first illustration, and so in the absence of information the legislator prefers to abstain. Now, however, the lobbyist wants the legislator to vote for the bill more than he wants her to vote against the bill, more than he wants her to abstain on the bill. There is some common interest: the lobbyist least prefers that the legislator abstain, and rather than abstain the legislator prefers to vote for the bill if it is good and vote against the bill if it is bad. But if the legislator always believed the lobbyist's statement that the bill is good, the lobbyist would prefer to say the bill is good whether or not that were true, in which case the legislator should abstain.

Rather, suppose the following equilibrium of partial skepticism. The legislator should believe the lobbyist if he says the bill is bad and so vote against the bill; and if the lobbyist says the bill is good, the legislator should believe the lobbyist one-third of the time and thus vote for the bill and ignore him two-thirds of the time and thus abstain on the bill. If the legislator does that, then when the truth is that the bill is bad, the lobbyist can tell the truth and gain a payoff of 1 or lie and say the bill is good and gain a payoff of 1 (because $(\frac{1}{3})(3) + (\frac{2}{3})(0) = 1$). If the truth is that the bill is bad, the lobbyist is indifferent between telling the truth or lying, and the lobbyist lies half the time and says that the bill is good so that he can gain from the chance of tricking the legislator into voting for the bill. If the truth is that the bill is good, the lobbyist always says that the bill is good. The legislator knows when the lobbyist says the bill is good that altogether there is a two-thirds chance that the lobbyist is speaking the truth: the bill truly is good half the time and the lobbyist always says it is good then – $(\frac{1}{2})$; the bill truly is bad half the time but then the lobbyist lies and says it is good half of that time – $(\frac{1}{2})(\frac{1}{2}) = \frac{1}{4}$ – so when the lobbyist says "good," his statement is true $(\frac{1}{2})/((\frac{1}{2})+(\frac{1}{4})) = \frac{2}{3}$ of the time. Before hearing from the lobbyist, the legislator thought there was a one-half chance that the bill was good. Knowing that the lobbyist has some common and some conflicting interests, if the legislator hears the lobbyist say the bill is good, then the legislator is able to revise her estimate of the chance that the bill is good from one-half to two-thirds, but not to a sure thing, as in the common-interest case in Table 3.3.

These examples and the marvelous formal models they illustrate are, of course, logically valid. However, the extent to which the notations of the model actually represent things like lobbyists, legislators, and debates is a contestable matter of interpretation. As a former lobbyist, legislative aide, and legislative journalist, I must say that the results of the costless signaling model of political deliberation do not correspond well to my experiences. When I was a lobbyist, the informal but prominent institutional norm made clear to me by legislators was that discovered deception would mean professional death; and I witnessed the norm enthusiastically enforced to end the career of a major lobbyist caught in a single deception of only mild importance. Generally, what legislators want to know from lobbyists, and from each other, is who is for the proposal, who is against the proposal, and what the arguments are on *each* side, and they pretty much expect to hear the truth. So what essential features of democratic reality are missing from the cost-less signaling model?

I think that the cheap-talk model would apply to something like buying a Bible from a door-to-door salesman, but that it does not apply to normal political discussion. Recurrent public interaction about knowable information among multiple senders and multiple receivers, not onetime private interaction about unknowable information in a dyad, is the characteristic structure of the *democratic forum*. I will discuss six problems with the costless signaling model: self-contradiction, single interaction, unverifiable and unprovable information, single sender, single receiver, and experimental disconfirmation.[37] First, there is a *contradiction* at the heart of the cheap-talk setup: the lobbyist and the legislator are in a one-shot interaction; they cannot believe one another unless they have some common interests, but the model assumes that preferences are transparent, that somehow they know perfectly one another's interests, common or conflicting. There was no interaction in the past; according to the model, there is only a single interaction. If preferences were *not* transparent, in a single interaction there would not be sufficient information from which to decide whether another person's interests were common or not, because in a single interaction an enemy would imitate a friend and thus conflicting interests would not be discovered. The finding that the sender might sometimes deceive depends on an assumption that the truth occurs often enough for the receiver to have confidently inferred the sender's incentives. Therefore, it is not possible to conclude that because deception is possible in any one instance it is possible in all instances taken together; that would be Riker's error repeated. The costless signaling model does not permit a *generalized* conclusion against the credibility of communication.

Second, what about reputation effects arising from *repeated interactions* between the sender and the receiver? The cheap-talk mixed-strategy equilibrium posits repetition, but it would seem that in a structure of repeated interaction a reputation for consistently providing accurate and valuable information would determine credibility. Reputation is absent from the cheap-talk model because there is something peculiar about the lobbyist's private information: the legislator does not know whether the bill is good or bad for most of her constituents and, according to the model, the legislator will *never* learn from any one or in any way (cheaper than relying on the lone, fleeting, and deceitful lobbyist), whether or not the lobbyist's statement about the bill being good or bad was true. If the lobbyist deceives, the deception will never be discovered; so the lobbyist has no reputation to protect in repeated interaction. Very few events of public interest are so purely private to one person as that, except sometimes perhaps with respect to another person's real preferences in a single instance (and that is the private information that the cheap-talk model assumes we know perfectly). To allow the lobbyist a reputation, we must allow that the lobbyist's statements are eventually verifiable by the legislator – for example, that after the vote the legislator hears from her constituents as to whether the enacted bill is good or bad. If repeated interactions are permitted, and if the legislator is unsure of the lobbyist's real preferences, then what would legislator and lobbyist do?

The model of credibility by reputation is much closer to my central intuitions about democratic debate than the cheap-talk model.[38] There is a series of interactions between the receiving legislator and the sending lobbyist. The legislator does not know the lobbyist's preferences; the legislator is unsure whether the interests of the lobbyist are common or conflicting. The lobbyist makes a statement relevant to a vote, and sometime after the vote the legislator discovers whether or not the statement was true. Let some votes be more important than others to the lobbyist. In this sort of situation, the friendly lobbyist with common interests always tells the truth, of course; the enemy lobbyist with conflicting interests always tells the truth until a vote comes along with a stake so high that he lies in order to cash in on the reputation he developed by telling the truth. The legislator believes whatever a lobbyist says until he discovers a lie, and after that he ignores anything that a lying lobbyist might say. Because others' preferences are normally not transparent to us, we interpret discovered deception as evidence of conflicting interest, and then act accordingly. "When Aristotle was once asked, what a man could gain by uttering falsehoods; he replied, 'not to be credited when he shall tell the truth.' "[39]

The equivalent of a receiver being able to verify a message is a sender being able to prove a message. Third, then, the basic cheap-talk model above assumed complete *unverifiability and unprovability* of a sender's private information. The reputation model above assumed that the receiver could, after a voting action, completely verify a sender's private information provided before that action.

Now assume an informed sender and an uninformed receiver in a single interaction with no reputation incentives, but now the private information of the sender is completely provable. If the receiver is strategically sophisticated and is well informed about the relevant decision variables and about the preferences of the sender, then the receiver can extract the truth by the strategy of disbelieving the sender unless the sender proves his claim.[40] Someone might dismiss this result as obvious or trivial, but its intellectual glamour is not what counts; what counts is the scope of its relevance. Much private information about states of the world relevant to public issues is provable. The scope of the result, therefore, is not trivial.

Fourth, the simple cheap-talk model assumes a *single sender,* but in a democratic forum there are usually multiple senders of relevant information. Return to the case of the deceptive lobbyist. One morning our legislator, with the astuteness of a Sherlock Holmes able to discern effortlessly people's innermost desires but frustrated thinking about her upcoming encounter with the deceptive lobbyist, is reading up on cheap-talk models of communication. Suddenly she realizes the solution to her information problem. "Watson," she tells her aide, "find the deceptive lobbyist and the honest lobbyist and show them into my study at four o'clock." The legislator knows that the deceptive lobbyist, whose common and conflicting interests were portrayed in Table 3.4, would not be completely truthful with her. She also knows that the honest lobbyist, whose common interests were portrayed in Table 3.3, would be completely truthful with her. The two lobbyists are seated. Recall that if she had to rely on the deceptive lobbyist alone, she would disbelieve the deceptive lobbyist and abstain from voting two-thirds of the time when he says "bad," so as to force some truth out of him. With the honest lobbyist available, she need no longer follow that strategy; all she has to do is believe the honest lobbyist. What would the deceptive lobbyist do in the presence of the honest lobbyist and the legislator? Incredibly, the deceptive lobbyist would randomize between saying "good" and saying "bad"; in other words, he would become the perfect liar. The deceptive lobbyist would know that the honest lobbyist was telling the truth and that the legislator believed the honest lobbyist; the legislator would believe that the deceptive lobbyist was a perfect liar and the deceptive lobbyist would know that she believed that, but he would lie anyway – all according to the unrealistic assumptions of the cheap-talk model. By going to the honest lobbyist, the legislator did what I try to do when I find myself confronted with mixed-motive, incomplete, cheap-talk information – the situation *does* occur: she tried to find better information from someone she could better believe. This may be an obvious or trivial point, but remember we are assessing the *general* credibility of communication for the normative purposes of constitutional design.

The fact of multiple senders with conflicting interests may compel a discipline of truthfulness among them, because each has an incentive to correct the other. Samuel Johnson concluded that most falsehoods must originate in vanity, since other opportunities for deception are so well circumscribed:

> To the lye of commerce, and the lye of malice, the motive is so apparent, that they are seldom negligently or implicitly received: suspicion is always watchful over the practices of interest; and whatever the hope of gain, or desire of mischief, can prompt one man to assert, another is by reasons equally cogent incited to refute.[41]

Johnson's common sense now has the seal of approval from economic theory. Return to the case of complete provability of private information. Now assume multiple informed senders, competing to provide private information sequentially to one uninformed receiver, in a single interaction with no reputation incentives. The strategically sophisticated receiver well informed about decision variables and sender preferences, as before, can compel the truth from a single sender. If the receiver is not sophisticated or well informed, and either if multiple senders' interests are sufficiently opposed or if the receiver wants to advance the senders' general welfare, then the receiver will hear a believably true message from one of the senders: from the one sender who prefers that the decision be based on true information. The combination of skepticism and multiple senders is available for tougher situations.[42] What if the private information held by multiple senders is not completely provable but rather only partially provable? *Partial provability* is when a sender can prove only part but not all of what she knows, as when time is too short for a complete demonstration or when one asserts a statement like "I am not a traitor."[43] If the sequential messages of senders with conflicting preferences over the receiver's actions are *refutable,* then the receiver will uncover the truth by following a simple strategy: believe a claim unless it is refuted.[44]

Fifth, do the strategies of a single sender change if there are *multiple receivers* instead of a single receiver? Montaigne noticed that this was a problem for the clever lobbyists of his acquaintance:

> Such men are prepared to make their honor and conscience slaves to present circumstances: but circumstances are liable to frequent change, and their words must vary with them. They are obliged to call the very same thing first grey then yellow, saying one thing to this man, quite another to another. If the persons who receive such contrary advice happen to compare their haul, what becomes of their fine diplomacy? . . . In my time I have known several men who hankered after a reputation for this fine sort of prudence: they can never see that to have a reputation for it renders it ineffectual.[45]

The structure of multiple receivers, depending on the configuration of payoffs, may compel a sender of costless unverifiable claims to convert from falsehood in private to truth in public. Such cheap talk with two audiences is analyzed by Farrell and Gibbons.[46]

Say there is one sender and two receivers – I will vary the sender's name by situation, but call the receivers "City Mouse" and "Country Mouse" – together as a public. If the interests of each of the receivers – both City Mouse and Country Mouse – in an outcome under consideration are coincident with those of the sender – perhaps the sender is President Mouse – then there is *full communication*. If the interests of each of the receivers conflict with those of the sender – perhaps Generalissimo Cat – then there is *no communication*. It may be that the interests of a sender, Mayor Mouse, coincide with receiver City Mouse's interests but conflict with receiver Country Mouse's interests. Mayor Mouse would lie to Country Mouse in private and would tell the truth to City Mouse in private; when all three are together, if Mayor Mouse has more to gain from City Mouse hearing the truth than he has to lose from Country Mouse hearing the same truth, then he will tell the truth in public, dubbed *one-sided discipline* by Farrell and Gibbons. If likable but dim-witted Country Mouse asked Professor Goose to recommend him for a job with City Mouse, the sender Professor Goose would tell his acquaintance City Mouse in private the truth about his friend Country Mouse's incompetence, but he would have to tell a lie if he was sitting together in the pub with both City Mouse and Country Mouse; this is called *subversion*. Finally, another sender, Senatorial Candidate Pig, might be unbelievable about budgetary priorities in private to either City Mouse or Country Mouse, but credible when they are joined in public audience; this is known as *mutual discipline*. Public assembly can transform private truth into public falsehood in the case of subversion, or can transform private falsehood to public truth in the case of one-sided discipline or mutual discipline.

Sixth, the hypothesis that humans act and communicate in an exclusively self-concerned and isolated payoff-motivated fashion is robustly *disconfirmed* by numerous controlled *experiments* in decision making. An incentive structure such that the best choice for each individual as an individual is also the worst choice for all of the individuals as a group is known as a prisoners' dilemma or a social dilemma. The game-theoretic predictions are that individuals will defect from rather than cooperate with the best choice for the group and that cheap-talk discussion, including mutual promises to cooperate, will make no difference whatsoever to the decision. Human-subject experiments consistently falsify those predictions. A meta-analysis of thousands of subjects in tens of experiments over three decades found a mean cooperation rate of about 50 percent (standard deviation about 25 percent); the game-theoretic prediction is zero percent. According to one measure in the meta-analysis, frequency of discussion increased the cooperation rate by 40 percent and promise making by 30 percent; the game-theoretic prediction is zero percent.[47] The experimental results do not disturb the tautologies of formal game theory, but they are relevant to any evaluation of the general credibility of communication and of the desirability of a deliberative democracy.

The basic cheap-talk model is wonderfully elaborated and undoubtedly accounts for some fragments of political communication, but necessarily does not account for the whole of political communication, I have argued. I have tried to show that rational choice models that more fully capture aspects of the characteristic structure of the democratic forum – recurrent public interaction about knowable information among multiple senders and multiple receivers – are closer to our commonsense notions of democratic life. Truth may not triumph in the marketplace of ideas, but it does survive in the public forum.

4. Is Democracy Deception?

A great deal can be learned from the unexceptionable assumption that credibility depends on incentives. For instance, the claim of a sidewalk panhandler one will never see again is quite different from the claim of a reputable fellow speaker in a democratic forum. The speaker's success depends on her credibility, and her credibility is most easily established by a reputation for consistency among her beliefs, desires, and actions. The beliefs and the desires asserted in today's debate cohere with the rest of her expressed beliefs and desires, so cannot be dismissed as opportunistic; her promises and threats are believed, because her words correspond to her deeds; and there are good reasons for exceptions. Credibility by consistency is possible within the structure of the democratic forum, and works largely as a matter of costly signaling: credibility is hard to win and easy to lose. Austen-Smith acknowledges the costly consistency argument, but argues that the relevant polar case is when speech making is cheap talk, because,

> if it is relatively costless for others to determine whether or not any legislator was deliberately misleading in debate, then presumably it is similarly costless for all legislators to obtain all the information, that is, there is no rationale for asymmetries in private information.[48]

In other words, if detecting lies were costless, then everyone would know everything, and there would be no informational reason for communication. However, it is not the case that humans are variably informed because deception is too costly to uncover; rather, humans are variably informed because different individuals lead different lives. Communication is how we learn from each other enough about those different lives so that we can try to live together in peace. One interprets others' actions and statements by means of the consistency assumptions, and makes oneself known to others by displaying consistency; there is simply no alternative. Even among mafiosi (but not to their victims), there is an "absolute obligation to tell the truth."[49]

Unlike the more honorable mafiosi, the cheap-talk lobbyist says to the legislator, "You know me well; I'm honest three-fourths of the time; you can count on that." But it is precisely randomization that we take to be deception, not mere negation. If the lobbyist always makes true statements, then the legislator knows that the lobbyist's statements are true. If the lobbyist always makes false statements, then the legislator knows that the negations of his statements are true.[50] A professor of politics at the Grand Academy of Lagado misunderstood the randomizing nature of deception: he directed that every senator in the council of a great nation, after he had delivered his opinion, and argued in the defence of it, should be obliged to give his vote directly contrary; because if that were done, the result would infallibly terminate in the good of the public.[51]

If the lobbyist sometimes makes true statements and sometimes makes false statements, then the legislator can't make enough sense of the lobbyist's incentives to decide how much he is lying and how much he is not, except on the unlikely assumption that the legislator already confidently knows the deceitful lobbyist's incentives. There is no meaningful difference between someone who lies to us one-fourth of the time and someone who lies to us three-fourths of the time; both are liars and we don't want any further dealings with either of them. In real life we tend to follow the bright-line rule that a single truth does not make someone honest, but that a single deception does make someone a liar. That is because the beliefs and desires of other minds cannot be known directly; they must be figured out from initial assumptions of consistency. A conspicuous inconsistency on the part of the sender, an inconsistency that results in a loss for the receiver, induces the receiver to conclude that the sender is either useless or malicious. Either the sender was not responsible when he performed one of the two inconsistent actions, because he was afflicted with weakness of will or his agency was damaged in some other way, in which case he is unreliable, or the sender acted as though he wanted the receiver to suffer a loss that she would not have suffered in the absence of the sender's message. As Hume put it, "A man delirious, or noted for falsehood and villainy, has no manner of authority with us."[52]

One's first and most important approximation of someone else's incentives is an assessment of whether the other player is benevolent, indifferent, or malevolent to one's own welfare. Deception is evidence of malevolence, and the malevolent are best not tested further, or neutralized if avoidance fails. Indeed, it is not untruth itself that repels us, but the malevolence it reveals. Even a malevolent truth is abhorred:

> A truth thats told with bad intent
> Beats all the Lies you can invent[53]

And a benevolent untruth might be deeply appreciated:

> When my love swears that she is made of truth
> I do believe her, though I know she lies.[54]

Deception resembles violence: "Both can coerce people into acting against their will. . . . But deceit controls more subtly, for it works on belief as well as action."[55] And when the coercion is malevolent, so much the worse: "If a mafioso does not respect the obligation to tell the truth in the presence of another man of honor, it is a sign that either one or the other of them is soon to die."[56]

Malevolent coercion is required against enemies in a state of war. As for the state of peace, since liars don't want to get caught, the fact that they err requires explanation. Some lies fail through miscalculation: Montaigne's courtier did not expect his victims to compare notes. Most lies are born of temptation, I think, from the human tendency to form a temporary preference for the poorer but earlier of two goals when the poorer goal is close at hand.[57] This self-defeating sacrifice of durable reputation for temporary advantage must be the case wherever, given individuals facing the same incentive structures, we are able to distinguish honest from dishonest people, such as in the democratic forum. Some cheap-talk lies go undiscovered. Deception is always possible in human affairs. But political science does not prove that democracy is inaccurate and meaningless. We do not suffer from deception as the consequence of democracy. Rather, we aspire to democracy as the best way to subdue deception.

Notes

1. As to voting, Riker (1982). As to discussion, Austen-Smith and Riker (1987, 1989); Austen-Smith (1990a,b, 1995).
2. Riker strongly influenced the political science profession as well, having published more refereed articles in its premiere journal, the *American Political Science Review*, than any other figure (Miller, Tien, and Peebler 1996).
3. Aranson and Ordeshook (1985).
4. Riker (1982); Riker and Weingast (1988).
5. Miller (1992); Knight and Johnson (1994); Przeworski (Chapter 6, this volume).
6. Updating Schmitt ([1926] 1985).
7. Riker (1982).
8. Riker (1982: 5).
9. Habermas (1984, 1988).

10. "Habermas manages to combine an enormous genius for architectonics with an equally extraordinary disregard for detail. The reader is left with a constant sense of hyperopia – the project seems clear from afar, but becomes fuzzier as one approaches" (Heath 1995: 146).
11. Elster (1986).
12. Manin (1987).
13. Cohen (1989: 19).
14. Austen-Smith and Riker (1987, 1989); Austen-Smith (1990a, b).
15. Austen-Smith and Riker (1987: 907).
16. Austen-Smith (1990a: 75, 93).
17. Austen-Smith (1995).
18. Riker (1982: 236), emphasis added.
19. Ibid., 237.
20. Ibid.
21. Ibid.
22. Mackie (1997).
23. On the last point, compare Hinich and Munger (1994).
24. Riker seems to think that "revealed choices" are directly observed. However, direct observation is of bodily movements, from which intentional actions such as "revealed choices" are inferred. Without this initial confusion of behavior with action, Riker's "meaninglessness" argument wouldn't get off the ground.
25. Shapin (1994); Coady (1992).
26. Davidson (1991a: 193).
27. Davidson (1991b: 160).
28. Davidson (1980: 222).
29. Davidson (1986: 208).
30. Riker (1982: 227).
31. Riker (1986: 118–22).
32. Ibid., 85.
33. Spence (1973).
34. Incentives and solution adapted from Farrell and Rabin (1996); the story is mine.
35. Austen-Smith (1990a, b, 1992, 1995).
36. Austen-Smith (1992: 46).
37. Austen-Smith's (1990b) formal model of committee debate has three sending and receiving legislators (engaged in pivotal-voter reasoning), and thus is more realistic with respect to the fourth and fifth problems. However, recall that elsewhere pivotal-voter reasoning leads to the false prediction that no one would vote in elections where the electorate was larger than committee size (e.g., Mueller 1989: 350).
38. I am summarizing and adapting Sobel (1985).
39. Johnson ([1753] 1963: 361).
40. Milgrom and Roberts (1986).

41. Johnson ([1753] 1963: 363).
42. Milgrom and Roberts (1986).
43. I have never been to Iceland. I can't *prove* that I have never been to Iceland, but I can refute each of an accuser's particular allegations, say, that I have gone to Iceland every Christmas for the past five years.
44. Lipman and Seppi (1995).
45. Montaigne ([1592] 1987: 1592: 34–35; I:9), "On Liars."
46. The following summarizes some of Farrell and Gibbons (1989); the animal examples are entirely my fault. There are conditions involving similar prior beliefs among the receivers that might result in noncommunication from the sender in the discipline cases.
47. Sally (1995).
48. Austen-Smith (1990b: 129).
49. Falcone and Padovani (1993: 58–61). Thanks to Federico Varese for the reference.
50. Compare Lewis's (1969: 147–51) convention of truth.
51. Swift ([1726] 1955: 207).
52. Hume ([1777] 1975: Section X, Part 1).
53. "Auguries of Innocence," in Blake (1978: 1313).
54. Sonnet 138 in Shakespeare (1985).
55. Bok (1978: 18).
56. Falcone and Padovani (1991: 57).
57. Ainslie (1992).

References

Ainslie, George. 1992. *Picoeconomics*. Cambridge University Press.

Aranson, Peter H., and Peter C. Ordeshook. 1985. "Public Interest, Private Interest, and the Democratic Polity." In Roger Benjamin and Stephen L. Elkin (eds.), *The Democratic State*. Lawrence: University Press of Kansas, 87–177.

Austen-Smith, David. 1990a. "Credible Debate Equilibria." *Social Choice and Welfare* 7:75–93.

1990b. "Information Transmission in Debate." *American Journal of Political Science* 34(1): 124–52.

1992. "Strategic Models of Talk in Political Decision Making." *International Political Science Review* 16(1): 45–58.

1995. "Modeling Deliberative Democracy." Notes written for the Workshop on Deliberative Democracy, University of Chicago, April 28–30.

Austen-Smith, David, and William H. Riker. 1987. "Asymmetric Information and the Coherence of Legislation." *American Political Science Review* 81(3): 897–918.

1989. "Asymmetric Information and the Coherence of Legislation: A Correction." *American Political Science Review* 84(1): 243–5.

Blake, William. 1978. *William Blake's Writings*, ed. G. E. Bentley, Jr. Oxford: Clarendon, vol. 2.

Blunt, John Henry, ed. [1662] 1866. *The Annotated Book of Common Prayer*. London: Rivington, vol. 2.

Bok, Sissela. 1978. *Lying: Moral Choice in Public and Private Life*. London: Quartet Books.

Coady, C. A. J. 1992. *Testimony: A Philosophical Study*. Oxford: Clarendon Press.

Cohen, Joshua. 1989. "Deliberation and Democratic Legitimacy." In Alan Hamlin and Phillip Pettit (eds.), *The Good Polity*. Oxford: Basil Blackwell, 17–34.

Davidson, Donald. 1980. *Essays on Actions and Events*. Oxford: Clarendon Press.

1986. "Judging Interpersonal Interests." In Jon Elster and Aanund Hylland (eds.), *Foundations of Social Choice Theory*. Cambridge University Press, 195–211.

1991a. "Epistemology Externalized." *Dialectica* 45: 191–202.

1991b. "Three Varieties of Knowledge." In A. Phillips Griffiths (ed.), *A. J. Ayer Memorial Essays*. Cambridge University Press, 153–66.

Elster, Jon. 1986. "The Market and the Forum: Three Varieties of Political Theory." In Jon Elster and Aanund Hylland (eds.), *Foundations of Social Choice Theory*. Cambridge University Press, 103–28.

Falcone, G., and M. Padovani. 1993. *Men of Honour*. London: Warner Books.

Farrell, Joseph, and Robert Gibbons. 1989. "Cheap Talk with Two Audiences." *American Economic Review* 79(3): 1214–23.

Farrell, Joseph, and Matthew Rabin. 1996. "Cheap Talk." *Journal of Economic Perspectives* 10(3): 103–18.

Habermas, Jürgen. 1984, 1988. *Theory of Communicative Action*. 2 vols. Boston: Beacon Press.

Heath, Joseph. 1995. "Review Essay: Habermas and Speech-Act Theory." *Philosophy and Social Criticism* 21(4): 141–7.

Hinich, Melvin J., and Michael C. Munger. 1994. *Ideology and the Theory of Political Choice*. Ann Arbor: University of Michigan Press.

Hume, David. [1777] 1975. *Enquiries Concerning Human Understanding and Concerning the Principles of Morals*. Oxford: Clarendon Press.

Johnson, Samuel. [1753] 1963. "The Adventurer, No. 50, Saturday 28 April 1753." In W. J. Bate, John M. Bullitt, and L. F. Powell (eds.), *"The Idler" and "The Adventurer."* New Haven, Conn.: Yale University Press, 363.

Knight, Jack, and James Johnson. 1994. "Aggregation and Deliberation: On the Possibility of Democratic Legitimacy." *Political Theory* 22(2): 277–96.

Lewis, David. 1969. *Convention*. Cambridge, Mass.: Harvard University Press.

Lipman, Barton L., and Duane J. Seppi. 1995. "Robust Inference in Communication Games with Partial Provability." *Journal of Economic Theory* 66:370–405.

Mackie, Gerry. 1997. "Science against Democracy: Where Social Choice Theory Went Wrong." Paper presented at American Political Science Association Convention, Washington, D.C., August.

Manin, Bernard. 1987. "On Legitimacy and Political Deliberation." *Political Theory* 15(3): 338–68.

Milgrom, Paul, and John Roberts. 1986. "Relying on the Information of Interested Parties." *Rand Journal of Economics* 17(1): 18–32.

Miller, Arthur H., Charles Tien, and Andrew A. Peebler. 1996. "The *American Political Science Review* Hall of Fame: Assessments and Implications for an Evolving Discipline." *PS: Political Science and Politics* 29(1): 78.

Miller, David. 1992. "Deliberative Democracy and Social Choice." *Political Studies* (special issue): 54–67.

Montaigne, Michel de. [1592] 1987. *The Complete Essays*, trans. M. A. Screech. Harmondsworth: Penguin.

Mueller, Dennis C. 1989. *Public Choice II*. Cambridge University Press.

Riker, William H. 1982. *Liberalism against Populism*. San Francisco: Freeman.

    1986. *The Art of Political Manipulation*. New Haven, Conn.: Yale University Press.

Riker, William H., and Barry R. Weingast. 1988. "Constitutional Regulation of Legislative Choice: The Political Consequences of Judicial Deference to Legislatures." *Virginia Law Review* 74(2): 373–402.

Sally, David. 1995. "Conversation and Cooperation in Social Dilemmas: A Meta-Analysis of Experiments from 1958 to 1992." *Rationality and Society* 7(1): 58–92.

Schmitt, Carl. [1926] 1985. *The Crisis of Parliamentary Democracy*. Cambridge, Mass.: MIT Press.

Shakespeare, William. 1985. *Shakespeare's Sonnets and "A Lover's Complaint."* Oxford: Oxford University Press.

Shapin, Steven. 1994. *A Social History of Truth*. Chicago: University of Chicago Press.

Sobel, Joel. 1985. "A Theory of Credibility." *Review of Economic Studies* 52: 557–73.

Spence, A. Michael. 1973. "Job Market Signalling." *Quarterly Journal of Economics* 87(3): 355–74.

Swift, Jonathan. [1726] 1955. *Gulliver's Travels*. Chicago: Great Books Foundation.

Chapter Four

Deliberation and Constitution Making

Constituent assemblies may involve deliberative democracy in two ways. On the one hand, deliberation among democratically elected delegates may be part of the process of adopting the constitution. On the other hand, promoting deliberative democracy may be one of the goals of the framers. In this essay I consider only the first aspect.[1] I shall proceed as follows. In Section 1, I present some stylized facts about constitutions and constitution making. In Section 2, I try to characterize the *deliberative setting* as an institutional structure. In Section 3, the substantive core of the essay, I consider deliberation in some early constituent assemblies. In Section 4, I draw some normative conclusions.

1. Constitutions and Constitution Making

I shall limit myself to the era of modern constitutions, from 1776 onward. They can be broadly characterized as a written set of laws with the following features. (a) The document is referred to as "the constitution" or some equivalent phrase. (b) It is adopted as a whole rather than piecemeal. (c) It regulates the most fundamental aspects of political life. (d) It is more difficult to amend the constitution than to enact ordinary legislation. (e) The constitution takes precedence in case of a conflict with ordinary legislation. These features do not always go together. Also, what is and what is not fundamental is to some extent a matter of judgment. For my purposes here, these complications do not matter.

This essay draws on numerous discussions with Stephen Holmes, Aanund Hylland, Claus Offe, Wiktor Osiatynski, Ulrich Preuss, and Cass Sunstein and on my earlier work on constitution making (Elster 1991, 1993a, b, 1994, 1995a,b,c,d,e,f, 1996a,b).

The processes by which constitutions are adopted vary widely. Not all involve deliberation, nor are all adopted by democratic procedures. A look at the history of constitution making suggests that the process may be nondemocratic and nondeliberative, democratic and nondeliberative, or democratic and deliberative. The fourth case, that of nondemocratic and deliberative procedures, is illustrated by various prerevolutionary French assemblies.[2] Since these were not constituent assemblies, I will not discuss them here. The making of the French Constitution of 1958 had an element of nondemocratic deliberation, but also included more genuinely democratic procedures, as explained later.

Before I discuss the other three cases, let me explain what I mean by democracy. I understand the idea in a minimal sense, as any kind of effective and formalized control by citizens over leaders or policies: "effective" to exclude ritual forms of participation, and "formalized" to exclude rebellion as a means of control. The *existence* of democracy does not depend on whether the control is ex ante or ex post, direct or representative, one-step or two-step, divided or undivided, or based on a narrow or broad electorate. Although the *extent* of democracy may depend on these features of the political system, I will not be concerned with these variations. The Federal Convention in Philadelphia illustrates deliberative democracy in spite of the fact that women, slaves, and many propertyless individuals were excluded from the process of selecting delegates to the Convention.[3]

A constitution may be imposed from above or from outside without any element of deliberation or democratic participation. The Prussian Constitution of December 5, 1848, was imposed by the king, the Japanese Constitution of 1946 by the U.S. occupying army. These constitutions were not sham documents. They regulated and constrained political life to a considerable extent, unlike Stalin's Constitution of 1936 or Yuan Shikai's "constitutional compact" for China of 1914. One might ask whether a constitution that is unilaterally imposed by an omnipotent power can protect the citizens against that power itself, given that "he that can bind, can release."[4] I think Hobbes got it wrong. Breaking a promise is worse than not making it, because a public act of promise creates expectations and therefore a potential for disappointment and rebellion. Autocrats can, if they want, bind themselves through this mechanism.

Documents adopted by democratic and nondeliberative processes include the French Constitutions of 1799, 1802, and 1804, written by and for Napoleon I, and the Constitution of 1852, written by and for his nephew Louis-Napoléon. Although their adoption went together with plebiscites or plebiscitary elections that supported the counterrevolutionary regimes, there was no democratic participation in the constitution-making process. A more recent example is the making of the French Constitution of 1958, written by and for de Gaulle.[5] Initially, he sought a free hand in preparing the new constitution and presenting it to ratification by referendum. When this idea met with resistance, he created a Consultative Constitutional Committee that discussed his draft and made nonbinding recommendations to him, virtually all of which he ignored. One might ask whether these are cases of *effective* ex post control, that is, whether the autocratic ruler would have respected the plebiscite had it gone against him. The antecedent of this counterfactual is so problematic, however, that the question may be meaningless.[6] If there had been a real chance of de Gaulle losing the referendum, he would never have gotten into a position where he could hold it in the first place.

There is another sense in which a constituent assembly might be democratic and yet not deliberative, namely if the delegates are sent with bound mandates and obey them rigorously. I discuss this case in Section 3. Here I shall only point to the tendency for constituent assemblies to claim what German scholars call *Kompetenz-Kompetenz*, the power to determine their own powers. They tend to resist, therefore, if the upstream powers that convene the assembly and select the delegates try to constrain their freedom of action.[7]

My interest is in constituent assemblies that are deliberative as well as democratic. They can be more or less democratic in two respects: with regard to the mode of election of delegates and with regard to their internal decision-making procedures. Democracy in the mode of electing delegates depends not only on the extent of the suffrage, but also on the choice of electoral system. Before the rise of political parties and the invention of proportional representation, there was no assurance that an assembly would be representative of its electorate. The Frankfurt assembly of 1848, for instance, although elected (in principle) by universal manhood suffrage, included no peasants, only a few small shopkeepers, virtually no manual workers, and no industrial workers at all. The Weimar assembly of 1919, by contrast, was elected by proportional representation. Also, an assembly is more democratic if delegates are chosen in one-step rather than two-step elections. The U.S. Constitution and the Bonn Constitution of 1949, for instance, were written by assemblies elected by the state legislatures.

Democracy in the internal function of the assembly depends notably on the decision whether to use individuals or supraindividual groups as the unit of vote. At the Federal Convention, each state cast one vote, regardless of population size. Although the Pennsylvanians wanted to refuse the smaller states an equal vote, their proposal was never put on the table.[8] When a committee was formed to forge a compromise on the upper house, James Wilson "objected to the committee because it would decide according to that very rule of voting which was opposed on one side,"[9] but to no avail. In the Assemblée Constituante of 1789, the nobility and clergy wanted the vote by estate, but the third estate, which had as many delegates as the other two taken together, successfully fought for vote by head.

2. The Deliberative Setting

The mere fact that an assembly of individuals defines its task as that of deliberation rather than mere force-based bargaining exercises a powerful influence on the proposals and arguments that can be made. Before I discuss the mechanisms involved, let me say a few words about the object of political deliberation.

With a few exceptions, the task of a political assembly is to choose among policy proposals. A member of the assembly will come to this task with a set of *policy preferences,* which derive from *fundamental preferences* and a set of *beliefs about ends–means relations.* As an illustration of the relation among these three elements, consider the debates over unicameralism versus bicameralism in the French Assemblée Constituante of 1789.[10] Very broadly speaking, the assembly contained three groups. The reactionary Right wanted to set the clock back to absolute monarchy, the moderate Center wanted a constitutional monarchy with strong checks on Parliament, and the Left wanted a constitutional monarchy with fewer and weaker checks on Parliament. On the issue of bicameralism, the positions were as shown in Table 4.1.

In the end, bicameralism was defeated by the alliance of reactionaries and radicals. (Some deputies may also have voted for unicameralism because they feared for their lives if they didn't.) This

Table 4.1. Views of Bicameralism in the Assemblée Constituante

	Fundamental Preferences	Beliefs	Derived Preferences
Reactionaries	Destabilize the regime	Bicameralism will stabilize the regime	Unicameralism
Moderates	Stabilize the regime	Bicameralism will stabilize the regime	Bicameralism
Radicals	Stabilize the regime	Bicameralism will destabilize the regime	Unicameralism

general phenomenon – agreement based on preference differences and belief differences that cancel each other – is quite common.[11] It implies that when deliberation reduces disagreement either about ends or about factual matters, it may increase disagreement about the decision to be taken. "Arguing to consensus" is an ambiguous phrase.

Whether argument is about ultimate ends or about the best means to realize them, it is constrained to be formally impartial. For various reasons it may be difficult for a member to cast a vote without justifying it before the other members or his constituency. Nor can he justify it by saying, "We should do X because that is what I want" or "P is true because that is what I believe" and expect others to be persuaded. In fact, doing so would not only be pointless but costly. As James Coleman writes, if "members [of an assembly] appear hesitant to bring up self-interest and sometimes express disapproval when another member does so," it is because there is a social norm "that says that no one should take a position that cannot be justified in terms of benefits to the collectivity."[12] The norm does not induce members to become impartial, only to appear to be so.

This is one source of misrepresentation of preferences: a speaker may find it in his interest to present himself as not moved by interest. First, he might want to *deceive* others about his real motivation. This case has two subcases, depending on what he hopes to achieve by the deception. On the one hand, he may want to avoid the opprobrium associated with the overt appeal to private interest in public debates. On the other hand, he might want to present his position as based on principle in a way that precludes compromise or bargaining. This amounts to using rational argument as a precommitment device. Second, he might want to *persuade* others if he believes they are susceptible of being swayed by impartial argument.

For specificity, imagine that we are dealing with an assembly debating and voting before a public audience or voters. The first subcase of the first motive for substituting impartial reasoning for interest could exist even when all members of the assembly are and know one another to be motivated exclusively by interest. In order to deceive their audience, they might still pretend to be motivated by the public interest, assuming that they care about reelection and that voters penalize naked appeals to interest. Vote-trading deals in Congress, for instance, are routinely dressed up in public-interest language.[13] By contrast, the second subcase can exist only if the speaker believes that other members might believe his claim to be motivated by genuinely impartial concerns. The second motive can exist only if he believes that other members might themselves be motivated by such concerns. He does not have to believe that they believe him to be so motivated, although he is more likely to persuade them if they do.

Concerning the first motive, we run into a snag. If the impartial justification corresponds *perfectly* to the speaker's interest, the disguise may be too transparent to work. Suppose that a conservative party proposes a tax cut for the wealthy by appealing to the trickle-down argument that the cut will ultimately benefit everybody. If the immediate effect is to produce benefits for all the rich and only for the rich, it is quite likely to be met with derision and might produce electoral defeat. The party would do well, therefore, to dilute its proposal so that it will benefit most but not all of the rich, and not only the rich. In these cases, there is an obvious trade-off. On the other hand, the proposal has to be sufficiently diluted to deflect suspicions (the *imperfection constraint*). On the other hand, it must not be so much diluted that the interest in question is harmed rather than promoted. A tax cut proposal only for the poor would appear eminently disinterested, but would hardly appeal to conservative voters.

Passion and prejudice, too, may dress themselves up as reason. The recent constitutions in Central and Eastern Europe, for instance, contain impartially worded clauses whose origin is unambiguously found in ethnic prejudice. All the constitutions in the region include clauses that ban (negative) discrimination on grounds of race, nationality, ethnicity, sex, religion, and many similar grounds. Only three constitutions – those of Bulgaria, Romania, and Slovakia – also contain explicit bans on reverse or positive discrimination, that is, affirmative action. These are also the countries in the region with the largest minority populations[14] and the strongest history of ethnic conflict. In the Romanian document, the ban covers only reverse discrimination on ethnic grounds. Bulgaria and Slovakia did at least try to satisfy the imperfection constraint by extending the ban on positive discrimination to *all* the criteria that are enumerated in the bans on negative discrimination. Yet in these countries, too, the clauses are due to the prejudices of an ethnic majority in the constituent assembly against various minorities. The biases against ethnic minorities would have been even stronger had not delegates to the Council of Europe intervened in the constitution-making processes. The first draft of the Romanian Constitution, for instance, contained an impartially worded ban on ethnically based parties that was directly aimed at the large Hungarian minority.

In deliberative contexts, force-based threats are inadmissible, not because they are necessarily based on self-interest but because the only force that is supposed to count is "the force of the better argument" (Habermas). To get around the norm that prevents him from making a threat, a speaker may present or misrepresent it as a warning. Rather than saying, "If you do X, I shall punish you by doing Y," he can say, "If you do X, you will bring about Y, which you do not want." Warnings, unlike threats, can be assessed as true or false and thus as subject to rational argument. Using this stratagem the speaker overcomes not only the norm against threats,[15] but also the problem of making his threat seem credible. A trade union leader whose behavior is not guided by the norm might still prefer saying, "If you do not give me what I ask for, I won't be able to control my members" rather than "If you do not give me what I ask for, I'll order my members to strike." The former is a matter of plausibility, the latter of credibility.

Chaim Perelman and Lucie Olbrechts-Tyteca offer an amusing anecdote that can be used to illustrate the threat–warning distinction: "In Belgium in 1877 when the Catholic Minister of Justice decided, despite a law which protected the freedom of the voter, not to prosecute the priests who had threatened the punishments of Hell against their parishioners who had voted for the liberal party, Paul Janson ridiculed the Minister: by raising doubts about the gravity of such threats, he was 'really committing religious heresy.' "[16] If the priests (as I suspect) had only been warning their parishioners, there would be no heresy. Similarly, a president standing for reelection may legitimately warn the voters that if they vote for his opponent, they will suffer economically, but not threaten to use the time between early November and late January to make them suffer.

The main argument I have tried to make is that a *deliberative setting* can shape outcomes independently of the motives of the participants. Because there are powerful norms against naked appeals to interest or prejudice, speakers have to justify their proposals by the public interest. Because there are powerful norms against the use of threats, they have to disguise them as warnings. Moreover – and this is the key point from the behavioral point of view – the proposals will be *modified as well as disguised*. The disguise of private interest or prejudice is subject to two constraints. First, as I mentioned, there is the *imperfection constraint*. Because a perfect coincidence between private interest or prejudice and impartial argument is suspicious, self-interested or prejudiced speakers have an incentive to argue for a position that differs somewhat from their ideal point. Second, public speaking is subject to a *consistency constraint*. Once a speaker has adopted an impartial argument because it corresponds to his interest or prejudice, he will be seen as opportunistic if he deviates from it when it ceases to serve his needs.[17] For these reasons, one cannot dismiss impartial arguments as ex post rationalizations with no independent efficacy. Also, this reductionist attitude is ultimately incoherent: if all appeals to the public interest were hypocritical and were known to be so, they could not persuade anyone and nobody would bother to make them.

The substitution of warnings for threats may also affect the substance of the proposals, because not all threats have perfect "warning equivalents." The substitute for saying, "If you do X, I shall punish you by doing Y" may be "If you do X, you will bring about Z" or "If you do W, you will bring about Y." The reason is that warnings, unlike threats, are subject to *plausibility constraints*.

The trade union leader might obtain a 15 percent wage increase if he could make a credible strike threat, whereas a warning might not be plausible above the 5 percent level. It is hard to make the employer believe that the workers will become uncontrollable unless they get a huge raise, because that is not how these emotions work. By contrast, the trade union leader can plausibly assert that his members will be uncontrollably angry if they feel they are being unfairly treated – for example, by getting lower wages than workers in comparable firms.

In deliberative settings, too, warnings are subject to plausibility constraints. The Polish and Hungarian Round Table talks between the regime and the opposition offer an example.[18] On a continuum from bargaining to arguing, the Polish talks were probably closer to the former and the Hungarian closer to the latter. Yet even in Poland the talks had a deliberative element, and overt use of threats might have caused them to break down. Also, a threat would not have been credible, because intervention would have been ruinously bad for the Communists, too. The Communists, therefore, presented the possibility of Soviet intervention as a warning rather than a threat.[19] The warning had some, although limited, plausibility and efficacy.[20] In the Hungarian Round Table talks that took place a few months later, the warning-equivalent of the threat had virtually no plausibility, largely because of the lack of Soviet intervention after the victory of Solidarity in the Polish elections.

3. Deliberation in Constituent Assemblies

Deliberation about constitutions requires the creation of what I called a deliberative setting. The procedure must go beyond the simple recording of votes and allow for communicative interaction. Also, the setting must steer this interaction toward arguing and away from threat-based bargaining. In discussing these issues, I shall rely heavily on the proceedings of the Federal Convention, the French constituent assemblies of 1789–91 and 1848, and the Frankfurt assembly of 1848. The proceedings of these assemblies – both in plenum and in committee – are very well documented. Also, because of the dramatic circumstances surrounding them, they bring out the interplay of reason, interest, and passion in the constitution-making process.

By and large, as I said, constituent assemblies refuse to be bound by upstream authorities. They assert the right to deliberate freely without any prior constraints on procedure or substance, ignoring mandates from their constituencies as well as instructions from the convening authority. The Assemblée Constituante of 1789 is the best illustration of this proposition. Many of the delegates had instructions from their constituencies to vote for voting by estate rather than by head, for an absolute veto for the king in the new constitution, and against any new taxes or loans before the constitution had been passed. Once the delegates met, they threw off these constraints, partly for reasons of expediency – a new loan was too urgent to be postponed – but mainly for reasons of principle.[21]

Although the reactionary Abbé Maury hypocritically invoked Rousseau's authority in favor of bound mandates,[22] he was in a minority. Pétion accepted bound mandates in ordinary legislative matters, but not for constitutional matters, "when it is a question of uprooting a number of abuses and prejudices, of introducing a whole new order and, as it were, of creating everything."[23] As I explained in the introduction to this volume, Sieyès argued that the desire of the nation could not be determined simply by consulting the *cahiers* of complaints and wishes the delegates had brought with them to Versailles. Mirabeau invoked the same idea when discussing the voting rules in the assembly. Replying to a proposal that the quorum be set at half the total number of delegates, he said that this would amount to giving a veto to the absent. "However, this kind of veto is the most fearsome and the most certain. While one can hope to influence and convince individuals who are present, by the use of reasons, what influence can one have on those who reply by not appearing?"[24] One cannot argue with the absent.

In the 1789 assembly, demands to respect the mandates of the deputies came mainly from the nonliberal nobility. Procedurally, they supported bound mandates because they were the traditional method. Substantively, they favored them because most of the instructions coincided with their views. The Left had not yet adopted what was to become the standard radical demand for quasi-direct democracy, to be ensured through bound mandates, short terms of election, and the option to recall representatives at any time. By the time of the Frankfurt assembly, this demand had come to the forefront:

> Whereas the moderates regarded themselves as members of an elected assembly free to vote in the light of discussion and not as delegates, the Left demanded that members should obey the gen-

eral will of the people. The vagueness of Rousseau's concept allowed the Left to set itself up as interpreter of this general will, but it was far more than simply a matter of furthering the interests of one's party. At other times the Left insisted that members should obey the instructions of their constituents. Any demands of the Left for the recall (*Abberufung*) of particular members were firmly resisted by the moderates on the Burkean grounds that members were not delegates and that they had been elected for the duration of the parliament.[25]

In spite of such attempts by the Right or the Left to impose bound mandates, constituent assemblies have consistently rejected this procedure and insisted on free communication before voting. The nature of the communication – its location on the continuum between arguing and bargaining – depends on several variables. The most important are *size* (small vs. large), *publicity* (open vs. closed proceedings), the presence or absence of *force*, and the importance of *interest* as a motivation of the framers. Although analytically and to some extent empirically distinct, the first three variables are closely related to each other. Large assemblies usually debate before a public that can, on occasion, resort to force or threats of force against the deputies. Also, as we shall see, the effects of size and the effects of publicity are closely related to each other.

Consider first size. Bargaining is necessarily a small-number phenomenon; in large, fragmented assemblies interaction must take the form of arguing. Modern constituent assemblies are not fragmented, of course. They usually consist of a small number of political parties whose leaders can and do engage in bargaining and logrolling. Before the rise of political parties, however, the individual member was the effective unit of interaction. In Philadelphia, the votes cast by the 12 state delegations were often split, sometimes resulting in a tie. In the 1789 French assembly, the 1,200 delegates can be roughly assigned to one of six groups, ranging from extreme Left to extreme Right, with Mirabeau forming a category of his own.[26] In Frankfurt, the 596 delegates consolidated into five groups, from Right to extreme Left.[27] Yet in both assemblies these subdivisions were fluid and unstable. In Paris, "given the lack of parties, opinion leaders . . . and speakers such as Maury, Barnave, Thouret, Mirabeau, Clermont-Tonnerre, Cazalès, Grégoire or le Chapelier, all capable of improvising a solid verbal rejoinder, strongly influenced their colleagues."[28] In Frankfurt, "a considerable number of representatives at any one time did not attach themselves firmly to any grouping. Although there was ample discussion in the clubs, many issues were so complex that members did not make up their minds until they were about to vote following the plenary debate. The parliamentary groups were not straitjackets for the views of members."[29]

In such contexts, no political leader could credibly promise to deliver a bloc of votes. This fact may be one of the explanations why Mounier, the leader of the moderates in the 1789 assembly, refused a vote-trading proposal made by three radicals, Barnave, Duport, and Alexandre Lameth. They offered Mounier both an absolute veto for the king and bicameralism if he in return would accept (a) that the king gave up his right to dissolve the assembly, (b) that the upper chamber would have a suspensive veto only, and (c) that there would be periodic conventions for the revision of the constitution. Mounier refused outright. According to his own account, he did not think it right to make concessions on a matter of principle, but he would also have been justified in doubting the ability of the three to deliver on their promise.[30]

Yet even if the assembly is large and the political subdivisions fluid, other subdivisions may be more stable. The French assemblies of 1789 and 1848 as well as the German assembly of 1848 were initially broken down in *bureaux*, randomly formed (and in the 1789 assembly frequently renewed) subcommittees that deliberated in parallel on the same matters before making their recommendations to the plenary assembly. In the French 1848 assembly this system was maintained until the end, but in the two other assemblies the *bureaux* were soon replaced by specialized committees. In Frankfurt, "as soon as the assembly got under way, the [*bureaux*] were overshadowed by the political clubs and the parliamentary committees. They were purely accidental groupings and could not stand up to the competition of bodies consisting either of like-minded people or of men set a common task."[31]

This description applies verbatim to the French assembly of 1789.[32] Yet before the replacement of the *bureaux* by the committees, a great debate took place over the respective roles of the *bureaux* and the plenary debates. For Mounier, leader of the moderates, the *bureaux* favored "cool reason and experience," by detaching the members from everything that could stimulate their vanity and fear of disapproval.[33] For the patriot Bouche, committees tended to weaken the revolutionary fervor. He preferred large assemblies, where "souls become strong and electrified, and where names, ranks and distinctions, count for nothing."[34]

The system of *bureaux* had obvious disadvantages. In debating any given subject, those who actually knew something about it would be in a minority. At the same time, however, the random composition of the group was likely to promote impartiality. Those who know a great deal about a subject also tend to have an interest in it or to be moved by strong passions; otherwise they would not have bothered to become informed about it. Ignorance is a good vaccine against these motives. Although it would be dangerous to entrust the final decision to the *bureaux*, they might play a useful role in structuring the debate and in making recommendations to the assembly. The proposal has in fact been made to have U.S. congressmen randomly assigned to committees.[35]

The dynamics of large assemblies, small *bureaux*, and small specialized committees are likely to be very different. In a large assembly, it is not possible to pursue an argument in a coherent and systematic fashion. The debates tend to be dominated by a small number of skilled and charismatic speakers, a Mirabeau or a Lamartine, who count on rhetoric rather than argument. The outward form of the debates is that of deliberation, but the force motivating the decisions is passion rather than reason. Although the speakers themselves need not be swayed by emotion, they hope to gain cause by playing on the emotions of the audience.[36] In the *bureaux*, one is more likely to observe the substance and not only the form of deliberation. The small size reduces the scope for demagogy and allows all speakers to be heard. Their random composition makes it less likely that interest and passion will dominate. In functionally specialized committees, the technical quality of whatever deliberation takes place, especially on factual matters, is likely to be higher than in the *bureaux*. Yet because the members are less likely to adopt an impartial attitude, there will be less deliberation and more bargaining.

The absence or presence of an audience is a second important determinant of the location of communication on the arguing – bargaining continuum. The four cases I have singled out vary considerably in this respect. At the Federal Convention, the sessions were closed and secret, a procedure that Madison later justified as follows. "Had the members committed themselves publicly at first, they would have afterwards supposed consistency required them to maintain their ground, whereas by secret discussion no man felt himself obliged to retain his opinions any longer than he was satisfied of their propriety and truth, and was open to the force of argument."[37] This is certainly one effect of secrecy: it enhances the quality of whatever deliberation takes place. Madison neglected, however, another effect of secrecy, that of shifting the mode of the proceedings toward the bargaining end of the continuum. There was a great deal of high-quality argument at the Federal Convention, but also a great deal of hard-nosed bargaining.[38]

In the three other assemblies the plenary proceedings were open to the public, which, moreover, played a very active role. In Paris in 1789 the galleries accommodated between 300 and 600 persons,[39] in Frankfurt between 1,500 and 2,000.[40] In both assemblies, the decision to admit the public was split on Left–Right lines. On the one hand, the Left had a theory of popular representation that went beyond the mere right to vote. In Paris, Camille Desmoulins compared the "incorruptible gallery" to "the tribunes of the people who attended the deliberations of the Roman Senate."[41] In Frankfurt, "[t]he public gallery for the radicals was a necessary link with the people represented by the assembly. The democrats did not believe in insulating members from the outside world to ensure undisturbed and impartial discussion."[42] The moderate and conservatives took the opposite view. In Paris, Abbé Maury said, "The Nation, when sending its representatives to the assembly, did not intend to elect actors who would be at the mercy of popular applause or boos." For the Frankfurt moderates, the people "had every right to hear but none to be heard in the chamber, as has been the English custom."[43]

On the other hand, the Left also believed that its substantive claims could benefit from public pressure. An important device to implement this pressure was to demand voting by roll call. The standard form of voting in Paris in 1789 as well as in Frankfurt in 1848 was by "sitting and rising" – those in favor of a motion stood up while those who were against remained seated (*culocratie*). This procedure could be defended or preferred on two grounds. First, it made it difficult to know exactly *how many* had voted for or against a given motion and, in case of a motion that passed, the exact majority for it. Given the prevailing ideology that when the majority had spoken, its opinion ipso facto became the general will,[44] an exact vote count was seen as incompatible with the duty of the minority to let its will merge with that of the majority.[45] Second, the procedure made it difficult to know exactly *who* had voted against the motion, a consequence that might be greatly desired if it was known to have strong popular support. Precisely for this reason, as one might expect, the Left in both assemblies often insisted on vote by roll call. In Paris, lists were made and circulated with the names of those who voted against popular measures. The fear of being on one of these lists contributed to the defeat of bicameralism and the absolute veto for the king. Some deputies feared for their lives, and those of their families, if they went against prevailing opinion in Paris.[46] In Frankfurt, too, an "instrument of the Left to make representatives responsive to public opinion was the demand for voting by name. This swayed votes, according to some observers."[47]

Let me try to assess the actual effects of publicity on the quality of debates and decisions, as distinct from these ideological and self-interested claims. Generally speaking, the effect of an audience is to replace the language of interest by the language of reason and to replace impartial motives by passionate ones. The presence of a public makes it especially hard to appear motivated merely by self-interest. Even if one's fellow assembly members would not be shocked, the audience would be. In general, this *civilizing force of hypocrisy* is a desirable effect of publicity.[48] It is not entirely accurate to say with Judge Brandeis that "[s]unlight is the best disinfectant." I prefer La Rochefoucauld: "Hypocrisy is the homage that vice pays to virtue." Publicity does not eliminate base motives, but forces or induces speakers to hide them.

On the other side of the balance sheet, the greater difficulty of backing down from a position one has stated in public has several undesirable effects. It makes it less likely that speakers will change their mind as a result of reasoned objections, and encourages the use of publicity as a precommitment device. Also on the negative side of the sheet is the fact that large audiences serve as a resonance box for rhetoric. In Frankfurt, the six hundred members would presumably have been less vulnerable to oratory had they only debated among themselves without two thousand present in the gallery. A further negative effect of publicity is that it may distort the democratic process, namely if it enables crowds to impose their will on a majority of democratically elected deputies. Paris should not rule France.

The last remark can serve to introduce the third variable, the use or threat of force in the constitution-making process. In Philadelphia, the delegates never went beyond the threat of force. In the debates over representation of the states in the Senate, the small states wielded the threat of an alliance with foreign powers, and the large states countered with reference to their own might.[49] In the three other assemblies, actual force played a major role. In Frankfurt, "the work of parliament was . . . threatened by the hunt of the crowd for unpopular members of the assembly."[50] One member of the Right Center was beaten up and two killed. In the two French assemblies, which I now discuss in more detail, the threat and use of force were decisive for the outcome.

The debates of 1789 were suspended in a field of force created by two extraparliamentary actors: the king's troops and the crowds of Paris. After the king reluctantly agreed on June 23 to the merging of the three orders into a national assembly, he reinforced the presence of troops near Versailles. The implied threat to the assembly escaped nobody. Mirabeau's replies to the king's challenge provide a nice illustration of the threat–warning ambiguity. In his first speech on the subject he spoke in quite general terms: "How could the people not become upset when their only remaining hope [i.e., the assembly] is in danger?"[51] In his second speech he became more specific. The troops "may forget that they are soldiers by contract, and remember that by nature they are men."[52] Furthermore, the assembly cannot even trust itself to act responsibly: "Passionate movements are contagious: we are only men, our fear of appearing to be weak may carry us too far in the opposite direction."[53] Of these statements, the first is a regular warning, the second what one might call a "self-fulfilling warning," and the third a thinly disguised threat.

In his brief intervention in the same debate, Sieyès mentioned that in all deliberative assemblies, notably in the Estates of Brittany, the assembly refused to deliberate if troops were located closer than twenty-five miles from where it was sitting.[54] However, when the assembly asked for the removal of the troops, the king in his response pretended that they had been brought to control Paris rather than to terrorize the assembly.[55] If the assembly took objection to the presence of troops in the vicinity of Paris, he would be perfectly happy to move the assembly to Noyon or Soisson, and to move himself to Compiègne so as to facilitate communication between them. However, the assembly could not accept a proposal that would deprive them of the threat–warning potential of Paris. The decision was made to send a delegation to the king, asking him to recall the troops, "whose presence adds to the desperation of the people."[56] If the king agreed, the assembly would send a delegation to Paris "to tell the good news and contribute to a return of order." There was no need to say what they would do if he failed to accommodate them. The next day the Bastille fell, and the king agreed to send the troops away.

As the balance of power shifted, the moderates came to believe that the main threat to the assembly now were the radical sections of the Paris Commune rather than the king's troops. On August 31 Clermont-Tonnerre proposed that the assembly leave Versailles for some other place in case the authorities in Paris were unable to keep the peace. "You did not give in to armed despotism; will you now yield to popular effervescence?"[57] A few days later the other moderates and part of the nobility joined him, the former believing that the move would save the assembly, the latter hoping it would destroy it.[58] Inexplicably, the king refused. Instead, he called in a regiment from Flanders for a show of force, thus starting the countdown for a confrontation on October 5 and 6 that would force him to move to Paris.

The Constitution of 1848, like that of 1791, was written in a force field defined by government troops and the people of Paris. In 1848, however, the movement was in the opposite direction. After the initial victory of the revolutionary forces in February 1848, the defeat of the June insurrection ushered in the counterrevolutionary movement that eventually brought Louis-Napoléon to power. As in 1789, the making of the constitution was heavily shaped by extra-parliamentary events. As Tocqueville (a member of the Constitutional Committee) wrote, "Had the Committee met on the 27th June instead of the 16th May, its work would have turned out to be entirely different."[59]

The Constituent Assembly was elected on April 23 and met in Paris on May 4. Between May 12 and May 17, the assembly discussed the procedure for electing the Constitutional Committee. In the middle of these deliberations, on May 15, a large crowd invaded the assembly to demand support for Polish independence, frightening many of the deputies. The eighteen members of the Constitutional Committee, whose composition may have owed something to the events of May 15[60] began their work on May 19 and delivered a first draft on June 19. On June 23 the government announced the closing of the national workshops that had been created in the wake of the February revolution, thus provoking an insurrection that was repressed after four days of bloody struggle. In July and August, the *bureaux* of the assembly deliberated on the project and submitted their comments to the committee, which delivered its final draft to the assembly on August 30. In September and October the assembly discussed the draft, which was adopted with only one significant change (discussed later) on November 4.

The two drafts were clearly written under the shadows respectively of the February and June insurrections. The first draft included not only a general proclamation of the right to work, but also institutional guarantees for the exercise of this right. It prohibited the practice of buying replacements for military service and opened the doors for progressive taxation. On these and other points, the debates in the Constitutional Committee contain numerous references to the need to respect public opinion.[61] The second draft abolished the right to work and constitutionalized proportional taxation. The ban on replacement was maintained, but dropped in the final version that was adopted by Parliament. Although the 1848 constitution retained the principle of manhood suffrage – as in Frankfurt, it would have been embarrassing to abandon the procedure by which the framers themselves had been elected – it was otherwise very much a counterrevolutionary document.

Consider finally the role of interest in constitution making. We have seen that in a deliberative setting it is difficult for the framers to *express* their interest openly and that they have to present it in a public-interest disguise. Although I have argued that this constraint is a shackle on feasible policy proposals and not only what can be said in their favor, it need not be a very powerful limitation. In most constituent assemblies, individuals, groups, and institutions argue for positions that manifestly benefit themselves.

The personal interest of the framers in the future political system was a factor to reckon with in Philadelphia, as shown by the pains that several speakers took to show that impartial proposals could also be embraced as being in the long-term interest of family lines. This idea that *self-interest can mimic impartiality* was strikingly expressed by George Mason:

> We ought to attend to the rights of every class of people. He had often wondered at the indifference of the superior classes of society to this dictate of humanity & policy, considering that however affluent their circumstances, or elevated their situations, might be, the course of a few years, not only might but certainly would distribute their posteriority through the lowest classes of Society. Every selfish

motive therefore, every family attachment, ought to recommend such as system of policy as would provide no less carefully for the rights and happiness of the lowest than of the highest orders of Citizens.[62]

Gouverneur Morris used similar veil-of-ignorance reasoning when he argued that "State attachments, and State importance have been the bane of this Country. We cannot annihilate, but we may perhaps take out the teeth of the serpents. He wished our ideas to be enlarged to the true interest of man, instead of being circumscribed within the narrow compass of a particular spot. And after all how little can be the motive yielded by selfishness for such a policy. Who can say whether he himself, much less whether his children, will the next year be an inhabitant of this or that state."[63] This argument refers to the thirteen states then in existence, but it was also used to cover the accession of future states. Against Gerry's proposal to "limit the number of new states to be admitted into the Union, in such a manner, that they should never be able to outnumber the Atlantic States,"[64] Sherman replied that "we are providing for our posterity, for our children and grand children, who would be as likely to be citizens of new Western states as of the old states."[65]

The role of group interest in Philadelphia is strikingly illustrated in the debates between the small and large states over their respective representation in the Senate. Although this confrontation involved some threats of force, as mentioned earlier, impartially phrased argument had a more central place. Both sides, in fact, were able to defend their views by appeals to fairness and justice.[66] There were obvious arguments from equality – equal representation of the states versus equal representation of individuals. Also, there were opposing arguments based on the nature of contracts. According to Sherman the time had now come to undo the inequality created at the birth of the republic. "That the great states acceded to the confederation, and that they in the hour of danger, made a sacrifice of their interest to the lesser states is true. Like the wisdom of Solomon in adjudging the child to its true mother, from tenderness to it, the greater states well knew that the loss of a limb was fatal to the confederation – they too, through tenderness sacrificed their dearest rights to sacrifice the whole. But the time is come, when justice will be done to their claims."[67] Patterson turned the argument on its head. "It

115

was observed . . . that the larger State gave up its point, not because it was right, but because the circumstances of the moment urged the concession. Be it so. Are they for that reason at liberty to take it back? Can the donor resume his gift without the consent of the donee."[68] For Sherman, justice requires contracts to be binding even if they are unfair. For Patterson, justice requires contracts to be undone if they are unfair.

Whereas the ideas of personal interest and group interest are clear enough, that of institutional interest may require clarification. When a body such as a parliament is involved in shaping the constitution that among other things is to regulate the role of that body, it may have a tendency to write an important role for itself into the constitution.[69] The French framers of 1789 were aware of this problem and took precautions against it, by voting themselves ineligible for the first ordinary legislature. It was Robespierre, in his first great speech, who won the assembly for this "self-denying ordinance."[70] Louis XVI had no such qualms: he offered to give up his veto *over* the constitution in order to obtain a veto *in* the constitution.[71] His reneging on that bargain was an important cause of the confrontation on October 5–6.[72] In Frankfurt, the unicameral constituent assembly created a bicameral constitution, thus offering an apparent counterexample to the claim that constitutions are shaped by institutional interest. Yet by having the members of the upper house elected by proportionality rather than equality, the constituent assembly effectively imposed the federal interest – represented by itself – over the state interests.

4. Some Normative Conclusions

I have tried to indicate how size, publicity, force, and interest may promote or hinder the creation of a deliberative setting – a framework that is conducive to genuinely impartial deliberation about the common good. In this conclusion I shall draw on these causal arguments to make some normative propositions about the optimal design of the constitution-making process. By "optimal design" I do not mean the design most likely to yield an optimal constitution, as defined by independent criteria. Rather, what I have in mind is the design most likely to create optimal conditions for deliberation. In Rawls's terminology, I shall discuss "pure procedural justice" rather than "perfect procedural justice."[73]

1. To reduce the scope for institutional interest, constitutions ought to be written by specially convened assemblies and not by bodies that also serve as ordinary legislatures. Nor should legislatures be given a central place in the process of ratification.
2. More generally, other institutions or actors whose behavior is to be regulated by the constitution ought not to be part of the constitution-making process. These include most obviously the executive, but also the judiciary and the military.
3. The process ought to contain elements of both secrecy (committee discussion) and publicity (plenary assembly discussions). With total secrecy, partisan interests and logrolling come to the forefront, whereas full publicity encourages grandstanding and rhetorical overbidding. Conversely, secrecy allows for serious discussion, whereas publicity ensures that any deals struck are capable of withstanding the light of day.
4. Elections to the constituent assembly ought to follow the proportional system rather than the majority system. Whatever the advantages of the majority system may be in creating ordinary legislatures, a constituent assembly ought to be broadly representative, for reasons similar to those adduced for representativeness in jury selection.
5. To reduce the scope for threats and attempts to influence the deliberations by mass demonstrations, the assembly should not convene in the capital of the country or in a major city. Nor should armed forces be allowed to sojourn in the vicinity of the assembly.
6. The constitution ought to be subject to popular ratification by referendum.
7. To overcome short-term or partisan interest, the assembly might impose on itself the principle that the constitution should not come into force until, say, twenty years after it is adopted. This procedure would amount to creating an artificial veil of ignorance and force each framer to put himself "in everybody's place."

The first and last of these proposals are highly unrealistic. A country can rarely afford to have two sets of elites, one for writing the constitution and another for governing the country. And if constitutions tend to be written in times of crises, delays are rarely affordable. The last observation points to an inherent paradox in the constitution-making process. On the one hand, because they are written for the indefinite future, constitutions ought to be adopted in maximally calm and undisturbed conditions. On the other hand, the call for a new constitution usually arises in turbulent circumstances. The task of constitution making demands procedures based on rational argument, but the external circumstances of constitution making generate passion and invite resorts to force.

These comments suggest a final, tentative generalization. Whereas ordinary legislatures are dominated by interest, constituent assemblies tend either to rise above interest or to fall below it. Theirs are "the best of times, the worst of times."[74] The nature of their task may inspire them to be guided by reason and ignore their interest, and the circumstances of their task may induce anger and fear that override interest.

Notes

1. With regard to the second aspect, Cass Sunstein (1986: 895, 1988: 1559) argues that the American framers, notably James Madison, set out to create a system of deliberative democracy. Note, however, Pétion's opinion, cited in Section 3, that deliberation is more important in constitution making than in ordinary legislation.
2. Castaldo (1989: 73 ff.).
3. For a similar comment on Greek democracy, see Ober (1989): 6–7.
4. Thomas Hobbes, *Leviathan* (1640), part II, ch. 26.
5. See Denquin (1988) and Elster (1995f).
6. Elster (1978: ch. 6.)
7. Elster (1993a).
8. Farrand (1964): 1:19.
9. Ibid., 515.
10. The following draws on Egret (1950).
11. It is also identified by Perelman and Olbrechts-Tyteca (1969: 20).
12. Coleman (1990: 393).
13. Posner (1982); Macey (1986).
14. The percentages are Albania, 2%; Bulgaria, 15%; the Czech Republic, 5.5% (not counting Moravians); Hungary, 8.6%; Poland, 2%; Romania, 10.5%; Slovakia, 14.4% (Bugajski 1994).
15. Perelman and Olbrechts-Tyteca (1969: 487): "There are arguments that can be referred to only by insinuation or allusion, or by a threat to use them. The threat may actually be one of these forbidden arguments."
16. Ibid., 207.
17. For an example, see Elster (1989a: 241).
18. Elster, ed. (1996).
19. Osiatynski (1996).
20. See also Zielinski (1995) and Elster (1996b).

21. The following draws on Castaldo (1989: 139 ff).
22. *Archives Parlementaires. Série I: 1789–1799* (Paris 1875–1888), 13: 112.
23. Ibid., 8: 582.
24. Ibid., 299.
25. Eyck (1968: 156).
26. Castaldo (1989: 29).
27. Eyck (1968: 150).
28. Castaldo (1989: 29–30).
29. Eyck (1968: 174).
30. For details about the negotiations, see Egret (1950) and Mounier (1789).
31. Eyck (1968: 113).
32. Castaldo (1989: 202–3).
33. Mounier (1789: 564).
34. *Archives Parlementaires*, 8: 307.
35. Thaler (1983); compare the idea of instituting a "deliberative opinion poll" – discussion among a group of citizens selected by random sample – advocated by James Fishkin (1991). For the benefits of randomization, see also Elster (1989b: ch. 2).
36. Aristotle's *Rhetoric* remains in many ways unsurpassed. The best modern treatment is Perelman and Olbrechts-Tyteca (1969).
37. Farrand (1964: 3:479).
38. Elster (1994).
39. Castaldo (1989: 305 n80).
40. Eyck (1968: 156).
41. Castaldo (1989: 303–4), who also cites many other claims in the same vein.
42. Ibid., 120.
43. Eyck (1968: 157).
44. This view was notably defended by Sieyès (Manin 1997: ch. V.4).
45. Castaldo (1989: 351 n192).
46. Egret (1950: 154, 158).
47. Eyck (1988: 157).
48. Elster (1995a).
49. For references, see Elster (1996a).
50. Eyck (1968: 312).
51. *Archives Parlementaires*, 8: 209.
52. Ibid., 213.
53. Ibid.
54. Ibid., 210. The constitution adopted on September 3, 1791, contained a clause that forbade troops to come closer than thirty-seven miles to the assembly.
55. Ibid., 219.

56. Ibid., 229.
57. Ibid., 513.
58. Mathiez (1898: 272).
59. Tocqueville ([1893] 1987: 169).
60. Cohen (1935: 49).
61. Craveri (1985: 120, 131, 135, 199, 205).
62. Farrand (1964: 1: 49).
63. Ibid., 530.
64. Ibid., 2:3.
65. Ibid.
66. See, e.g., Madison (ibid., 1:151) versus Dickinson (ibid., 159).
67. Ibid., 1: 348. The argument rests on the idea that *urgency tends to equalize bargaining power*, further developed in Elster (1996a).
68. Farrand (1964: 1: 250–1).
69. If one believes, as I do, in methodological individualism, talk about group interest and institutional interest can never be more than shorthand for individuals' motivations. If members of a parliamentary caucus, for instance, do not follow the party line, they may fail to get renominated or reelected, or suffer financial sanctions. In other cases, legislators seem to *identify* with the institution to which they belong. Independently of reelection, they tend to feel pride in their institution because of a need for cognitive consonance ("This must be an important institution since I am a member of it") or through socialization.
70. *Archives Parlementaires*, 26:124.
71. Mathiez (1898: 268, 278 ff).
72. Castaldo (1989): 278–9.
73. Rawls (1971: 85–8 ff). My argument is close to the spirit of Ely (1980).
74. See also Tocqueville ([1835–40] 1969: 199).

References

Bugajski, J. 1994. *Ethnic Politics in Eastern Europe*. London: Sharpe.

Castaldo, A. 1989. *Les méthodes de travail de la constituante*. Paris: Presses Universitaires de France.

Cohen, J. 1935. *La préparation de la Constitution de 1848 (pouvoirs législatif et exécutif)*. Paris: Jouve.

Coleman, J. 1990. *Foundations of Social Theory*. Cambridge, Mass.: Harvard University Press.

Craveri, P. 1985. *Genesi di una costituzione*. Naples: Guida Editori. (This volume contains the complete transcripts, in French, of the *procés-verbaux* of the Constitutional Committee of 1848.)

Denquin, J.-M. 1988. *1958: La genèse de la Ve République*. Paris: Presses Universitaires de France.

Egret, J. 1950. *La révolution des notables*. Paris: Armand Colin.

Elster, J. 1978. *Logic and Society*. Chichester: Wiley.

1989a. *The Cement of Society*. Cambridge University Press.

1989b. *Solomonic Judgments*. Cambridge University Press.

1991. "Constitutionalism in Eastern Europe: An Introduction." *University of Chicago Law Review* 58: 447–82.

1993a. "Constitutional Bootstrapping in Paris and Philadelphia." *Cardozo Law Review* 14: 549–76.

1993b. "Rebuilding the Boat in the Open Sea: Constitution-Making in Eastern Europe." *Public Administration* 71: 169–217.

1993c. "Majority Rule and Individual Rights." In S. Hurley and S. Shute (eds.), *On Human Rights*. New York: Basic Books, 175–216, 249–56.

1994. "Argumenter et négocier dans deux assemblées constituantes." *Revue Française de Science Politique* 44: 187–256.

1995a. "Strategic Uses of Argument." In K. Arrow et al. (eds.), *Barriers to the Negotiated Resolution of Conflict*. New York: Norton, 236–57.

1995b. "Limiting Majority Rule: Alternatives to Judicial Review in the Revolutionary Epoch." In E. Smith (ed.), *Constitutional Justice under Old Constitutions*. The Hague: Kluwer, 3–21.

1995c. "Transition, Constitution-Making and Separation in Czechoslovakia." *Archives Européennes de Sociologie* 36: 105–34.

1995d. "The Impact of Constitutions on Economic Performance." In *Proceedings from the Annual Bank Conference on Economic Development*. Washington, World Bank, 209–26.

1995e. "Forces and Mechanisms in the Constitution-Making Process." *Duke Law Review* 45: 364–96.

1995f. "Executive–Legislative Relations in Three French Constitution-Making Episodes." In *Revolusjon og Resonnement*. Oslo: Norwegian University Press, 67–99.

1996a. "Equal or Proportional? Arguing and Bargaining over the Senate at the Federal Convention." In J. Knight and I. Sened (eds.), *Explaining Social Institutions*. Ann Arbor: University of Michigan Press, 145–60.

1996b. Introduction to Elster, ed. (1996).

Elster, J. (ed). 1996. *The Round Table Talks in Eastern Europe*. Chicago: University of Chicago Press.

Ely, J. H. 1980. *Democracy and Distrust*. Cambridge, Mass.: Harvard University Press.

Eyck, F. 1968. *The Frankfurt Parliament, 1848–49*. London: Macmillan Press.

Farrand, M. 1964. *Records of the Federal Convention*, vols. 1–4. New Haven, Conn.: Yale University Press.

Fishkin, J. 1991. *Democracy and Deliberation*, New Haven, Conn.: Yale University Press.

Macey, J. 1986. "Promoting Public-Regarding Legislation through Statutory Interpretation: An Interest-Group Model." *Columbia Law Review* 86:223–68.

Manin, B. 1997. *Principles of Representative Government*. Cambridge University Press.

Mathiez, A. 1898. "Étude critique sur les journées des 5 & 6 octobre 1789" (part I). *Revue Historique* 67: 241–81.

Mounier, J.-J. 1789. "Exposé de ma conduite dans l'Assemblée Nationale." *Archives Parlementaires* 9: 557–88.

Ober, J. 1989. *Mass and Elite in Democratic Athens*, Princeton, N.J.: Princeton University Press.

Osiatynski, W. 1996. "The Round Table Talks in Poland." In Elster, ed. (1996), 21–68.

Perelman, C., and L. Olbrechts-Tyteca. 1969. *The New Rhetoric*. Notre Dame, Ind.: University of Notre Dame Press.

Posner, R. 1982. "Economics, Politics, and the Reading of Statutes and the Constitution." *University of Chicago Law Review* 49: 263–91.

Rawls, J. 1971. *A Theory of Justice*. Cambridge, Mass.: Harvard University Press.

Sunstein, C. 1986. "Government Control of Information." *California Law Review* 74: 889–921.

1988. "Beyond the Republican Control." *Yale Law Journal* 97: 1530–90.

Thaler, R. 1983. "The Mirages of Public Policy." *Public Interest* 73: 61–74.

Tocqueville, A. de. [1835–40] 1969. *Democracy in America*. New York: Anchor Books.

[1893] 1987. *Recollections*. New Brunswick, N.J.: Transaction Books.

Zielinski, J. 1995. "The Polish Transition to Democracy: A Game-theoretic Approach." *Archives Européennes de Sociologie* 36: 135–58.

Chapter Five
Pathologies of Deliberation

The dominant view among contemporary political theorists, including some theorists writing in this volume, is that deliberation improves the quality of decisions and enriches democracy. In this essay I turn a more skeptical eye on deliberation and its effects. I do so not as an advocate of closed, authoritarian collective decision making. Instead, my intention is to identify scenarios in which deliberation produces outcomes that are perverse from the perspective of democratic theory. These pathologies of deliberation, like their physiological counterparts, must be understood if we are to immunize ourselves against them.

I accept Przeworski's broad definition of deliberation, offered in Chapter 6, this volume, as the endogenous change of preferences resulting from communication. I am particularly interested in the influence of public communication on the preferences and identities of citizens in democratic settings, and the influence of citizens' preferences on government policy.

Information produced as societies collectively consider how to organize themselves influences what people believe is best for them and for others. These beliefs in turn often depend on the causal models we have in our minds about the effect of a given course of action on our well-being and that of others. Public communication influencing these causal beliefs is as important as deliberation over normative matters, and perhaps more subject to manipulation. It may be hard for me to convince you of the normative correctness of spending money on public education if you are dedicated to an extreme version of laissez-faire, just as it is hard to convince someone to invert his or her preference for chocolate versus strawberry ice cream. But I may be able to convince you that larger expenditures on education will increase the gross national product and leave us both better off. Public communication in democracies often concerns such causal matters.

Public communication – deliberation – may induce people to hold causal beliefs that are both inaccurate and promote the interest of the sender of the message. It is not a new point that this may occur and may entail substantial social cost. But the manipulation of causal beliefs and hence of induced preferences is a potential pathology of the democratic process that must be considered in discussions of deliberation. Similarly, we must consider the potential for deliberation to influence citizens at a deeper level: to mold their very sense of who they are and what their capabilities are. It is common for those who celebrate deliberative democracy to argue that deliberation can give rise to such transformations of the self. And yet rarely do these discussions consider the potential of deliberation to reduce the subject's sense of his or her capabilities or to foist on them a sense of self at odds with his or her real needs and interests. Without consideration of the potential of public communication to induce beliefs that appear contrary to our more authentic interests, and identities that undermine our capacities, discussions of deliberation ring hollow.

In this essay I do not more than offer some instances of public communication with pathological results. I begin with instances in U.S. politics in which deliberation induces preferences that appear to be more in line with the interests of the communicator than with those of recipients of the messages communicated. Or, stranger still, deliberation creates the public belief that preferences have been transformed, a belief that is false but politically consequential. Finally, I offer examples from the United States and from a democracy in a developing country – one of substantial social inequality – where public communication produces identities that are politically debilitating for those who hold them.

1. Deliberation and Induced Preferences

The prevailing view in political science is that citizens have preferences over policies and these preferences drive the actions of politicians and governments. Citizens elect representatives whose policy positions are closest to their own preferences. The representatives, who wish to retain office in the future, implement policies consistent with these preferences. The sequence is laid out in simplified form below: citizens' preferences "cause" politicians' policy proposals (in that politicians anticipate citizens' preferences, or try to do so, when they make proposals in campaigns), and these proposals become the policies of the winning politician, who wishes to be reelected next time around (see Sequence 1).

Sequence 1

Citizens' preferences → Politicians' proposals →
  Government policy

Scattered but impressive empirical research seems to support this model. A line of studies finds that, in the United States, the policy actions of legislators mirror the preferences of their constituents (Miller and Stokes 1966; Page and Shapiro 1992; Jackson and King 1989; Bartels 1991). Stimson, Mackuen, and Erikson (1995) have uncovered evidence of "dynamic representation": shifts in public opinion along a Left–Right dimension are followed in the next period by shifts in the same direction by members of the U.S. House of Representatives and by presidents. Outside the United States, the Comparative Manifestos Project concludes that in ten advanced industrial democracies voters' preferences are embodied in party programs, which in turn shape government actions (see Budge, Robertson, and Hearl 1987; Klingeman, Hofferbert, and Budge 1994).

But these studies are not without ambiguities. Stimson and associates show that members of the U.S. Senate are in fact not responsive to changes in public opinion; the body as a whole is responsive only because individual senators are voted out when the public mood shifts and they fail to adjust. And in an earlier study Stimson (1991) finds a reaction effect, whereby public opinion reacts against changes in policy undertaken by policy makers (see also Durr 1993). Either the policy makers are overdoing it or the public mood is partly endogenous to government actions. Page and Shapiro (1983: 183–4) note but have difficulty explaining their finding that Congress is more responsive to leftward shifts in public opinion than to rightward ones; if Congress is a mirror of the public's mood, it is not a smooth mirror. Still in the U.S. context, Achen (1978) reported that losing candidates in the 1958 elections were on average closer to the policy position of the median voter in their constituency than were winners; the same was true in the 1984 presidential election. In turn Klingeman et al.'s interpretations of their statistical results have been subjected to stinging criticisms (see King and Laver 1993), and the reader must accept on assertion their view that party programs are the embodiment of citizens' wishes. Contrary evidence is supplied by Iversen (1994), who finds party leaders and militants occupying more extreme positions than voters in seven European countries.

An alternative view of the role of citizen preferences is that these preferences are themselves the product of deliberation, broadly conceived: they change endogenously in response to communication. And communication, rather than taking place from the bottom up, from citizens to politicians via elections, movements, lobbying, polls, and so on, is from the top down: elites shape citizens' views on matters of public concern by framing them in persuasive ways or through sheer intensity of exposure (see Sequence 2). Hence, Zaller (1992) shows public opinion to be a function of elite debate. When governments do things and the opposition does not object, neither do citizens. When governments do things and the opposition objects, citizens who share the party identification of the opposition follow suit. (Of course, the opposition may object because it anticipates that its partisan followers will have some substantive reason for not liking what the government is doing; perhaps Zaller leaves some room for a less docile citizenry.)

Sequence 2

Elite debate → Public opinion → Government policy

As in the citizen-preference-driven model, it matters to politicians that public opinion supports them, presumably because the next election is at stake. But having public opinion behind one entails not responding to citizens' autonomously shaped preferences by producing outcomes they like, but "framing information properly" (see, e.g., Kinder and Sears 1985). Granted, information properly framed will interact with "values" or "predispositions," which are formed through socialization and personal experience and are less prone to elite shaping. Still, the prominent role that scholars of public opinion assign to the public communications of presidents, parties, legislators, experts, anonymous others, polls, and the news media in determining how citizens think about politics should lead us to doubt the view of citizen preferences as exogenous to political communication. Hence, deliberation, far from being a complement, perhaps a desirable one, to the democratic process is an inextricable part of that process, for good or ill.

The recent emphasis on framing and elite guidance of mass opinion may be overstated. One may agree that elite debate shapes public opinion without agreeing that this is the only force acting on public opinion. Zaller's study leaves the impression that Americans do nothing but expose themselves to the messages of politicians and the news media and then answer surveys, and his empirical tests do not allow us to assess the impact of political information generated in workplaces, shopping malls, churches, chance encounters, and so forth. And we need to know more about why some messages sink in and others do not, as well as the sociology of political attentiveness. A normative assessment of the fact that opinions, and perhaps induced preferences, are endogenous awaits a fuller theory of endogenous preferences formation.

Other deliberation-induced deviations from the classical model are even more perverse. In the following discussion I will focus on two deviations. One is relatively straightforward but nonetheless troubling: self-interested private actors intervene in public debates to convince the public of erroneous causal effects of policies; the public thus primed lobbies legislators, who act on the erroneous public beliefs. The second is more complex: politicians act on misperceptions of public preferences; they are guided not by preferences but by pseudo-preferences, preferences falsely imputed to electorally significant segments of the public – the majority of a legislator's constituents, for example. These misperceptions may extend to the public itself: people may think that a majority wants A when in fact it wants B. Pseudo-preferences can have a causal impact on policy. Sometimes misinterpretations of the public's mood occur by mistake, but they may also be manufactured by special interests that exploit the complexity of modern contexts of political communication to cover their trail.

An apt example of the first phenomenon comes from the public debate about environmental legislation. In 1990, lobbyists financed by the automobile industry mobilized "grassroots" opposition to convince wavering senators to vote against rules that would have tightened emission standards. The lobbyists put together a loose coalition of farmers, police, and citizens' groups by making the specious claim that the legislation would have the effect of limiting the size of all vehicles manufactured in the United States to that of sub-compacts:

> Vans and station wagons, small trucks and high-speed policy cruis-
> ers, they were told, would cease to exist. The National Sheriffs As-
> sociation was aroused by the thought of chasing criminals in a
> Honda Civic. The Nebraska Farm Bureau said rural America would
> be "devastated" if farmers tried to pull a trailer loaded with live-
> stock or hay with a Ford Escort. (Greider 1992:37)

Lobbyists who were agents of special interests created an erroneous causal belief, which in turn engendered an induced preference against the clean-air legislation, and wavering senators,
who received thousands of calls and letters from citizens, voted
against the bill.

In this sequence, instead of citizens' preferences generating
government policy via party programs chosen in elections, organized interests shaped citizens' preferences over policies, and those
endogenously formed policy preferences in turn caused a shift in
government policy (see Sequence 3). The ultimate cause of government action is the preferences of economic interests. That the
communication was self-interested would appear not to have in-
oculated citizens against believing it.

Sequence 3

Special interests communicate against policy A → Citizens turn
   against policy A → Policy A dies

If senators and other legislators in well-established democracies
care intensely about being reelected, and mold their actions in deference to the future retrospective judgment of voters (Mayhew
1974; Manin 1997), it is not clear why the lobbyists' efforts were
effective. If the causal beliefs that special interests promoted were
obviously false, and if a majority of citizens would in fact benefit
from cleaner air, why would the senators not ignore manipulated
induced preferences? One answer is that they might themselves be
unsure about the causal impact of the bill – could they really be
sure that police departments would be able to drive the cars they
needed under tighter emission standards, and at a reasonable
price?

Other possible explanations are more disturbing. If the prospective judgment by citizens of a piece of legislation is manipulable, perhaps their retrospective judgments will be as well. By the next election car prices may have risen for reasons that have nothing to do with the legislation in question; won't the same special interests attempt to convince the public that the clean-air bill is at fault? In this particular case Greider suggests a third explanation, no more appealing than the second. Some senators want to vote against the legislation because they receive campaign contributions from the affected industry. The mobilization of grassroots or pseudo-grassroots opposition gives them a cover, allowing them to claim that their actions were in line with public sentiment.

A similar story can be told about deliberation over the financing of health care in the United States. Early in the Truman administration the American Medical Association derailed Democratic efforts to create a health insurance fund. The AMA spent $1 million in advertising, it endorsed candidates, and doctors sent literature out with their bills claiming that the fund would reduce the quality of care and patient choice. The perception was that the AMA changed the outcome of some races in the 1950 midterm elections. By the 1952 presidential election the insurance fund was off the agenda (Mayhew 1974: 44).

Or perhaps, even more perversely, the intervention of special interests had the effect of misleading legislators about citizens' preferences rather than of actually changing those preferences. Senator Paul Douglas (D-Ill.) reflected on the process: "Legislators *accepted the conclusion* that the voters were opposed to all forms of health insurance and that they should *avoid an open conflict* with the AMA" (cited in Mayhew 1974: 44; emphasis added). Douglas suggests that legislators were acting on a misperception of public preferences. (He also hints at a second, in this case reinforcing, causal mechanism: economic interests' direct leverage on legislators, quite apart from their ability to influence citizens.)

If he was right, the causal sequence was as follows: economic interests intervened so as to change the public perception of voter preferences – a perception shared by politicians and perhaps by many voters themselves. Legislators modified their behavior in deference to the preferences they mistakenly imputed to the public (see Sequence 4). (And powerful private actors brought pressure to bear on legislators using a threat that was not directly electoral, or not electoral via the mechanism of shaping voter preferences.)

Sequence 4

Special interests communicate against policy A → Representatives misperceive public as against policy A → Policy A dies

If Douglas's sequence is correct, deliberation on health care in the 1950s bore a strong resemblance to deliberation in the 1990s. Bill Clinton promised health care reform in the 1992 presidential campaign. The issue resonated with many voters, and polls found that health care ranked among respondents' top concerns (see Shapiro, Jacobs, and Harvey 1995). (Note that the saliency of health care was itself in part the product of Clinton's campaign focus and that of Pennsylvania Senator Harrison Wofford before him; already we have departed from the Downsian world of exogenous voter preferences.) When Clinton introduced his health care plan in September 1993, it was greeted with widespread support and generated relatively little opposition from Republications in Congress.

The insurance industry then injected into the public debate the view that reform would reduce quality and limit patient choice. The medium of communication was paid TV advertisements, costing $60 million out of an estimated $100 million spent by organizations opposed to the administration's proposals (West, Heith, and Goodwin 1996). The AMA's literature sent out with patients' bills in the 1950s seems quaint by comparison. Public opinion eventually, in 1994, turned against the administration's proposed reforms.

The common perception, perpetuated by much press reporting at the time, was that ads sponsored by the drug and insurance industries turned the public against the president's plan, which in turn gave courage to congressional Republicans to block the plan (a variation on Sequence 3). Particularly influential, again in the common view, were the "Harry and Louise" ads, sponsored by the Health Insurance Association of America, in which an affluent couple discussed the failings of the Clinton health care plan. The ads themselves became a media event. Nightly news programs devoted significant time to reporting on the ads during the first half of 1994, and they received extensive coverage in the newspapers, including front page coverage in the *New York Times* (Kathleen Jamieson, cited in West et al. 1996:48).

Recent research demonstrates that the perception that ads changed public opinion is probably wrong. Although public opinion eventually turned against the Clinton health care plan, exposure to antireform ads contributed little to this opposition (West et al. 1996: 22–6). In 1993, before the debate among politicians became heated, the public remained supportive of the reforms. Then came industry-sponsored ads. The ads were interpreted by politicians and the news media as changing public opinion, which in turn encouraged partisan and ideological opposition in Congress. Indeed, the drug and insurance industries' strategy was to show the ads in places where reporters and editors lived so that they would be reported by the media, creating the impression among members of Congress that the ads were reaching, and persuading, normal citizens (West et al. 1996:45). Republicans in Congress thought, mistakenly, that the ad campaign had turned the public against reforms. Republicans, encouraged by this supposed change in public sentiment, mobilized vigorously against the reforms, and the ensuing debate in turn scared large segments of the public away from Clinton's proposals (Shapiro et al. 1995). Hence, the public's shift against health care reform was a combined result, first of a mistaken interpretation of the public's mood, which animated Republican elite opposition, followed by a "Zaller effect" of elite debate generating citizen opposition.

Shapiro et al. (1995) capture the smoke-and-mirrors quality of public deliberation over health care:

> The high levels of elite disagreement produced conflicting messages that contributed to the public's confusion and hesitation. . . . The near continual reference to the results of the latest opinion polls themselves added an additional set of messages, reinforcing uncertainty as uncertainty itself was reported in the news, making it no easier for the public to sort out a clear direction for national policy.[1] (14–15)

In the following midterm elections, health care reform was absent from campaign rhetoric, despite polls that continued to reveal a preponderant public concern with health care.

As may have been the case forty-five years earlier, misperception of changed public preferences was the politically relevant outcome of deliberation. In more abstract terms, the sequence was as follows: a politician argues for a policy in a campaign, with some resonance; the candidate wins, and the government proposes policies in line with the campaign proposal; the government proposal generates only mild partisan opposition and public acquiescence; special interests, aided by the press, intervene, creating the erroneous view that the public has turned against the government's proposal; in response to these pseudo-preferences the opposition vigorously criticizes the government's proposal; large segments of the public, responding to elite confrontation, withdraw support; the proposal is defeated.

Sequence 5

Government proposes A → Opposition, citizens acquiesce →
  Special interests communicate → Press reports public
  opposition to A → Opposition believes press, argues against
  policy A → Citizens oppose policy A → Policy A dies

The power of pseudo-preferences to displace real preferences in shaping government action gives the feel of a shadow play to this deliberative process.

Assume that there is nothing strategic about reporters misrepresenting public opinion: in this example we can suppose that, in search of a good story, they just mistook slick ads for persuasive ones and didn't bother to wait for public opinion data or weren't adept at interpreting those data. Why would politicians, who have an interest in knowing their constituents' preferences, be taken in?

Perhaps politicians' hypersensitivity to preferences, even to those that turn out to be false, should not surprise us given what research has demonstrated about voters' sensitivity to the preferences of impersonal "others." Mutz (1992) finds that respondents to public opinion polls are likely to follow the putative opinion of others – anonymous "experts" or "public opinion" – on matters about which their own commitments are weak.[2] Politicians in a Downsian democracy ought to be like voters with ill-formed preferences, since the politicians merely represent, or even merely reflect, the preferences of their constituents. They should shift quickly in response to apparent shifts in public opinion.

In a more rationalistic vein, Austen-Smith (1992) shows that politicians should believe lobbyists only under restricted conditions; otherwise, lobbyists' interests should lead legislators to disregard the information lobbyists supply. But Austen-Smith assumes that legislators know where their information is coming from. In the case I have been discussing, the lobbyists' messages and their ostensible effects on public opinion were recycled through a relatively disinterested source (the press). The anonymity of all of this communication works against actors' – politicians' and citizens' – assessing the strategic positions of sources. For example, U.S. lobbyists have shifted from face-to-face techniques to manufacturing pseudo-grassroots movements. They run TV ads the sponsorship of which is vague. For example, in 1994 several large corporations sponsored an ad campaign to limit lawsuits by consumers and board members. Viewers of the ads learned only that the sponsor was an organization called "Citizens for a Sound Economy." (This lobbying technique is known in Washington as "Astroturf.")

Politicians may have acted in accord with pseudo-preferences because of the "Geider effect": the public belief that grassroots opinion had turned against the legislation may have allowed them to respond to special interests while appearing to respond to public opinion.

Arnold (1993) attributes to interest groups a central role in assuring accountability in democracies like the United States: they alert voters, who lack the resources and inclination to follow the government's every move, when it goes astray. The foregoing scenarios take us a long distance from Arnold's model. Unlike interest groups that alert the public when the government implements bad policies, providing information about policies and their likely nefarious effects, in the health care scenario special interests provided self-interested information and distorted public perceptions about the public's preferences.

Imagine that, in the health care reform scenario, the public's preferences had not eventually shifted in the direction that they were mistakenly reported to have shifted – that elite discord about health care had not produced "confusion and hesitation." In this case would we not expect voters to punish politicians who misperceived their preferences by voting them out of office? Even this safety mechanism is uncertain. Several conditions must be in place for voters to thus hold politicians accountable. Voters must be able to identify who has enacted (or failed to enact) policies they like (Powell 1990). Majority governments make this task easier; minority and divided governments make it more difficult (but see Anderson 1995 and Mayhew 1991). If issue cycling is possible, voters must measure the politician's performance against a sociotropic standard (Ferejohn 1986); voter control may be enhanced by a focus on prior campaign promises (see Ferejohn 1995; Stokes 1997).

When citizens cannot hold politicians accountable, politicians'

133

incentives to gather accurate information about the identity of lobbyists or the mood of the public are diminished.

2. Identities and Pseudo-identities

Other examples stray even further from the Downsian model of autonomous preferences and from the liberal model of deliberation revealing the truth. Public communication may change not only preferences but indeed identity. Political parties manufacture identities in accord with party ideology and strategy (see, e.g., Przeworski and Sprague 1986), and states manufacture identities in accord with the need to defend and rule. Perhaps some identities are the result of primordial ties and slowly evolving self-definitions, but we learn more and more about the elite forces that purposively craft them.

Crafted identities may nevertheless serve some useful purpose for those who bear them. But some identities, call them "pseudo-identities," seem to work against the needs, interests, or character that their bearers would express if left to their own devices. Consider instances in which abstract narratives concerning a category of people, narratives tailored for political ends, are believed by people whom the narrative is about, even though their own experience would lead them to believe a different narrative. These narratives are one way of thinking about "conceptions of the world," Gramsci's (1971) phrase for the beliefs about how society functions, about our own capacities and those of others. Because it is common to attach excessive importance to our personal experience (Elster 1989: 38), it is startling that public communication might actually lead us to deny our own experience in constructing conceptions of the world.

The recent debate in the United States about Aid to Families with Dependent Children, food stamps, and other entitlement programs for the poor offers an example. The welfare debate is, among other things, about causal sequences, competing stylized narratives about the kind of life that leads to a person's being on public assistance. The liberal narrative says that poverty perpetuates itself across generations; limited opportunities for education, racial prejudice, and the absence of publicly funded health and child care perpetuate poverty. The conservative narrative says that poor people fail to respond to opportunities; weaned from reliance on welfare, more recipients would become self-reliant.

The intended audience of these narratives is the white middle-class voting public. But the narratives are inevitably heard by people whose lives are their subject. An advocate for the homeless told the *New York Times*, "There's such a barrage of shame and blame and welfare recipient bashing in this country that some AFDC recipients believe some of it. . . . So as to have some self-esteem, women on AFDC want to say, 'I'm not like other women on welfare.' "[3] One welfare recipient interviewed, a mother of four who studied for her high school equivalency degree, echoed the conservative narrative: "Some people just like to sit at home and collect welfare. . . . Some people just don't care, they figure they've got an income coming in and they don't have to do nothing, while me, I'm out here trying to do something with myself and set an example for my children."[4]

In research in Lima, Peru, I found what looked like pseudo-identities among some shantytown community leaders (Stokes 1995). They reasoned: "Poor people are bad [lazy, stupid, etc.], I am good; therefore, I am different from other people in this community." One man lived in a shack in a very poor neighborhood, and he could barely bring in enough money to keep food on the table. He told me with conviction about how important it was for "professionals" like himself to dress well and avoid cantinas that poor people frequented; in this way he would guard his "social prestige."

The professional identity in the shantytown produced preferences that seemed at odds with interests. A dimension of the professional identity was a desire for decorum in relations between employers and workers. Decorum was inconsistent with forming labor unions and with engaging in strikes or other collective actions once unions were formed. Some workers I interviewed opposed unionization, even though they knew that unionized workers in the same sector earned more than they did. They preferred a *trato directo*, direct dealing, with management. "This way we don't go on strikes or marches. We don't create problems or anything public," one man told me (see also Cohen 1989; but for a conflicting view see Scott 1985, 1990).

3. Conclusions

If pseudo-preferences and pseudo-identities are not rare phenomena in democracies, then deliberation sometimes has normatively unpleasant results: it may allow policy to be driven by special interests that manipulate common citizens' notions of what they want the government to do; it can displace real citizen preferences with preferences that politicians, coaxed by interests and the press, mistakenly impute to citizens; and it can instill identities in citizens that they would probably otherwise not hold and which by any commonsense measure are not in their interests.

I am prepared to believe that deliberation has at least some of the good effects theorists attribute to it: drawing citizens out of their parochial interests, instilling community-mindedness, and increasing the amount and variety of data that inform collective decisions. If deliberation can be either salutary or pathological, what rules for deliberation are suggested in the foregoing discussion?

- If elite, specifically partisan, debate shapes citizen preferences, then we need parties that array themselves over a sufficiently broad spectrum to permit citizens a choice of the preferences to which they will cleave. Perhaps we need more than two.
- The press perpetrates misinterpretations of what people want, probably as often in pursuit of the facile "good story" as for political objectives. Competitive ownership structures of print and broadcast media reduce the herd mentality among the press and encourage dissonant analyses.
- Resource-poor citizens' associations should be capacitated so that they can compete effectively with resource-rich special interests in the expensive arena of public deliberation. Cohen and Rogers (1995) and Schmitter (1995) propose schemes for equalizing these resources.
- The public and politicians have to know where the information and points of view they are showered with come from. Most advanced industrial democracies have truth-in-labeling rules for the food we eat and the medicines we consume; we need such rules for trade associations and lobbies.

Notes

1. Shapiro et al. (1995) found that policy makers paid attention to polls not as a guide to the public mood but as a guide to how the public mood should be shaped so that it would conform with their own policy preferences and partisan positions. "[W]hen policymakers used opinion poll results, they sought to identify issues and matters in which the public

needed to be 'educated' – i.e., the public needed to be molded or directly influenced to fall in line with the legislator's or a coalition's position" (12–13).

2. This effect is reversed on matters about which respondents have strong opinions: knowing that expert or public opinion is against their preferences only reinforced respondents' commitment to their position. Mutz (1992: 98–9), following Petty and Cacioppo (1981), offers a single mechanism for these contradictory results. Upon hearing the position of "others," respondents mentally run through the arguments they associate with the "others' " position. This mental exercise persuades them of the "others' " position when they have few or unconvincing counterarguments to supply. But when they believe strongly in their own counterarguments, they only become more wedded to their position. See also West (1991) and Bartels (1988).

3. *New York Times*, March 5, 1995.

4. Ibid.

References

Achen, Christopher H. 1978. "Measuring Representation." *American Journal of Political Science* 22: 475–510.

Anderson, Christopher. 1995. "The Dynamics of Public Support for Coalition Governments." *Comparative Political Studies* 28(3): 350–83.

Arnold, Douglas. 1993. "Can Inattentive Citizens Control Their Elected Representatives?" In Lawrence C. Dodd and Bruce I. Oppenheimer (eds.), *Congress Reconsidered*, 5th ed. Washington: CQ Press, 401–16.

Austen-Smith, David. 1992. "Strategic Models of Talk in Political Decision Making." *International Political Science Review* 13(1): 45–58.

Bartels, Larry. 1988. *Presidential Primaries and the Dynamics of Public Choice*. Princeton, N.J.: Princeton University Press.

1991. "Constituency Opinion and Congressional Policy Making: The Reagan Defense Build-Up." *American Political Science Review* 85: 457–74.

Budge, Ian, David Robertson, and Derek Hearl (eds.). 1987. *Ideology, Strategy, and Party Change: Spatial Analysis of Post-War Election Programs in Nineteen Democracies*. Cambridge University Press.

Cohen, Joshua, and Joel Rogers. 1995. "Secondary Associations and Democratic Governance." In Erik Olin Wright (ed.), *Associations and Democracy*. London: Verso, 7–101.

Cohen, Youseff. 1989. *The Manipulation of Consent: The State and Working-Class Consciousness in Brazil*. Pittsburgh: University of Pittsburgh Press.

Durr, Robert H. 1993. "What Moves Policy Sentiment?" *American Political Science Review* 87: 158–70.

Elster, Jon. 1989. *Nuts and Bolts for the Social Sciences*. Cambridge University Press.

Ferejohn, John. 1986. "Incumbent Performance and Electoral Control." *Public Choice* 50: 5–25.

———. 1995. "The Spatial Model and Elections." In Bernard Grofman (ed.), *Information, Participation, and Choice: An Economic Theory of Democracy in Perspective*. Ann Arbor: University of Michigan Press, 107–24.

Gramsci, Antonio. 1971. *The Prison Notebooks*. Trans. and ed. Quintin Hoare and Geoffrey Nowell Smith. New York: International.

Greider, William. 1992. *Who Will Tell the People? The Betrayal of American Democracy*. New York: Simon & Schuster.

Iversen, Torben. 1994. "The Logics of Electoral Politics: Spatial, Directional, and Mobilizational Effects." *Comparative Political Studies* 27(2): 155–89.

Jackson, John E., and David C. King. 1989. "Public Goods, Private Interests, and Representation." *American Political Science Review* 83: 1143–64.

Kinder, Donald, and David Sears. 1985. "Public Opinion and Political Action." In G. Lindzey and E. Aronson (eds.), *Handbook of Social Psychology*, 4th ed. New York: Random House, 659–741.

King, Gary, and Michael Laver. 1993. "Party Platforms, Mandates, and Government Spending." *American Political Science Review* 87(3): 744–7.

Klingeman, Hans-Dieter, Richard I. Hofferbert, and Ian Budge. 1994. *Parties, Policies, and Democracy*. Boulder, Colo.: Westview.

Manin, Bernard. 1997. *The Principles of Representative Government*. New York: Cambridge University Press.

Mayhew, David. 1974. *Congress: The Electoral Connection*. New Haven Conn.: Yale University Press.

———. 1991. *Divided We Govern: Party Control, Lawmaking, and Investigations, 1946–1990*. New Haven Conn.: Yale University Press.

Miller, Warren E., and Donald E. Stokes. 1966. "Constituency Influence in Congress." In Angus Campbell, Philip E. Converse, Warren E. Miller, and Donald E. Stokes, *Elections and the Political Order*. New York: Wiley, 351–73.

Mutz, Diane. 1992. "Impersonal Influence: Effects of Representations of Public Opinion on Political Attitudes." *Political Behavior* 14(2): 89–122.

Page, Benjamin, and Robert Shapiro. 1983. "Effects of Public Opinion on Policy." *American Political Science Review* 77(1): 175–90.

———. 1992. *The Rational Public: Fifty Years of Trends in American Policy Preferences*. Chicago: University of Chicago Press.

Petty, R. E., and J. T. Cacioppo. 1981. *Attitudes and Persuasion: Classic and Contemporary Approaches*. Dubuque, Iowa: William C. Brown.

Powell, G. Bingham, Jr. 1990. "Holding Governments Accountable: How Constitutional Arrangements and Party Systems Affect Clarity of Responsibility for Policy in Contemporary Democracies." Paper presented at the meetings of the American Political Science Association, San Francisco.

Przeworski, Adam, and John Sprague. 1986. *Paper Stones: A History of Electoral Socialism*. Chicago: University of Chicago Press.

Schmitter, Philippe C. 1995. "The Irony of Modern Democracy and the Viability of Efforts to Reform Its Practice." In Erik Olin Wright (ed.), *Associations and Democracy*. London: Verso.

Scott, James C. 1985. *Weapons of the Weak: Everyday Forms of Peasant Resistance*. New Haven, Conn.: Yale University Press.

1990. *Domination and the Arts of Resistance: The Hidden Transcript*. New Haven, Conn.: Yale University Press.

Shapiro, Robert Y., Lawrence R. Jacobs, and Lynn K. Harvey. 1995. "Influences on Public Opinion Toward Health Care Policy." Mimeo.

Stimson, James A. 1991. *Public Opinion in America: Moods, Cycles, and Swings*. Boulder, Colo.: Westview.

Stimson, James A., Michael B. Mackuen, and Robert S. Erikson. 1995. "Dynamic Representation." *American Political Science Review* 89: 543–65.

Stokes, Susan C. 1995. *Cultures in Conflict: Social Movements and the State in Peru*. Berkeley: University of California Press.

1997. "Democratic Accountability and Policy Change: Economic Policy in Fujimori's Peru." *Comparative Politics*. 29(5): 544–65.

West, Darrell. 1991. "Polling Effects in Election Campaigns." *Political Behavior* 13(2): 151–63.

West, Darrell, Diane Heith, and Chris Goodwin. 1996. "Harry and Louise Go to Washington: Political Advertising and Health Care Reform." *Journal of Health Politics, Policy, and Law* 21(1): 35–68.

Zaller, John R. 1992. *The Nature and Origins of Mass Opinion*. Cambridge University Press.

Chapter Six

Deliberation and Ideological Domination

"I did not realize how sophisticated they [the opponents] would be in conveying messages that were effective politically even though substantively wrong."

Hillary Clinton, interview in the
New York Times, October 3, 1994

I

"Deliberation" is a form of discussion intended to change the preferences on the bases of which people decide how to act. Deliberation is "political" when it leads to a decision binding on a community. Discussion of a seminar paper is not political: participants may learn what to do individually but do not decide how to act collectively. Finally, "democratic political deliberation" occurs when discussion leads to a decision by voting. If a dictator listens to a discussion and then makes the decision, deliberation is political but not democratic.

In a democracy we want to persuade others because we know that they may vote on a decision that will bind us. We want to influence other people's views because these views will affect us.

What difference does it make if people deliberate before voting? Is the outcome of voting preceded by deliberation in some ways better than one without it? Is a democratic decision based on deliberation more likely to be based on true beliefs about the causal relations between policies and outcomes or about the beliefs of others? When people have a chance to persuade each other before voting, are they more likely to accept the outcome of voting? These are the questions I ask.

My central claim is that deliberation may lead people to hold beliefs that are not in their best interest. As indicated by the title of this essay, deliberation may lead to "ideological domination," in the sense of Gramsci (1971). I begin by arguing that deliberation theorists, notably Cohen (1989; see also Chapter 8, this volume), wish away the vulgar fact that under democracy deliberation ends in voting. I do agree that the aggregative conception of democracy is not only unattractive but also incoherent: voting is inevitably based on preferences that are endogenous to the political process. But, I claim, proponents of deliberation miss another plain fact, namely that most public discussion concerns not aims but means. If preferences change in the course of deliberation, it is largely because people change their beliefs, either the "technical" beliefs about the causal relations between policies and outcomes or the "equilibrium" beliefs about the political efficacy of alternative directions of collective action. I then inquire how these beliefs are induced. I analyze first a model of "indoctrination," in which people are duped into false technical beliefs. I opt for a different model, in which individuals are locked into a bad equilibrium because of their expectations about the beliefs of others. A brief conclusion follows.

II

According to Cohen (1989: 33), "deliberation aims to arrive at a rationally motivated consensus – to find reasons that are persuasive to all. . . ." Educated by Manin (1987), he admits, however, that such reasons may not be found, which means that deliberation must end with voting. He also observes that "[r]easons are offered with the aim of bringing others to accept the proposal . . ." (32). But "to accept the proposal" need not lead to voting for it if someone is hypocritical. I think that Cohen confuses two arguments: it is one thing to say that appealing to one's own interest is not persuasive to others and thus such appeals will not enter into a public discussion; it is another to claim that "the discovery that I can offer no persuasive reasons on behalf of the proposal of mine may transform the preferences that motivate the proposal" (34–5).[1] People may discover that their arguments are not sufficient to persuade others, listen to their arguments, and yet vote in favor of their interests. True, Cohen anticipates my skepticism by qualifying the foregoing sentences by assumptions, such as "a commitment to deliberative justification" (34) or "to settling the conditions of their associations through free deliberation among equals" (32). But to justify the normative ideal of deliberation, these should be conclusions, not assumptions. The challenge facing the proponents of deliberative democracy is to persuade us that people will indeed vote on the basis of good reasons if they participate in a free, equal, and reasoned public discussion.

The word "voting" does not appear once in Cohen's essay in this volume, where he claims that the participants "are prepared to cooperate in accordance with the results of such discussion, treating those results as authoritative." Yet under democracy, deliberation ends in aggregation. And it is the result of voting, not of discussion, that authorizes governments to govern, to compel. In the end, some people must submit to an opinion that is different from theirs or to a decision that is contrary to their interest.[2] If all the reasons have been exhausted and deliberation does not lead to unanimity, some people must behave against their reasons. They are coerced to do so, and the authorization to coerce them is derived from the sheer force of numbers, no longer from the validity of reasons. Deliberation may lead to a decision that is reasoned: it may enlighten the reasons the decision is taken and elucidate the reasons it should not be taken. Even more, these reasons may guide the implementation of the decision, the actions of the government. But the authorization for these actions, including coercion, originates from voting, counting heads, not from discussion.

III

The conception of democratic deliberation as any kind of public discussion that leads to a binding decision appears to be broader than Cohen's (1989; see also Chapter 8, this volume). If it is, then I think that his is far too narrow.

Cohen distinguishes "deliberation" from "discussion" by arguing that the former makes recourse to "reasons," while the latter may be restricted to a mere pooling of information. But we must ask, as he does, what counts as "reasons." One understanding is normative: having defined a reason as a "consideration that counts in favor of something," Cohen clarifies that "[t]he relevant sense of 'counts in favor' is itself normative" (Chapter 8). To the extent to which I can interpret his text, he seems to see deliberation as a discussion about goals.[3] His problem (1989, 1993; see also Chapter 8) is to see how conceptions of common good can emerge under conditions of pluralism, obviously pluralism of values. But, and here I am making an empirical claim, if this is what deliberation is about, then we rarely deliberate. The large part of political discussion concerns not goals but means, not the question whether motherhood is good but whether the best way to promote motherhood is indeed to throw mothers and children on the street.[4]

To explain how I see the role of deliberation in the democratic process, let me consider a model that ignores it altogether: the spatial theory of voting. In this model, voters have ready-made preferences over "outcomes": states of the world, individual or collective, that result at least in part from policies of governments they elect. Candidates or parties compete by offering policies. Citizens vote for a party or a candidate who offers policies that are closest to their preferences.

This theory is flagrantly incoherent. Consider a summary of the spatial theory of voting offered by Enelow and Hinich (1984):

> [W]hat spatial theory assumes is that the voter has a given stake or interest in the outcome of the vote, which he recognizes, and which leads him to vote as he does. The form of this self-interest is subjectively determined by the voter. Spatial theory does not explain the source or form that this self-interest takes. The theory merely assumes that the voter recognizes his own self-interest, evaluates alternative policies or candidates on the basis of which will best serve this self-interest, and casts his vote for the policy or the candidate most favorably evaluated. (3)

Voters have preferences over outcomes, yet parties do not propose outcomes, only policies. But how are voters, whose utility is derived from *outcomes,* to decide among parties that offer *policies?* Something is obviously missing.

If individuals are to be able to choose among policies, they must have beliefs about the consequences of their vote for the outcomes about which they care. These beliefs are of two kinds: (a) technical beliefs, that is, models of causal relations between policies and outcomes (Vanberg and Buchanan 1989; Austen-Smith 1992: 47), and (b) equilibrium beliefs, that is, beliefs about other people's beliefs.[5] To be able to decide among policies, individuals must anticipate the effect of policies on outcomes and they must anticipate others' beliefs about these effects. In Gramscian language, a system that comprises both classes of beliefs is called "ideology." Ideology, in this conception, is a cognitive map that orients people's actions, and this map comprises both theories of causal relations and beliefs about others. This is how I will use this term.

Even if preferences over outcomes are exogenous to the political process, voters decide not on the basis on these exogenous preferences but on the basis of preferences induced by their beliefs. If preferences over outcomes are exogenous – people just want to consume more, work less or more pleasantly, walk safe streets, and see their kids learn – these are not the operative preferences. The preferences on which people act politically are contingent on their beliefs about the consequences of their actions.[6]

And, indeed, parties and candidates competing for office do not offer merely policies: they explain to the electorate how these policies will affect the outcomes, trying to persuade citizens that their policies, as distinct from those of their opponents, will lead to outcomes citizens want. Hence, the preferences on which people act in politics are endogenous to the political process. They are shaped by a discussion about reasons. These reasons appear to satisfy all of Cohen's criteria but one: they are "considerations that count in favor"; the process through which they are adduced may satisfy the norms of freedom, reciprocity, and formal (but perhaps not substantive) equality; this process may aim at a rationally motivated consensus. Yet these are reasons one course of action is better than another in reaching goals, whether or not these goals themselves have resulted from a public reasoning. They are "technical," not normative, reasons.

IV

Just to clarify the role of substantive equality in deliberation about means, assume a Condorcet-tradition setup in which everyone has access to some privately observed information of equal quality and an equal ability to process this information. A group is to decide by a majority vote if a particular coin is biased. Everyone observes privately a series of realizations and then individuals exchange messages about them. If everyone observed the same number of realizations and if everyone had the same reasoning capacity, then they should aggregate private information directly, rather than modify their beliefs by exchanging their information (Ladha 1992).[7]

I posit this setup only to argue that if these two conditions are true – if everyone has information of the same quality and the same capacity to interpret this information – then deliberation should not modify beliefs. If beliefs are altered as a result of communication, therefore, it must be because either (a) individuals have unequal access to information or (b) they see themselves as having unequal reasoning capacity. If I observe one toss and I know someone else observed a hundred, I will use the other person's information. If I am not sure if I can count as well as someone else, I may do the same. Hence, deliberation about technical reasons inevitably entails a recognition of inequality: either of information or of the ability to process it.

V

Inequality of information, however, may be just a matter of division of labor. Drug companies conduct research on their effectiveness, and as a result they know what other people do not. In the Condorcet world, this specialization would be innocuous: if we all want only to do the right thing, we should all believe whatever drug companies tell us. But in a world in which there are conflicts of interests this is no longer true: now we have to examine arguments critically, through the optic of the interests of the speakers.

Now, as I read accounts of deliberation, I am struck that they never allow the cognitive quality of the democratic process to suffer from this process. Specifically, no account I know of permits a person already holding a true technical belief to acquire a false belief as a result of communication.[8]

In the entire literature on "strategic talk," summarized by Austen-Smith (1990, 1992), it is possible that (a) even though some people hold true beliefs while others have none, truth cannot be credibly communicated, since speech predictable from the interest of the speaker is not credible, or (b) someone who held no beliefs about a particular matter can be told and accept falsehood. If someone knows that he or she does not have the (costly) information and that someone else has it, then some false beliefs can be communicated and accepted. But even in these Bayesian equilibria, more people hold true beliefs as a result of communication than without it.

But is it really impossible that someone who already holds a true belief could be persuaded to accept a false one? And is it impossible that more people would hold false beliefs as a result of deliberation?

I realize that these are separate questions. One calls for specifying micro mechanisms by which individual beliefs are altered as a result of discussion. The second calls for statistics: how often does it happen? As is often true, the second question may be easier to answer than the first.

VI

I think it must happen often. Let me first introduce a distinction between two ways of holding a false belief (and being duped into holding one): I may know correctly who I am but hold a false belief about actions that promote my interests, or I may hold correct technical beliefs but identify myself with a group of which I am not a part. I am a worker who would benefit from increasing the tax burden but I incorrectly believe that growth is driven by saving and therefore that income should be transferred, in the words of the *Wall Street Journal,* to "those who save." Or I may be a worker and believe correctly that growth is driven by consumption but see myself as a member of "the middle class." Some ideological battles, therefore, are about technical beliefs and some about identity.

The recurrent battle about technical beliefs concerns the model of economic growth. This is not the place to go over the history of economic ideologies:[9] basically, between the mid-1930s and mid-1970s many people believed that growth was stimulated by increasing the income of those who consume, and now most people believe that it is promoted by giving income to those who save. In the 1930s, Léon Blum could say that "a better distribution . . . would revive production at the same time that it would satisfy justice," while Bertil Ohlin (1938: 5) could claim, "In recent years it has become obvious that . . . many forms of 'consumption' – food, clothing, housing, recreation – . . . represent an investment in the most valuable productive instrument of all, the people itself." But then, by 1976, we could read on the editorial page of the *New York Times* (May 6, 1976) the following message paid for by the Mobil Oil Company:

Corporate earnings have to rise to levels substantially above those of the recent years if our country is not to get into even deeper trouble. [If this does not occur] every group will begin fighting for a larger piece of that static pie. Women, blacks, and other racial movements, and young people of all backgrounds will be the hardest hit. College graduates will find job hunting even tougher. More and more of them will have to take jobs lower in the economic scale. This will further squeeze every minority and everybody else. Economic growth is the last, best hope for the poor and for all the rest of us. Sheer redistribution of income cannot do the job. We must create a steadily larger income pie. This can be done only through economic growth. And only profitable private businesses can make the capital investments that produce economic growth and jobs and tax revenues.

Battles about identity are also perennial. Gramsci (1971: 260) noted that the revolution the bourgeoisie introduced into the realm of ideology was to portray itself as the future of all humanity, "capable of absorbing the entire society." In turn, one of the persistent socialist themes at the turn of the century (Karl Kautsky, *The Class Struggle* [1971]) was that the petite bourgeoisie and peasants were "future proletarians," who might as well immediately embrace the interests of the proletariat. The image of society as composed of individuals with harmonious interests repeatedly hurls itself against various maps of particularistic identities with conflicting interests.

VII

I snuck in the Mobil Oil ad for a surreptitious purpose. One-eighth of the *New York Times'* editorial page costs money: why would a private firm spend it? Is it because readers of this distinguished newspaper do not have information about the consequences of a "sheer distribution of income" and need to acquire correct beliefs so that they will be better off? If so, they are the ones who should have paid for it: this information is valuable to them and costly. Or was this ad expected to further the interests of Mobil Oil?

In a society in which interests are in conflict, the fact that various economic agents spend money to persuade others constitutes prima facie evidence that someone is irrational. Either those who spend money to communicate are throwing it away or these costly messages persuade others to hold beliefs that are not in their best interest.

Deliberation can occur – a public discussion can take place – only if someone pays for it. Even if someone who knows the truth seeks to share it with an ignorant or misinformed person for the sake of that person's best interest, communication is costly. Private corporations have money that they can use; political parties need to raise it just to be heard.

VIII

It is time to put 2 and 2 together. Deliberation can occur only if someone pays for it. Deliberation (again, about technical reasons) can be effective only if there is inequality, either of access to specific information or of calculating capacity. Add a dose of self-interest, and the mixture will reek of "manipulation," "indoctrination," "brainwashing," whatever one wants to call it.

I believe that Mobil Oil knew that its arguments were self-serving (and did not care if they were true). It must have also thought that they would be persuasive; otherwise, it would not have paid for the ad. But I am not willing to believe that people ended up believing them just because they were exposed to this and thousands of similar messages. Something else must be involved.

IX

To approach the question of micro mechanisms, more preliminaries are needed. Boudon (1994) makes useful distinctions: people can hold a belief because it is true, for a reason, or they can hold it for a cause. He points out that our explanations of why people hold a particular belief tend to be asymmetric: if people believe the truth, it is for a reason; if they believe a falsehood, it is for a cause. Boudon's central point is that people can believe a falsehood for a reason if they reason badly: they can have all the correct information and use some rules of inference, but either these rules of inference can be invalid or people can make mistakes using them. That people have a limited cognitive and inferential capacity is not an earth-shaking discovery: George Bernard Shaw once remarked, "Common sense is that which tells us that the earth is flat." But what is strange for a book written by a sociologist is that Boudon never asks himself why someone who knows the truth would not correct the calculating mistakes of someone who arrives at falsehood: his is a society in which people do not communicate. Characterizing what he calls the "Simmel model," he writes that

> when we, whether as scientists or laypersons, construct a theory to explain a phenomenon, we always introduce, as well as explicit statements to which reasoning is applied, implicit statements which do not appear directly in the field of our consciousness. Moreover, Simmel says, *it may very well happen that the structure of the theory is modified as soon as these statements are made explicit.* (56; emphasis added)

Hence, it would appear that although individuals can make mistakes in their reasoning, these are easily corrected by communication: it is enough that someone points out the mistake and false beliefs evaporate. To explain why false beliefs survive in a society in which individuals communicate, Boudon would have had to show that some of Simmel's implicit a prioris are universally shared, so that no one could make them explicit. But then he could not have written his book.

It is easy to adduce causal mechanisms that would explain why deliberation could lead ignorant or even truthfully informed individuals to believe in falsehood. Think of Ash's (1952) classical conformity experiments. Seven individuals enter a room, to be shown several lines of equal length, one marked differently from the rest. Six stooges of the experimenter declare the differently marked line to be longer and the experiments show that the seventh person, the experimental subject, is very likely to embrace this view even if this person would have recognized this line to be of equal length without having been exposed to communication.

The problem with explanations by causes, however, is that they do not provide micro foundations, but enclose them within a black box. I am thinking of Althusser's (1971) *appelation:* A person is walking down the street and hears from behind someone calling, "Hey, you!" This person recognizes him or herself to be the addressee of this appeal, and this is all we know about the mechanism by which ideology appeals to individuals. In the Ash experiments we also get only a label: "conformity."

As Boudon argues, in many cases explanations by causes can be replaced by ones by reasons. If I am uncertain about my perceptions and if I believe that people with whom I discuss are motivated only by the truth, it is rational for me to discount some of my own impressions. If I know that other people have observed more coin tosses or are better at counting their realizations, I might as well defer to their views. "Deference," the recognition that only some people are, in the words of Winston Churchill, "fit to govern," can be a perfectly rational posture. Indeed, in Manin's (1995) view, our representative institutions were built on this assumption.

Whether one takes the "hot" or the "cold" version of this model, "indoctrination" is easy to describe. Some people are stooges: they know better and are complicit in misleading others. Others are either caused to believe them or have good reasons to believe that others know better.

In this indoctrination model, ideological domination can be deduced from the ownership of the means of production, including the means of intellectual production. This is what Anderson (1977) does in his interpretation of Gramsci. The Stigler–Peltzman–Becker model is even more straightforward about it: votes are bought with money (Stigler 1975; Peltzman 1976; Becker 1983). Money is used to persuade and it does.[10]

X

I never liked this story of indoctrination (Przeworski 1985: 135). It requires that some people know the truth and that they know that it is not good for them if other people know it, that they are complicit in propagating falsehood, and that other people believe them. This may happen when a particular piece of information is costly and therefore access to it is highly specialized: Austen-Smith's story of drug companies and legislators. But I find it unpersuasive as an account of dominant ideologies – complex and somewhat coherent sets of beliefs on the basis of which people tend to act in their everyday lives. Even in the Austen-Smith story, unless they collude, will not lobbyists for rival drug companies claim that their competitors' remedies are ineffective?

To be plausible, accounts of indoctrination must allow individuals to have some independent knowledge and to be exposed to conflicting information. Condorcet's belief in reason may be exaggerated, but individuals do acquire in their daily pursuits a knowledge that limits their gullibility: one source of information is simply one's own experience. And under democracy, even if access to the media of communication is regulated to some extent by money, competing ideologies do sneak through. So even if we assume that some agents deliberately seek to dupe others, they face two constraints: private knowledge of the individuals and the counterarguments that enter into the public domain.

XI

Ironically, what Boudon has to say does not differ from Althusser (1970, 1971). The latter believed, with Gramsci, that individuals acquire some kind of spontaneous, uncritical, knowledge in their everyday life: a "lived" or "spontaneous" experience. This knowledge is valid in the sense that it successfully orients individuals' everyday actions: indeed, success in everyday life is what validates this knowledge. Marx's English shopkeepers believe that value is added by buying cheap and selling dear, and this belief is perfectly valid as a guide for their actions. Theirs is a local knowledge[11] or, if we are to put it in the framework of Aumann's (1987) model, the knowledge of participants.[12] Althusser then went on to distinguish this spontaneous local knowledge of participants from scientific knowledge, which is "critical" precisely in the sense that Boudon attributes to Simmel: it bares the hidden assumptions.[13] This critical knowledge, which is the knowledge of an observer, adds up what the English shopkeepers pay and what they sell for and comes up with zero: value is not generated by exchange. But this true, critical, global knowledge is not an effective guide for individual action: even if the shopkeeper plowed through *The Capital,* as a participant he would still have to buy cheap and sell dear. Hence, revealing the "hidden a priori" may change mental states of individuals without modifying the causal model on the basis of which they act: Marxist shopkeepers must act like shopkeepers even if they attend revolutionary meetings at night. Revealing fallacies of composition or pointing out the suboptimality of equilibria is enlightening but not useful.

Take a one-shot prisoner's dilemma. Players have two beliefs: one about the mapping of their payoffs on their strategies and one about the welfare properties of the equilibria. The first concerns the consequences of their actions within the game and the second the consequences of the game. Judgments about the welfare consequences of the game entail out-of-equilibrium beliefs: what will happen if we all cooperate.

Many Marxists and fellow sympathizers reasoned that once individuals know the game is no good, they will alter their behavior within it, so that individual actions can be transformed by changing individual consciousness. Yet the knowledge that the equilibrium has bad properties does not affect individual behavior within it; cooperating will just make you a sucker.[14] So even if shopkeepers have correct beliefs about everything, they are revolutionary shopkeepers but shopkeepers nevertheless.

XII

But beliefs matter. Suppose I am a physician and I wonder if I should raise my fees. I may think that if I do others will not and I will lose enough patients for my income to diminish. If these expectations are fulfilled, there will emerge a virtuous noninflationary equilibrium. But suppose I believe that if I raise my fees so will others, so that my market share remains the same. Everyone coordinates on the past or expected rate of inflation, and these expectations are fulfilled: we get a bad, inflationary equilibrium.[15] To simplify this story, think of a coordination game with equilibria that can be Pareto-ranked. Here beliefs are crucial: if the beliefs support an inferior equilibrium, the agents are locked into it. They have true beliefs: it is true that deviating from the bad equilibrium would be disastrous for an individual even if adhering to it were collectively suboptimal. And to get where I need to get, suppose now that these coordination equilibria are asymmetric and no longer comparable by the Pareto criterion:

		Joe Smith	
		Does C	*Does D*
	Does A	2,1	0,0
Mobil Oil			
	Does B	0,0	1,3

Suppose that Mobil Oil says to Joe, "If you strike, no one will support you," or that Mr. Smith says to Mobil Oil, "If you fire me, we will tax you." In this game, it matters who believes what. Whichever is the (pure strategy) equilibrium, agents are locked into it. The knowledge that the {B, D} equilibrium is superior by the compensation criterion to the {A, C} equilibrium is immaterial, and Mobil Oil is better off in {A, C}. The Mobil Oil message that Joe Smith would be worse off replying with D to A is true, and so is the message from Joe Smith about replying with B to C. The question is which equilibrium will prevail, and this is a question about my beliefs about the beliefs of others. If Smith believes that Mobil Oil will persuade others that a "sheer redistribution of income" is bad, he must go along. If Mobil Oil believes that people will believe that a redistribution of income, à la Léon Blum, promotes not only justice but also development, it must go along.[16]

Let me provide a more fleshed-out example. Suppose there are three groups, W, a net fiscal contributor, and P_1 and P_2, net fiscal beneficiaries, respectively, of programs 1 and 2. W's announce that they want to pay lower taxes. P_1's figure that if W's pay lower taxes and P_2's continue to get their benefits, it will be at their cost. P_1's can then either ally with W's against P_2's or with P_2's against W's. The crucial belief is whether P_1's think that P_2's will cooperate with them or with W's. If each of the P's expects that the other would come to their help in the case W's want to reduce their contribution, the equilibrium will entail no reduction of programs; if either of the P's thinks the other would not help them, the W's can in two steps reduce both programs. (The formal structure of this game is discussed by Weingast 1994.)

XIII

To begin concluding, let me posit two facts. One is the Mobil Oil ad. The second is that many Americans today have lower incomes than they had in 1978 and yet they appear to support beliefs, incarnated in politicians and implemented in policies, that made them worse off. My question was whether there exists a causal connection between these two facts: "Why do masses of people support ideas that made them worse off than they could be?"[17]

I think that there is such a connection and that this connection is established and maintained by a self-interested manipulation of public opinion, but that this manipulation is distinct from the indoctrination described earlier. I sought to provide a nonmentalistic account of ideological domination, what Ferejohn and Satz (1993) would have considered an "externalist" theory. Different equilibria can be sustained by different mutually consistent beliefs. And the crucial beliefs, it turned out, are not one's own "technical beliefs" but one's expectations about the technical beliefs of others. Ideological domination is thus established in my story not by duping individuals about objective causal relations between an individual action and its consequences for one's own welfare but by manipulating mutual expectations, the theories isolated individuals have about the beliefs of others.

153

Technical beliefs must be difficult to manipulate.[18] They are true or false and individual experience is a source of independent knowledge about their validity.[19] But equilibrium beliefs are endogenous: they are true only if they are shared and individuals have little direct knowledge about the beliefs of others. In my account, everyone holds true technical beliefs: Joe Smith in our coordination game knows correctly that he would have been better off under another equilibrium, and he knows correctly that if he does not go along with the Mobil Oil message he will be worse off than under either equilibrium. What he does not know is which equilibrium will prevail. This he cannot know a priori: this is not an objective datum but an endogenous effect of deliberation. If he believes that Mobil Oil can convince others, he must go along; if he believes that Léon Blum can, he must not. Such beliefs are thus not subject to validation through everyday experience but call for experiments, mental or perhaps political. They thus appear easier to manipulate.

What does matter in my story is not whether Joe Smith believes Mobil Oil but whether he expects others to believe Mobil Oil. What is prior to this game are beliefs about who can be a credible Stackelberg leader: this is the position that Mobil Oil claims with "Corporate earnings have to rise to levels substantially above those of the recent years if our country is not to get into even deeper trouble," and "only profitable private businesses can make the capital investments that produce economic growth and jobs and tax revenues." If Joe Smith expects others to believe this, he is stuck, even if he thinks that Mobil Oil will take the money and run with it to Venezuela.

I could go on, since an important question remains open: can we, as observers, predict whether Mobil Oil will prevail? I think we can. (a) Because private control over investment decisions gives firms control over the future of the entire society, business is in a privileged position in conditioning everyone's interests on their own (Lindblom 1977; Przeworski and Wallerstein 1988). (b) Because individuals can communicate only via mass media and access to them is to a large degree regulated by money and education, chances to coordinate beliefs are unequally distributed. (c) Because individuals do not know who thinks what and are uncertain what and whom to believe, they must use heuristics to assess the credibility of the conflicting claims to which they are exposed and these heuristics have an independent causal effect.[20]

I also think that my account of deliberation explains the crucial role of identity in the transmission of information. What matters in coordinating beliefs is not just what they are but who holds them: what the beliefs are of people "like me." Gramsci tells a story of a city slicker who speaks to an assembly of peasants. The orator presents arguments that appear convincing, but the peasants do not believe him because they vaguely recall that "one of them," a peasant, once argued to the contrary. "Identity" thus plays a role in deliberation. But I am not sure which way it cuts. Perhaps hearing "one of us" is more persuasive, but we also have evidence that people accept the authority of those they view as superior: "they" can know better.

I still have one caveat to address.

XIV

Does all of the above imply that individuals are not the best judges of their interests?[21] I want to hide behind "democratic skepticism," a principle that says, "When you think others are wrong, convince but do not override." There is little in this essay that I am certain about: I know that those of a different political persuasion will just dismiss my problem with the claim that the American people hold beliefs that are in fact good for them. Since I know no objective way of resolving this, albeit empirical, controversy, the only datum is what people actually do. I am prepared to claim that individual beliefs are endogenous with regard to the distribution of income, with regard to political institutions, and with regard to the mechanisms that regulate the access of money to political institutions. Hence, I believe that if these conditions changed, beliefs on the basis of which people act in politics would also change. But endogenous beliefs cannot be used to make normative evaluations of counterfactual states of the world (Przeworski 1991: 101–2).

In turn, I fail to see why deliberation would induce legitimacy.[22] Deliberation coordinates beliefs and locks individuals into equilibria. But these equilibria have distributional consequences: the idea that majority rule is just an expedient substitute for unanimity should be stored in the archives of eighteenth-century thought. Indeed, these equilibria can be collectively suboptimal even by the Pareto criterion. Individuals are locked into such equilibria, unable to deviate. But it does not mean that they do not know that they could be better off.

Notes

1. Not long ago I participated in a meeting in which no one disagreed with the recommendation of a committee and yet two persons voted against it in a secret ballot.
2. This sentence is a paraphrase of Condorcet ([1785] 1986:22): "Il s'agit, dans une loi qui n'a pas été votée unanimement, de soumettre des hommes à une opinion qui n'est pas la leur, ou à une décision qu'ils croient contraire à leur intérêt. . . ."
3. The only example of deliberation I could find in Cohen's text is a reference to the principles of justice that are compatible with the ideal of deliberative democracy.
4. Note that I do not dispute that people can be induced to change their views about desirable goals (which Knight and Johnson [1992] do), only that public discussion is often couched in terms of deliberation about goals.
5. In the experimental literature, the distinction seems to be between "evidence" information, which concerns facts relevant to the matter to be decided, and "opinion information," which concerns other people's positions or votes (Hastie 1986: 132).
6. Manin (1987: 350) argues that "during political deliberation, individuals acquire new perspectives not only with respect to possible solutions, but also with regard to their own preferences." Yet it is not clear whether he has in mind some basic preferences or only those induced by beliefs.
7. This assertion is neutral with regard to the issue of whether individuals should use their information directly or, à la Austen-Smith and Banks (1994), anticipate the fact that their vote makes a difference only when it is pivotal.
8. Some experimental evidence, reviewed by Hastie (1986: 148), indicates, however, that when two subjects were paired, one with the correct and the other with the incorrect answer to a question, "if the correct individual was very confident of his or her judgment, the pair was likely to succeed in solving the problem. However, if the incorrect individual was more confident, the pair tended to fail."
9. See Przeworski and Wallerstein (1982).
10. McKelvey and Ordeshook (1986) as well as Miller (1986) argue, in different ways, that the absolute level of information does not affect the quality of collective decisions. But there is a caveat: "provided some strong symmetry conditions hold with regard to the resources of such [interest] groups" (McKelvey and Ordershook 1986: 909), "Of course, this optimistic conclusion cannot be sustained if there are substantial inequalities. . . ." (Miller 1986: 191).

11. Elster (1985: 487–90) also interprets "fetishized" knowledge as local knowledge.

12. In Aumann's model observers may have true knowledge of the entire system, but if outcomes are strategically interdependent, each participant must anticipate the beliefs of other participants about his or her beliefs about the system. And if I suspect that others do not know that I have correct knowledge of the system, then my knowledge as an observer will not be a valid guide to my actions.

13. Gramsci (1971), for example, says at one point, "For *the individual workers,* the junction between the requirements of technical development and the interests of the ruling class is 'objective' " (202; emphasis added). From the individual point of view it appears that social organization of production is necessitated by technological requirements.

14. Note that the only possibility of change I am entertaining is one of beliefs, not of basic preferences. Altruism would do it.

15. This is one story of inertial inflation. It is motivated by the observation of one of the authors of this theory, Luiz Carlos Bresser Pereira, who told me that in Brazil the rate of inflation was higher in the price-taking than in the price-making sectors.

16. These are "warnings" rather than "threats" in Elster's (no date: 23) language, but they are "once-removed" warnings: the claim is not "If you do this, I will be forced to . . . ," but "You will be left alone by the action of third persons." I am not sure that such warnings fit the dichotomy between "arguing" and "bargaining" or, in Vanberg and Buchanan's (1989: 58) language, "agreement as compromise versus agreement as truth-judgement." They constitute claims that have a truth-value ex post but are indeterminate ex ante: whether they are true depends on whether they are believed.

17. I have not studied the transformations of public opinion concerning economic issues, and I may be unduly influenced by the Republican claims about the mandate they received in elections. According to the data summarized by the *New York Times,* there has been little transformation in voting patterns over the past decade. Hence, perhaps what has changed are the beliefs of the median voter but not of the mass of citizens.

18. Experimental evidence summarized by Hastie (1986) shows that when the validity of a solution to an experimental problem can be easily demonstrated (such problems are called "Eureka brainteasers"), truth will win in a group discussion. When, however, solutions are difficult to demonstrate, member status or role and the confidence with which the member holds an opinion will influence others. As Hastie remarks, there is strangely little experimental research in which

individuals must pool private, nonredundant information: a situation one would expect to find frequently in natural settings. In turn, Panning's (1986) summary of knowledge about information pooling in nonexperimental settings has nothing to say.

19. I once took a taxi ride from O'Hare Airport to Hyde Park with a driver who, on finding that I am a professor, pitied me for having to read books. The only book he read was the Bible and, he said, "Everything this book says is true." But then, as we were passing the Sears Tower, he corrected himself: "Everything except the story of the Tower of Babel. If God had confounded the tongues of those who were trying to construct the Tower of Babel, he certainly would have done it for the Sears Tower, which is much, much higher."

20. I have in mind such rules as: "Make others better off when it is costless to me," "Discount purely selfish appeals," "Think about the future," "Be careful of plunging into the dark," "Do not trust what you cannot understand." Manin (1987: 358) observes, for example, "In order to increase its support, each party has an interest in showing that its point of view is *more general* than the others." Elster (no date: 13) cities impartiality as a persuasive attribute of arguments.

21. Bernard Manin pushed me to confront this implication.

22. This is perhaps the claim most frequently made with regard to deliberation. It is reviewed skeptically by Knight and Johnson (1992).

References

Althusser, Luis. 1970. *For Marx*. New York: Vintage Books.

　　1971. "Ideology and Ideological State Apparatuses." In *Lenin and Philosophy*. New York: Monthly Review Press.

Anderson, Perry. 1977. "The Antinomies of Antonio Gramsci." *New Left Review* 100: 5–78.

Ash, S. E. 1952. *Social Psychology*. Engelwood Cliffs, N.J.: Prentice-Hall.

Aumann, Robert. 1987. "Correlated Equilibrium as an Expression of Bayesian Rationality." *Econometrica* 55: 1–18.

Austen-Smith, David. 1990. "Credible Debate Equilibria." *Social Choice and Welfare* 7: 75–93.

　　1992. "Strategic Models of Talk in Political Decision Making." *International Political Science Review* 16: 45–58.

Austen-Smith, David, and Jeffrey S. Banks. 1994. "Information Aggregations, Rationality and the Condorcet Jury Theorem." Unpublished manuscript, University of Rochester.

Becker, Gary S. 1983. "A Theory of Competition Among Interest Groups for Political Influence." *Quarterly Journal of Economics* 98: 371–400.

Boudon, Raymond. 1994. *The Art of Self-Persuasion*. Cambridge: Polity Press.

Cohen, Joshua. 1989. "The Economic Basis of Deliberative Democracy." *Social Philosophy & Policy* 6: 25–50.

1993. "Moral Pluralism and Political Consensus." In David Copp, Jean Hampton, and John Roemer (eds.), *The Idea of Democracy*. Cambridge University Press, 270–191.

Condorcet. [1785] 1986. "Essai sur l'application de l'analyse a la probabilité des décisions rendues a la pluralité des voix." In *Sur les élections et autres textes. Textes choisis et revus par Olivier de Bernon*. Paris: Fayard.

Elster, Jon. 1985. *Making Sense of Marx*. Cambridge University Press.

No date. "Strategic Uses of Argument." Unpublished manuscript, University of Chicago.

Enelow, James M., and Melvin J. Hinich. 1984. *The Spatial Theory of Voting: An Introduction*. Cambridge: Cambridge University Press.

Ferejohn, John, and Debra Satz. 1993. "Rational Choice and Social Theory." Unpublished manuscript, Stanford University.

Gramsci, Antonio. 1971. *Prison Notebooks*. Ed. Quntin Hoare and Geoffrey Nowell Smith. New York: International Publishers.

Grofman, Bernard, and Guillermo Owen (eds.). 1986. *Information Pooling and Group Decision Making*. Greenwich, Conn.: JAI Press.

Hastie, Reid. 1986. "Experimental Evidence on Group Accuracy." In Bernard Grofman and Guillermo Owen (eds.). *Information Pooling and Group Decision Making*. Greenwich, Conn.: JAI Press, 126–66.

Kautsky, Karl. 1971. *The Class Struggle*. New York: Norton.

Knight, Jack, and James Johnson. 1992. "Aggregation and Deliberation: On the Possibility of Democratic Legitimacy." Unpublished manuscript, Washington University and University of Rochester.

Ladha, Krishna K. 1992. "The Condorcet Jury Theorem, Free Speech, and Correlated Votes." *American Journal of Political Science* 36: 617–34.

Lindblom, Charles E. 1977. *Politics and Markets: The World's Political-Economic System*. New York: Basic Books.

McKelvey, Richard D., and Peter C. Ordeshook. 1986. "Information, Electoral Equilibria, and the Democratic Ideal." *Journal of Politics* 48: 909–37.

Manin, Bernard. 1987. "On Legitimacy and Political Deliberation." *Political Theory* 15: 338–68.

1995. *Principes du gouvernement représentatif*. Paris: Calmann-Lévy.

Miller, Nicolas R. 1986. "Information, Electorates, and Democracy: Some Extensions and Interpretations of the Condorcet Jury Theorem." In Bernard Grofman and Guillermo Owen (eds.), *Information Pooling and Group Decision Making*. Greenwich, Conn.: JAI Press, 173–92.

Ohlin, Bertil. 1938. "Economic Progress in Sweden." *Annals of the American Academy of Political and Social Science* 197: 1–7.

Panning, William H. 1986. "Information Pooling and Group Decision Making in Nonexperimental Settings." In Bernard Grofman and Guillermo Owen (eds.), *Information Pooling and Group Decision Making*. Greenwich, Conn.: JAI Press, 159–66.

Peltzman, Sam. 1976. "Toward a More General Theory of Regulation." *Journal of Law and Economics* 19: 211–40.

Przeworski, Adam. 1985. *Capitalism and Social Democracy*. Cambridge University Press.

1991. *Democracy and the Market*. Cambridge University Press.

Przeworski, Adam, and Michael Wallerstein. 1982. "Democratic Capitalism at the Crossroads." *Democracy* 2: 52–68.

1988. "Structural Dependence of the State on Capital." *American Political Science Review* 82: 11–29.

Stigler, George. 1975. *The Citizen and the State: Essays on Regulation*. Chicago: University of Chicago Press.

Vanberg, Viktor, and James M. Buchanan. 1989. "Interests and Theories in Constitutional Choice." *Journal of Theoretical Politics* 1: 49–62.

Weingast, Barry. 1994. "The Political Foundations of Democracy and the Rule of Law." Paper presented at the Sixth Villa Colombella Seminar, Dijon, France, September 7–10.

Chapter Seven

Arguing for Deliberation: Some Skeptical Considerations

1. Introduction

Political theorists regularly lament the absence or the demise of deliberation within U.S. political institutions.[1] Would-be political reformers of various persuasions urge deliberation upon us.[2] Yet in their pleadings such theorists and reformers frequently invoke deliberation in an uncritical manner. They proceed as though the ways in which deliberation might operate and the effects we can expect of it are not just obvious, but attractively so.[3] I, in fact, find deliberation intuitively appealing. But intuition is insufficient and I am skeptical of uncritical invocations. I here explore some important points at which the intuitive attraction of deliberation needs to be supported by arguments.

Advocates of deliberation, usually tacitly, sometimes explicitly, presume that deliberation, because it centrally involves reasoned discussion, obviously is superior to other modes of political decision making. "The alternatives to deliberation," we are told in one forthright endorsement of this view, "are less moral or more authoritarian ways of dealing with fundamental moral conflicts concerning social justice, by a presumed cultural consensus, non-deliberative procedures, political deals, or threats of violence."[4] How are we to make sense of claims of this sort? My aim

This is a revised version of remarks originally prepared for the Workshop on Deliberative Democracy held at the University of Chicago April 28–30, 1995. My thinking on deliberation has been greatly influenced by my ongoing collaboration with Jack Knight. I thank Jack, David Austen-Smith, and Annabelle Lever for comments and discussion about the present essay. They, however, are absolved from responsibility for any errors or infelicities.

in this essay is to suggest that the answer to that question is not obvious.

The case for deliberative democracy, as typically formulated, comes in two main variants. First, there are exercises in retrieval, which seek to interpret or reinterpret existing legal and political arrangements in ways that highlight their tacit or suppressed deliberative dimensions.[5] Second, there are philosophical essays, which aim to clarify and justify deliberation as an ethical ideal.[6] Each approach has virtues. But each approach, almost by its very nature, *presumes* that deliberation is normatively and practically superior to aggregation, and so each neglects issues that are crucial to the task of formulating a persuasive defense of democratic deliberation. In particular, neither approach is, in my estimation, sufficiently attentive to issues of political and social theory. By this I mean that they do not treat deliberation primarily as a mode of political decision making.

In the remainder of this essay I suggest that extant arguments for deliberation are incomplete, and so, unpersuasive, in several important, related ways. They misconstrue the difficulties of "nondeliberative procedures" such as voting in what might be seen as self-serving ways (Section 2). They do not adequately justify the constraints they impose on the range of views admissible to arenas of deliberative decision making (Sections 3 and 4). And they do not specify adequately the mechanisms at work as parties to deliberation seek to persuade or convince one another (Section 5). I hope, by exploring these shortcomings, to arrive at a first approximation of what an adequate argument for deliberation might look like.[7] I offer a sketch of such an argument in the conclusion (Section 6).

2. What Is Wrong with Nondeliberative Procedures? Aggregation

Deliberation, most of its defenders will agree, is, in practical terms, incomplete. Hence, we are told that it need "not result in unanimity or even consensus."[8] As a result, what Gutmann terms "non-deliberative procedures," specifically aggregation devices, will be an unavoidable component of any democratic institutional arrangement.[9] Advocates of deliberation nevertheless tend to be deeply suspicious of political arrangements that rely exclusively or even predominantly on the aggregation of preferences or interests. They commonly suppose that, by comparison with deliberation, such arrangements lack the "moral resources" necessary to legitimate whatever collective decisions they generate.[10]

Cass Sunstein clearly articulates this complaint. Invoking Kenneth Arrow, he writes:

> To be sure, there are notorious difficulties in the claim that political outcomes can actually reflect the "public will." It is doubtful that private desires or even aspirations can be well-aggregated through the process of majority rule. Even if a process of aggregation were possible, it would not be entirely desirable in light of the broader goals of deliberation in producing reasoned agreement rather than simple aggregation.[11]

Sunstein makes two points in this passage. First, as social choice theorists have shown, under specifiable conditions, all known aggregation procedures suffer from important, unavoidable, endogenous difficulties.[12] Hence, aggregation may on its own terms be practically flawed, normatively objectionable, or both. Second, even if these difficulties might somehow be mitigated, deliberation, because it aims to inform our collective decisions with "reasoned" argument, remains normatively superior to the "simple aggregation" of expressed preferences or interests. Sunstein, however, moves far too quickly here. He invokes Arrow carelessly. And he presumes rather than demonstrates that, compared with aggregation, deliberation is normatively attractive. As a consequence, Sunstein unintentionally both subverts his own qualms about aggregation and accentuates several unresolved difficulties with common efforts to establish the comparative normative superiority of deliberation.

Recall Arrow's argument. He demonstrates that there exists no aggregation mechanism that simultaneously conforms to a set of several relatively unobjectionable normative criteria and generates coherent collective decisions. For present purposes it is important to recall in particular the first of Arrow's conditions, namely what has come to be called "unrestricted domain." This condition disallows any prior constraint on the content of the preferences or interests that a proposed aggregation mechanism must accommodate. So, for example, if we wish to reach a collective decision on some matter of U.S. race relations (and restricting ourselves solely to living, public figures), the preferences of, say, Larry Bird, Bill Bradley, Carol Mosely-Braun, Pat Buchanan, Bill Cosby, Mario Cuomo, David Duke, Louis Farrakan, Mark Furman, Lani Guinier,

Jesse Jackson, Michael Jordon, Nancy Kassebaum, Corretta Scott King, Stephen King, Spike Lee, Rush Limbaugh, Toni Morrison, Walter Mosley, Joyce Carol Oates, Colin Powell, Patricia Schroeder, and Clarence Thomas – *whatever* the substance of their preferences might be – must all be admissible.[13]

The first thing to notice is that the "notorious difficulties" that follow from the work of Arrow and other social choice theorists for any assessment of aggregative arrangements diminish considerably if we relax or lift the requirement of unrestricted domain.[14] The "impossibility" that Arrow demonstrated emerges from the task of designing a collective choice procedure that can simultaneously produce coherent outcomes and conform to all of the stipulated normative conditions. If we eliminate one of the conditions, we eliminate the impossibility, and, as a result, we eliminate a major basis for skepticism of the sort that Sunstein and other advocates of deliberation voice regarding the viability of aggregative arrangements. So, in the case at hand, relaxing or eliminating the condition of unrestricted domain would go a significant distance toward mitigating such skepticism.[15]

I am not concerned here, however, to examine the relative advantages and disadvantages of any of the wide variety of available aggregation mechanisms.[16] I wish instead to suggest that this brief discussion of Arrow highlights how common defenses of deliberation are severely hampered by two related difficulties.

First, advocates of deliberation operate with something of a double standard. While they regularly invoke Arrow's "impossibility" result to expose the problems associated with aggregation mechanisms, they do not subject their preferred deliberative methods to similarly exacting standards.[17] Instead of insisting that deliberative arrangements too must meet some stringent condition of access analogous to "unrestricted domain," advocates of deliberation regularly and, as I argue in Sections 3 and 4, unjustifiably, impose substantial prior constraints either on the behavior of parties to deliberation or on the range of views admissible to relevant deliberative arenas.

Second, having countenanced such constraints on admissibility, advocates of deliberation nevertheless still have considerable difficulty establishing the normative appeal of deliberation relative to aggregation. In particular, they have yet to establish adequately how deliberation derives normative force from the sort of "reasoned" argument in terms of which it is commonly defined. This is

especially important insofar as advocates of deliberation justify restrictions on the domain of admissible views by references to some
standard of reasonable behavior or discussion. In combination
these difficulties provide ample grounds for skepticism about even
the strongest current arguments for democratic deliberation.

3. Reasoned Argument

I start with a provocation. Consider the following, troubling
doubt voiced by Karl Mannheim:

> Political discussion possesses a character fundamentally different
> from academic discussion. It seeks not only to be in the right but
> also to demolish the basis of its opponent's social and intellectual
> existence. Political discussion, therefore, penetrates more pro-
> foundly into the existential foundation of thinking than the kind of
> discussion which thinks only in terms of a few selected "points of
> view" and considers only the "theoretical relevance" of an argu-
> ment. Political conflict, since it is from the very beginning a ration-
> alized form of the struggle for social predominance, attacks the
> social status of the opponent, his public prestige and his self-
> confidence. It is difficult to decide in this case whether the subli-
> mation or substitution of discussion for the older weapons of
> conflict, the direct use of force and oppression, really constituted a
> fundamental improvement in human life. Physical repression is, it
> is true, harder to bear externally, but the will to psychic annihila-
> tion, which took its place in many instances, is perhaps even more
> unbearable. It is therefore no wonder that particularly in this
> sphere every theoretical refutation was gradually transformed into
> a much more fundamental attack on the whole life-situation of the
> opponent, and that with the destruction of his theories one hoped
> also to undermine his social position.[18]

Mannheim here pretty clearly sanitizes academic discussion at
least as I have experienced it. He also obviously is writing in response to the particular circumstances of interwar German politics.
Mannheim nevertheless captures an important feature of much political discussion, namely that it frequently involves parties who
seek to challenge one another at a quite "fundamental," even "existential," level.

Advocates of deliberation conveniently never consider misgivings of this sort. The depth of this neglect becomes especially apparent when we turn to demands that the behavior or political

views of parties to deliberation, as a subset of political discussion, be "reasonable." A good first example is the practice of insisting that deliberation be governed by something like what John Rawls terms "precepts of reasonable discussion."[19] Such precepts, on Rawls's account, enjoin parties to political deliberation from accusing "one another of self- or group interest, prejudice or bias, and of such deeply entrenched errors as ideological blindness and delusion." Charges such as this amount, according to Rawls, to "a declaration of intellectual war." We must instead be prepared to countenance deep, perhaps insurmountable, disagreement while at the same time attributing to others "a certain good faith."

There are several reasons why one might object to this view. First, political actors may, in fact, be driven by self-interest, blinded by prejudice, or deluded by ideology. It very plausibly is among the desirable features of democratic deliberation that it allows participants to raise this possibility, to challenge those to whom the charge in fact applies, and to do so publicly.[20] Thus, if, in a deliberative decision-making process, a participant presses claims that, knowingly or not, are prejudiced, ideologically biased, or unjustifiably self-interested, others must be allowed not only to contest those claims but, Rawls's precepts notwithstanding, to characterize them as prejudiced, ideological, or selfish as part of their reason for so doing.

Second, there surely are points when "unreasonable" factors such as anger, frustration, humor, fear, joy, and humiliation quite reasonably and justifiably enter political argument. Should political actors motivated by such emotions be disallowed, for that reason, from participating in democratic deliberation? Should we ground our vision of deliberation on the sort of conceptual gerrymandering that draws hard and fast boundaries between reason and emotion when such boundaries likely would banish not only obstreperous demands and angry shouts but tears and laughter from the deliberative arena?[21]

Finally, consider the sort of political practice that might be disallowed under this sort of constraint. Civil disobedience, for example, seems, and indeed often is designed to be, paradigmatically "unreasonable." But it surely is plausible to see civil disobedience as part of an ongoing process of political deliberation. "Outrageous" and "unreasonable" acts of civil disobedience might, by demonstrating the depth of grievances or of outrage, prompt relevant political actors to reconsider and perhaps revise an otherwise binding collective decision.[22]

These objections suggest that there are deep problems with the "precepts of reasonable discussion" that Rawls advances. Yet his precepts confront a still deeper problem. The demeanor that those precepts characterize would certainly be conducive to reasonableness and civility. Even if parties to deliberation conform to them, however, Rawls's precepts do not ultimately mitigate the basic objective of political discussion as Mannheim depicts it. As I noted earlier, many advocates of deliberation acknowledge that it need not generate agreement or consensus. Once we relinquish the notion that deliberation ought to aim at, and is likely to generate, consensus, however complex, and see political disagreement as necessarily endemic to political debate and discussion, the extent to which we behave diplomatically or otherwise will not alter our ultimate aim. We still will be challenging not just our opponent's values, interests, or preferences, but the broader understandings and commitments – in short, the worldview – that sustain them.[23]

Consider, for example, political discussion in a society where some parties defend and others dispute the claim of members of some one among the society's constituent cultural, racial, or ethnic groups or religious denominations to a disproportionate share of the society's available material resources.[24] Or consider political discussions within a society about which sorts of political protections and opportunities are to be afforded to whom and under what circumstances.[25] The argument in either case is unlikely to revolve simply around the respective distributive interests or policy preferences of the contending parties. It also almost certainly will require those defending various positions to contest and hopefully subvert the basic vision of the world that sanctions competing claims.

Parties to the debate in the United States over abortion, for example, do not simply challenge the interests or dispute the theories of others with whom they disagree. They do, surely, do that.[26] But, more fundamentally, they subscribe to different worldviews and so they differ over the very conceptions of persons, of motherhood, and of the place of women in society more generally. It is *this* terrain upon which the entire debate proceeds.[27] The aim of each side is thus to challenge the worldview and, in so doing, to undermine "the whole life-situation" of those who defend competing positions.

This amounts to precisely the sort of "intellectual war" that Rawls hopes to excise from, and that Mannheim fears is endemic to, political discussion.

4. "Reasonable Pluralism"

Advocates of deliberation might object here. They might claim that while Mannheim characterizes political discussion generally, deliberation, as a mode of collective decision making, is characterized in the first instance by the particular sort of discussion that it involves. Deliberation on this view specifically consists of *arguments* that require parties to give and respond to *reasons*.[28] They might therefore seek to insulate deliberation from Mannheim's misgivings about political discussion by insisting that in order to be admissible to relevant deliberative arenas, political views must be "reasonable." Here I have in mind those who, again like Rawls, argue that public deliberation need not be responsive to "the fact of pluralism" per se but only to "the fact of reasonable pluralism."[29]

Such claims, in my estimation, prejudge in an unjustifiable way the question of which sorts of argument or value are legitimately admissible to the process of political deliberation and debate. A good example is recent work by Amy Gutmann.[30] Here the demand is not simply that the parties to deliberation behave with a certain civil demeanor. Rather, the demand is for some pre-political normative criteria to which parties to deliberation subscribe and that enable them to recognize as reasonable some range of possible claims or positions that they do not merely tolerate, but treat with respect. Other claims and views are inadmissible. So, on Gutmann's account, "actual deliberation" consists in "the give and take of argument that is respectful of *reasonable* differences."[31]

Mutual respect entails in particular ways both "integrity" in advancing one's own position and "magnanimity" in characterizing the positions of others.[32] This, however, leaves poorly defined the criteria we should use to determine what constitutes a position that is "reasonable" and hence deserving of respect.[33] I approach this issue indirectly by trying to ascertain the sort of claim or position that parties to deliberation might deem "unreasonable." Conveniently, Gutmann obliges: "There is no reasonable account of social justice among human beings as we know them that would justify routine murder of innocents, arbitrary arrests, systematic deception, and other common political practices."[34] It seems safe to say that, from this perspective, any view that endorses slavery would be "unreasonable" and so inadmissible to deliberative arenas.[35] This judgment, as I hope now to show, creates difficulties for the effort of defending deliberation.

In arguments against slavery, as in the contemporary U.S. debate over abortion, we encounter not just the interests, policy preferences, or even moral values of contending parties, but the sort of broader commitments and understandings that I earlier termed a worldview. The relation between masters and slaves is marked by three features: (a) an extreme asymmetry of power, (b) the abrupt, involuntary, and irreversible isolation of the slave from his family and community of origin, and (c) the pervasive dishonor visited on the slave.[36] The slave's distinctive, extreme powerlessness with respect to the master emerges from the fact that paradigmatically slavery constitutes a reprieve from death, usually of captives in war, but also in instances of those either convicted of capital crimes or rendered vulnerable by extreme physical or economic hardship. The reprieve, however, is conditional upon the slave continuously and manifestly yielding to the power of the master.

On this account, "the slave, however recruited" is "socially dead" and has "no socially recognized existence" independent of the master. In particular, the slave is denied ties to present or future communities or to any cultural heritage and so is "truly a genealogical isolate."[37] The crucial point here is that the slave's status is part of a symbolically constructed worldview.[38] Masters deploy symbolic practices to mark slaves as "socially dead" and situate them "outside the game of honor." Hence, "social death" initiates, and the outward markings of that status complete, the explanation for why slaves submit to, and uninvolved third parties accept without protest, what in other circumstances would amount to institutionalized evil, cruel, unjust, or inhumane treatment. In slave societies, symbolically marked categories of common sense define slaves as the sort of entity to whom notions of cruelty, injustice, and so on simply do not apply.[39]

The practice of slavery so characterized poses a deep dilemma for those who, like Gutmann, seek to identify legitimate participants in democratic deliberation by categorizing claims as reasonable or unreasonable. On the one hand, they might hold that anyone who sincerely advocates slavery is manifestly unreasonable and hence not a legitimate party to deliberation. We might, according to this line of argument, be required to tolerate the views of those who defend the practice of slavery but we need not respect them in the sense that we allow them access to relevant deliberative arenas.

This response would tightly and perhaps unduly circumscribe the domain of deliberation. It would remove disagreements over deep moral issues such as slavery – and others, like abortion – from the political agenda because disagreement over such issues trades not merely on competing interests or values but on conflicting worldviews. Deliberation, then, would be impotent in the face both of what might (erroneously) be thought of as anachronistic examples like slavery and of the whole range of pressing issues raised by cultural pluralism in modern societies. For Gutmann in particular, and for many other advocates of deliberation, this would be an unacceptable price to pay. Her essays are explicitly, and in my view rightly, aimed at expanding the range and types of issue that we deem susceptible to democratic deliberation. She presents her arguments as correctives to those liberals who advocate strategies of "preclusion," which would remove issues from the democratic agenda.[40]

On the other hand, those who adopt the strategy of defining "reasonable pluralism" as a starting point for deliberation might admit defenders of slavery to relevant deliberative arenas and there attempt to persuade them that their position was deeply unjust. To do so they would have to challenge, and, in order to succeed, ultimately subvert, the defenders' basic worldview. This is because, within that worldview, slaves are socially dead and so not subjects of either justice or injustice. Consequently, in order to persuade defenders of slavery that that institution is unjust, it would be necessary to challenge their worldview in such a way that they rearranged the basic categories of personhood and moral agency within which they operated. In short, it would be necessary to attack defenders of slavery in precisely the "existential" manner that initially prompted Mannheim's apprehensions about political debate and discussion.

5. The Force of the Better Argument

Once again, advocates of deliberation might object. Deliberation, they might claim, evades Mannheim's strictures regarding political discussion because there is some feature of democratic deliberation, or, more specifically, about the way that language enters into it, that he overlooks and that, in addition, in some sense either induces or embodies reasonable discussion. This line of argument focuses our attention on neither the civility or otherwise of behavior nor the reasonableness or otherwise of claims, but on the mechanisms at work when parties to deliberation seek to persuade or convince one another. There are at least two possible classes of mechanism here. In my estimation both founder, albeit in different ways, because they trade upon inadequate characterizations of the "force" of the better argument.

First, the process of public debate in a deliberative forum may itself induce parties to adopt "reasonable" commitments or advance "reasonable" claims. This is among the ways that Sunstein, for example, believes that "public deliberation should produce better public decisions."[41] Consider two ways in which this might occur.

In the first place, public debate might induce parties to adopt reasonable positions or advance reasonable claims for straightforwardly strategic reasons.[42] This does not imply that there is no such thing as impartial argument in politics. I return to this possibility later. Even if we grant that political actors sometimes articulate principled arguments in an impartial manner, it nevertheless may be quite difficult empirically to distinguish between a speaker who sincerely invokes some principle and one who does so because he deems such an appeal to be strategically advantageous. Thus, when I announce, "It's not the money, it's the principle of thing!" I may be hoping to impress those with whom I am arguing with my resolve and unwillingness to compromise. I am trying to establish a credible commitment that might prompt others to concede rather than continue to argue in the face of my "principled" intransigence.[43] By contrast, I may wish, in the hope of securing a favorable agreement, to invoke principle in order to afford my opponent an honorable excuse for capitulating to my demands. In neither case does the force of the better argument, when deployed in this way for strategic advantage, bear the substantial normative weight that advocates of deliberation impose upon it.[44]

A second, similar line of argument might avoid this difficulty by offering an account of how, over time, those who invoke some principle for strategic reasons might sincerely come to embrace it. On this view public debate might generate psychological pressures toward "self-censorship." These pressures deter speakers from advancing claims that might be deemed "unreasonable" because they reflect a speaker's self-interest or because they articulate positions they suspect others consider morally objectionable. Such self-censorship expresses not so much genuine conviction as anticipation of disapproval or reproach. Yet, over time, something like dissonance reduction might induce such parties to actually adopt "reasonable" positions to which they earlier paid only lip service. This amounts to what Elster calls "the civilizing force of hypocrisy."[45]

The difficulty is that this view, while perhaps empirically plausible, trades on the existence and functioning of psychological mechanisms that first induce actors to engage in self-censorship and eventually cause them to embrace the resultant views. Over time, such mechanisms "might even bring about a transformation of preferences and values, simply by making venal or self-regarding justifications seem off-limits."[46] But this sort of causal process hardly affords the robust moral resources to which advocates of deliberation aspire. It does not so much generate a "reasoned agreement" as induce a conformity that is at once rather shallow and normatively suspect.[47] In cases of this sort what passes for the force of the better argument remains subject to Mannheim's strictures and, hence, does not afford a justifiable way of constraining the range of views admissible to the deliberative arena.[48]

Consider now the second class of mechanisms that could potentially animate democratic deliberation. The "strategic uses of argument" that I just canvassed are, after all, admittedly parasitic on the existence of and demand for impartial argument in politics.[49] This admission nevertheless leaves crucial questions unanswered. How widespread a role does impartial argument play in political debate? And what are the mechanisms at work in such argument? If advocates of deliberation could argue (a) that impartial claims are, even tacitly, quite widespread in public debate and (b) that such claims are animated by mechanisms other than the strategic calculation and attendant psychological pressures discussed earlier, they could simultaneously evade Mannheim's doubts about political discussion and justify constraints on the sort of views admissible to deliberative forums.

Here we might follow Habermas and argue that democratic deliberation embodies something like his concept of communicative reason.[50] A number of social and political theorists have recently adopted this approach.[51] On this view, parties to democratic deliberation necessarily rely on communicative reason and, by raising and challenging the validity claims (to truth, normative rightness, and sincerity) that constitute the pragmatic presupposition of all linguistically mediated interaction, aim to establish a shared understanding of the context of their interaction. In so doing they eschew strategic behavior and so, in principle at least, might avoid Mannheim's apprehensions. For Habermas, the crucial, categorical distinction here is between strategic and communicative action. The former is oriented toward success, at purposively inducing others to behave in particular ways. The latter aims at the cooperative search for mutual understanding. Whereas strategic action coordinates social interaction by external influence or force, communicative reason does so via "consent," where this involves arriving at an agreement that is justifiable solely by reasons in light of generalizable interests of the relevant parties.

The problem remains, however, of specifying the ways that language operates to coordinate social and political interaction. This perhaps is not so preposterous a prospect as skeptics might think.[52] Yet existing arguments are far from persuasive. In particular, Habermas does not adequately defend his categorical distinction between communicative and strategic action.[53] Without a cogent argument on this general point talk about "deliberative rationality," "communicative democracy," and so on, remains significantly incomplete, as much a promissory note as a warranted commitment. Such talk does not currently afford the basis for a persuasive reply to Mannheim.

6. Arguing for Deliberation

To this point I have been more or less relentlessly critical. My intent, however, is not entirely negative. As I mentioned at the outset, I find democratic deliberation intuitively attractive. So while I have been concerned to identify and explore deficiencies in what I consider to be some of the strongest extant arguments for deliberative democracy, my hope is that the exercise of highlighting those deficiencies will help to illuminate ways in which we might sketch a more persuasive defense of democratic deliberation. In closing I offer a (clearly nonexhaustive) list of five broad challenges that a plausible case for deliberation must meet.

In the first place, a plausible argument for deliberation cannot be utopian in the sense that it makes heroic assumptions about participants.[54] Although there is danger in embracing a cynical "realism" about political agents, their capacities, and their motivations, any defense of democratic deliberation nevertheless must itself be reasonable in the sense of accommodating itself to current knowledge about political motivation and practical reasoning. It thus is unreasonable, in my estimation, to anticipate that deliberation will massively transform the preferences, capacities, or character of participants in normatively attractive ways.[55] Similarly, it is unreasonable to demand that parties to deliberation subscribe in advance to anything like Rawls's "precepts of reasonable discussion." Rather than making some such precepts a condition of entry into deliberation, it seems more reasonable to hope that, where it is successful, deliberation might engender "good faith" by enabling participants to develop greater understanding of and trust in both one another and the deliberative process itself.[56] We must, in any case, recognize that deliberation by no means guarantees any such development.

Second, a plausible argument for deliberation must not – in the effort to differentiate deliberation from bargaining – categorically exclude either self-interested claims or the conflicts that such claims might generate from the range of admissible topics that participants to deliberation might address.[57] Members of previously excluded groups, for example, typically demand entry into relevant decision-making arenas precisely because, as long as they remain excluded, their *interests* are not adequately considered.[58] There is no reason to think that this should be any less true of deliberative arrangements than, for instance, of electoral systems.

It is similarly easy to envision situations where self-interest-based claims are justified even among long-established participants in deliberation. Consider a common problem of public goods provision modeled in simple game-theoretic terms as a "chicken" interaction. Here two or more actors are in a situation where any one of them can supply the requisite level of a public good.[59] If no one provides the good, the consequences are disastrous for all. Each player nevertheless prefers that someone else perform the required task. Indeed, the equilibria in such a game involve outcomes in which some actor provides the public good while others exploit her cooperative activity. Faced with a strategic situation of this sort, any party to deliberative proceedings aimed at resolving it clearly could, with justification, object to being exploited in this way.[60] This sort of objection surely represents a justifiable response to predictable demands that some particular actor simply should sacrifice in the common interest. And if the group were to try to arrange some "fair" resolution (e.g., rotation of burdens over time), any such resolution would have normative force precisely because self-interest-based claims provide, as it were, a significant part of the normative scaffolding in terms of which fairness can be defined.

Third, we here run up against the need to specify the mechanisms at work when parties to deliberation advance arguments in the hope that they might persuade or convince one other. In strategic settings like the chicken game I just discussed, each actor has a strong incentive to establish a credible commitment that she will not provide the public good in question. However, this can generate a collectively disastrous dynamic in which all try to commit themselves to such a noncooperative strategy. How can this dynamic be avoided? Game theorists offer some small hope here. They have demonstrated that under a range of conditions and even when it does not directly affect the payoffs of relevant players, communication can, if not entirely eliminate, significantly constrain the sort of indeterminacy players confront in strategic interactions.[61] What game theorists lack, and what no other social or political theorists currently provide, is a robust account of the "force" of language in social and political interaction.[62] For reasons I have already given, this is especially troubling for advocates of democratic deliberation.

Fourth, a plausible account of democratic deliberation must include an account of the institutional forms that deliberative processes might take. In this regard, advocates of deliberation have produced provocative work on the role of secondary associations in a deliberative arrangement. But this work is incomplete in at least two ways. In the first place, it pays relatively little attention to the shape and operation of those "encompassing formal institutions organizing representation along territorial lines" within which secondary associations operate and from which they derive legal standing and power.[63] A plausible account of democratic deliberation requires a clearer understanding of how deliberative arrangements relate to such formal institutions.[64] As noted earlier advocates of deliberation typically concede that it need not end in agreement. We thus, at a minimum, require an account of how deliberative processes interact with nondeliberative decision-making procedures like voting.[65]

In the second place, defenses of "associational democracy" need a clearer understanding of how deliberative procedures themselves might operate within both secondary associations and more formal political institutions. Here again, results from social choice and game theory are instructive. These results suggest, among other things, (a) that the outcomes of aggregation are ambiguous because different methods of counting votes can generate dramatically different outcomes from the same initial profile of preferences and (b) that, as a result, not only are the outcomes of aggregation especially vulnerable to manipulation, but we typically are unable to differentiate outcomes produced by agenda control or strategic voting from those that are not.[66] Analogously, there is very good reason to suspect that the outcome of deliberation depends heavily upon the sequence in which participants speak and the point at which debate is terminated.[67] If different deliberative procedures generate widely different outcomes from the same initial range of views, deliberation is susceptible to objections comparable to those that have been leveled at aggregation mechanisms.

All of this has implications not only for how we might design deliberative institutional arrangements, but also for whether and how we consider the outcomes of deliberation to be legitimate. Specifically, the inevitable and consequential contingencies of the deliberative process subvert Rousseauian notions that an agreement reached via democratic deliberation, when one is, is legitimate because it somehow embodies a unique, coherent, independently ascertainable "general will" that, in turn, reflects "*the* common good." These same contingencies suggest that a plausible defense of deliberative democracy requires a more pragmatist approach. On this view any agreement reached through deliberation is necessarily conditional, tentative, and revisable. And any such agreement represents "*a* common good" that is fashioned rather than discovered by parties to the deliberative process and that is only as legitimate as that process itself. So a plausible case for democratic deliberation must treat deliberative procedures themselves, and not just the outcomes they generate, as tentative and revisable.

Finally, a plausible argument for deliberative democracy must include an account both of the sort of effects that we might anticipate from deliberation and of how we might justify those effects. It is simply not sufficient to insist that any outcome that does emerge from deliberation will be, in Sunstein's words, a "reasoned agreement." A plausible argument for deliberation, in short, would acknowledge that substantive agreement on preferences or values is neither practically realistic nor normatively appealing in a large, pluralist constituency. It would recognize that the demand for such agreement is too strong if we are looking to deliberation, at least in part, as a remedy for the practical shortcomings (e.g., the instability) of outcomes generated by aggregation mechanisms. All we require in this regard is that deliberation induce what are called single-peaked preferences. This would ensure a shared understanding among participants of what is at stake in a particular political conflict even if they continue to disagree over how best to resolve it.[68] In this sense a plausible argument for deliberation would make "reasonable pluralism," if it were possible, an outcome of, rather than a precondition for, democratic deliberation. And it would acknowledge that inducing such "reasonable pluralism" will frequently involve the sort of "fundamental attack" on competing worldviews that prompted Mannheim's apprehensions.

An argument of this sort may seem overly skeptical and, for that reason, may be treated as implausible by those who strive to retrieve the suppressed deliberative dimensions of our political arrangements or who seek a philosophical vindication of democratic deliberation as part of a "fundamental political ideal."[69] It would, however, bring into clearer focus, in ways that extant arguments for deliberation do not, how deliberation might function politically, as part of a democratic process of reaching legitimate, binding collective decisions.

Notes

1. This lament is clear, for instance, in the now-familiar writings of Ben Barber and Jane Mansbridge. For more recent examples in the context of U.S. politics see Jeffrey Abramson, *We the Jury* (New York: Basic Books, 1994), and Joseph Bessette, *The Mild Voice of Reason* (Chicago: University of Chicago Press, 1994). On the vicissitudes of deliberation in the theory and practice of representative institutions more generally, see Bernard Manin, "The Metamorphoses of Representative Government," *Economy and Society* 23 (1994): 133–71.
2. See, again in the context of U.S. politics, James Fishkin, *Democracy and Deliberation* (New Haven, Conn.: Yale University Press, 1991); Thomas Mann and Norman Ornstein, *Renewing Congress* (Washington, D.C.: AEI / Brookings Institution 1992); and Lani Guinier, *The Tyranny of the Majority* (New York: Free Press, 1994).
3. I explore some other aspects of this presumption elsewhere. See Jack Knight and James Johnson, "Aggregation and Deliberation: On the Possibility of Democratic Legitimacy," *Political Theory* 22 (1994): 277–97.

4. Amy Gutmann, "The Challenge of Multiculturalism in Political Ethics," *Philosophy & Public Affairs* 22 (1993): 171–206, at 202.

5. Here I have in mind, for example, Cass Sunstein, *Democracy and the Problem of Free Speech* (New York: Free Press, 1993).

6. Gutmann, "The Challenge of Multiculturalism," and Joshua Cohen, "Deliberation and Democratic Legitimacy," in A. Hamlin and P. Pettit (eds.), *The Good Polity* (Oxford: Basil Blackwell, 1989), 17–34, are representative here.

7. I have begun this task more systematically elsewhere. See Knight and Johnson, "Aggregation and Deliberation." See also Jack Knight and James Johnson, "What Sort of Equality Does Democratic Deliberation Require?" forthcoming in J. Bohman and W. Rehg (eds.), *Deliberative Democracy* (Cambridge, Mass.: MIT Press).

8. Sunstein, *Democracy and the Problem of Free Speech*, 247. See also Cohen, "Deliberation and Democratic Legitimacy," 23. For an argument that this is not simply a contingent feature of deliberation see Manin, "The Metamorphoses of Representative Government."

9. I set aside the possibility that political decisions might be made by lot. There are interesting possibilities here. See, e.g., Richard Mulgan, "Lot as a Democratic Device of Selection," *Review of Politics* 46 (1984): 539–60; Fredrik Engelstad, "The Assignment of Political Office by Lot," *Social Science Information* 28 (1989): 23–50; and Akhil Reed Amar, "Choosing Representatives by Lottery Voting," *Yale Law Journal* 93 (1984): 1283–1308. Yet I suspect that the random, arbitrary nature of lotteries is unlikely to inspire those advocates of deliberation who seek to inject greater reason into democratic arrangements.

10. I borrow the quoted phrase from Claus Offe and Ulrich Preuss, "Democratic Institutions and Moral Resources," in David Held (ed.), *Political Theory Today* (Stanford, Calif.: Stanford University Press), 143–71. Seyla Benhabib offers a recent example of this view. "A mere aggregation of majority preferences could not claim legitimacy because the basis on which the preferences of the minority were discounted could not be stated; neither could such a procedure claim rationality, because no grounds could be given as to why the aggregation of majority preferences would result in a better and more enlightened decision than conclusions reached by some other procedure." Seyla Benhabib, "Deliberative Rationality and Models of Democratic Legitimacy," *Constellations* 1 (1994): 26–52, at 29.

11. Sunstein, *Democracy and the Problem of Free Speech*, 244.

12. Kenneth Arrow, *Social Choice and Individual Values*, 2d ed. (New Haven, Conn.: Yale University Press, 1963). For a brief survey of subsequent work in social choice theory see Amartya Sen, "Social Choice," in *The New Palgrave: A Dictionary of Economics*, vol. 4 (London: Macmillan Press, 1987). I leave aside the complaint that aggregative ar-

rangements are susceptible to influence by exogenous factors (e.g., power, wealth), for it is by no means clear that deliberation is any less susceptible to such influence. So one who hopes to defend deliberation as normatively superior to aggregation must show that the latter is susceptible to internal problems to which the former is not.

13. Arrow, *Social Choice and Individual Values*, 23–4, 18.

14. Recall that Arrow devotes Chapters 6 and 7 of *Social Choice and Individual Values* to this possibility.

15. Eliminating the demand for unrestricted domain does not *ensure* a meaningful, rational collective outcome. It does, however, make such an outcome possible.

16. This terrain is mapped by the contributors to "Symposium: Economics of Voting," *Journal of Economic Perspectives* 9(1) (1995).

17. Elsewhere I explore at some length the difficulties involved in specifying normative constraints on deliberative arrangements analogous to the conditions of unrestricted domain, anonymity, and neutrality that social choice theorists impose in an effort to ensure procedural equality in collective decision-making processes; see Knight and Johnson, "What Sort of Equality?"

18. Karl Mannheim, *Ideology and Utopia* (1936) (New York: Harcourt Brace Jovanovich, 1985), 38.

19. John Rawls, "The Domain of the Political and Overlapping Consensus," *New York University Law Review* 64 (1989): 233–55, at 238–9.

20. This need not be an illiberal position. See Richard Sinopoli, "Thick-Skinned Liberalism: Redefining Civility," *American Political Science Review* 89 (1995): 612–20.

21. For qualms regarding such gerrymandering see Amelie Rorty, "Varieties of Rationality, Varieties of Emotion," *Social Science Information* 24 (1985): 343–53.

22. Jürgen Habermas, "Civil Disobedience: Litmus Test for the Democratic Constitutional State," *Berkeley Journal of Sociology* 30 (1985): 95–116.

23. My use of the notion of worldview draws upon Clifford Geertz, *The Interpretation of Cultures* (New York: Basic Books, 1973). I understand it to be a symbolically constituted, comprehensive, and more or less coherent conception of social and natural order – of the way the world is, the sorts of entities that it contains, and the ways that relevant actors expect those entities to behave.

Talk of the way that a worldview sustains an actor's interests, preferences, or values need not automatically make rationalists uneasy. "On a causal-instrumental view of rationality, our standards of rationality must depend on our view of the character of this world and upon our view of what we are like, with our capacities, powers, disabilities and weaknesses. . . . Our view of the world and of ourselves, and our notion of what counts as rational are in continual interplay." Robert

179

Nozick, *The Nature of Rationality* (Princeton, N.J.: Princeton University Press, 1993), 134–5.

24. This may, but need not, involve an assertion of narrow self-interest. It may involve the assertion of principled claims. Thus, treating people equally may require that we distribute resources differentially among a population. John Roemer, "A Pragmatic Theory of Responsibility for the Egalitarian Planner," *Philosophy and Public Affairs* 22 (1993): 146–66.

25. So, for example, issues of this sort arise when we ask whether or not a society should ascribe rights to *groups*. For various positions on this issue see, e.g., Will Kymlicka (ed.), *The Rights of Minority Cultures* (Oxford: Oxford University Press, 1995).

26. Two caveats. First, I do not deny that there are interests at stake in the abortion debate; I only deny that that is all that is at stake. Second, abortion may seem to be an extreme example, but it does not, I think, differ qualitatively from other such debates over pornography and free speech, economic regulation, or affirmative action. And, after all, I assume that we want deliberation to have purchase on burning issues of the day, over what Gutmann in the passage cited earlier refers to as "fundamental moral conflicts," and not just over relatively more tractable issues.

27. Kristin Luker, *Abortion and the Politics of Motherhood* (Berkeley: University of California Press, 1984), and Faye Ginsburg, *Contested Lives: The Abortion Debate in an American Community* (Berkeley: University of California Press, 1989). I have discussed this example at greater length elsewhere. See Jack Knight and James Johnson, "Deliberative Democracy and Cultural Pluralism," paper presented at the American Political Science Association Meetings, Washington, D.C., August 1993.

28. Cohen, "Deliberation and Democratic Legitimacy," 22, offers a forthright statement of this view. See also Knight and Johnson, "Aggregation and Deliberation," 285–6.

29. Rawls attributes this distinction to Joshua Cohen, "Moral Pluralism and Political Consensus," in David Copp et al. (eds.), *The Idea of Democracy* (Cambridge University Press, 1993), 270–91; see especially 281–4. Elsewhere Cohen endorses a rather minimalist position, where "reasonable is defined . . . in terms of a willingness to entertain and respond to objections" and where "to be unreasonable" is, by contrast, to "favor institutions and policies that cannot be justified to others." Joshua Cohen, "A More Democratic Liberalism," *Michigan Law Review* 92 (1994): 1503–46, at 1537–8.

30. In addition to the article cited in note 4 above, see Amy Gutmann and Dennis Thompson, "Moral Conflict and Political Consensus," *Ethics* 101 (1990): 64–88, and Amy Gutmann and Dennis Thompson, "Moral

Disagreement in a Democracy," *Social Philosophy and Policy* 12 (1994): 87–110. I should say that, despite my criticisms, I think that Gutmann and Thompson are exactly correct when, in the latter article, they insist that "moral disagreement should be considered a condition with which we must learn to live rather than an obstacle to be overcome on the way to a just society" (91).

31. Gutmann, "The Challenge of Multiculturalism," 197; emphasis added.
32. Gutmann and Thompson, "Moral Conflict and Political Consensus," 78–82.
33. Rawls, of course, claims that his "political liberalism" requires an "overlapping consensus" on the principles of justice that govern the "basic structure" of society and that such a consensus need accommodate only "the fact of *reasonable* pluralism." In this sense, Rawls is concerned primarily with "matters of constitutional essentials and basic justice," while I am concerned with more mundane issues of deliberation over policy issues as well. Yet even Rawls concedes that his more ambitious theory of justice, because it accommodates only the "fact of reasonable pluralism" – in contrast to the "fact of pluralism" per se – "runs the danger of being arbitrary and exclusive." See John Rawls, *Political Liberalism* (New York: Columbia University Press, 1993), 36–7, 58–66. For the sorts of reasons I advance in the text, I suspect that, by building reasonableness into its conception of justice, such a Rawlsian view is unacceptably circular. For a further, more recent defense, however, see Cohen, "A More Democratic Liberalism," esp. Sec. IV.C.
34. Gutmann, "The Challenge of Multiculturalism," 195.
35. For some indication of the continuing relevance of this example in the contemporary world see "The Flourishing Business of Slavery," *The Economist* (September 21, 1996): 43–4.
36. My discussion of slavery is deeply indebted to Orlando Patterson, *Slavery and Social Death* (Cambridge, Mass.: Harvard University Press, 1983).
37. Ibid., 5.
38. "The master's authority was derived from his control over symbolic instruments, which effectively persuaded both slave and others that the master was the only mediator between the living community to which he belonged and the living death that his slave experienced.

"The symbolic instruments may be seen as the cultural counterpart to the physical instruments used to control the slave's body. In much the same way that the literal whips were fashioned from different materials, the symbolic whips of slavery were woven from many areas of culture. Masters all over the world used special rituals of enslavement upon first acquiring slaves: the symbolism of naming, of clothing, of hairstyle, of language, and of body marks. And they used, especially in the more advanced slave systems, the sacred symbols of religion." Ibid., 8–9.

39. Ibid., 11, 8.

40. For a defense of the latter strategy as precisely enabling the effective functioning of democratic arrangements see Stephen Holmes, "Gag Rules and the Politics of Omission," in J. Elster and R. Slagstad (eds.), *Constitutionalism and Democracy* (Cambridge University Press, 1988), 236–57. It should be noted that Holmes rightly insists that any such preclusion requires normative justification. Presumably this would require public deliberation.

41. Sunstein, *Democracy and the Problem of Free Speech*, 243.

42. Jon Elster, "Strategic Uses of Argument," in Kenneth Arrow et al. (eds.), *Barriers to Conflict Resolution* (New York: Norton, 1995), 247–8.

43. On the difficulties involved in making credible commitments see Thomas Schelling, *The Strategy of Conflict* (Cambridge, Mass.: Harvard University Press, 1960).

44. Advocates of deliberation typically draw a sharp distinction between it and bargaining. Thus, we are told in one representative statement that deliberation "ought to be different from bargaining, contracting and other market-type interactions, both in its explicit attention to considerations of the common advantage and in the ways that attention helps form the aims of the participants." Cohen, "Deliberation and Democratic Legitimacy," 17.

45. See Elster, "Strategic Uses of Argument." An earlier version of this argument appears in Jon Elster, "The Market and the Forum," in J. Elster and A. Hylland (eds.), *Foundations of Social Choice Theory* (Cambridge University Press, 1986), 113. There Elster attributes this view to Habermas. Although I do not see the basis for the attribution, the possibility seems provocative on its own merits.

46. Sunstein, *Democracy and the Problem of Free Speech*, 244.

47. For example, "Dissonance reduction does not tend to generate autonomous preferences." Elster, "The Market and the Forum," 113. See also Cohen, "Deliberation and Democratic Legitimacy," 25. Consequently, claims about the "civilizing force of hypocrisy" do not comport well with the effort to ground democratic arrangements on autonomy. For such an effort see Cass Sunstein, "Preferences and Politics," *Philosophy and Public Affairs* 20 (1991): 3–34.

48. Advocates of deliberation might suggest that the preceding argument trades upon a double standard. Earlier I questioned whether it is legitimate to define deliberation so narrowly that we categorically exclude "unreasonable" psychological factors such as emotion. Here I am arguing that we are wrong to invoke apparently similar psychological mechanisms as the grounds for our account of how actors might be "persuaded" to forsake some position they defend or claim they

advance. This complaint is misplaced. It overlooks a normatively relevant asymmetry between the sort of psychological mechanism (e.g., disappointment, anger, or fear) that might either prompt political actors to enter and advance claims in a deliberative arena or characterize their response to claims advanced there by others, and the sort of psychological mechanism (e.g., dissonance reduction) that might, in Sunstein's words, make certain sorts of claims "*seem* off-limits." The former expands the range of claims admissible in democratic deliberation while the latter curtails it.

49. Elster, "Strategic Uses of Argument," 248–9.
50. See, e.g., Jürgen Habermas, "Three Normative Models of Democracy," *Constellations* 1 (1994): 1–10, and Jürgen Habermas, "Further Reflections of the Public Sphere," in C. Calhoun (ed.), *Habermas and the Public Sphere* (Cambridge, Mass.: MIT Press, 1992), 421–61.
51. See, e.g., Benhabib, "Deliberative Rationality"; Iris Marion Young, "Justice and Communicative Democracy," in R. Gottlieb (ed.), *Radical Philosophy* (Philadelphia: Temple University Press, 1993), 123–43; and Thomas McCarthy, *Ideals and Illusions* (Cambridge, Mass.: MIT Press, 1991), ch. 7.
52. See James Johnson, "Is Talk Really Cheap?" *American Political Science Review* 87 (1993): 74–86. It is especially important to note that postmodern skepticism has little purchase here precisely insofar as postmodern writers such as Michel Foucault systematically, if tacitly, accord normative weight to relations of communication characterized by equality, symmetry, and reciprocity. I make an extended argument to this effect elsewhere. See James Johnson, "Communication, Criticism, and the Postmodern Consensus," *Political Theory* 25 (1997: 559–83.
53. See James Johnson, "Habermas on Strategic and Communicative Action," *Political Theory* 19 (1991): 181–201.
54. On this understanding of utopianism see Thomas Nagel, "What Makes a Political Theory Utopian?" *Social Research* 56 (1989): 903–20.
55. In any case, such a transformation – whatever its scope – would, at best, emerge as a by-product of deliberation aimed at attaining some tangible outcome. As a consequence, this possibility provides scant aid in the task of justifying democratic deliberation. On this point see Knight and Johnson, "Aggregation and Deliberation," 288, 295–6.
56. The emergence of trust in either others or institutions need not entail the sort of massive character transformation that I just discounted. See Russell Hardin, "Trusting Persons, Trusting Institutions," in R. Zeckhauser (ed.), *Strategy and Choice* (Cambridge, Mass.: MIT Press, 1991), 184–209.
57. In this sense it would help subvert the view that self-interested and moral claims are necessarily mutually exclusive and opposed. On this point see Nagel, "What Makes a Political Theory Utopian?" 909,914.

58. Anne Phillips, *The Politics of Presence* (Oxford: Oxford University Press, 1995).
59. See Michael Taylor, *The Possibility of Cooperation* (Cambridge University Press, 1987), 35–49.
60. I assume here that the relevant actors are equally endowed with the resources needed to provide the public good. That is, there is no obvious asymmetry of, for example, wealth, experience, or power. Obviously, inequalities on any of those dimensions (or others) might well justify the sort of exploitation depicted in the text.
61. For reviews of this research see Joseph Farrell and Matthew Rabin, "Cheap Talk," *Journal of Economic Perspectives* 10 (1996): 103–18, and Vincent Crawford, "Explicit Communication and Bargaining Outcomes," *American Economic Review* 80 (1990): 213–19. I offer an interpretation of these results in Johnson, "Is Talk Really Cheap?"
62. Jim Bohman is a recent exception to this remark. He offers an admittedly partial list of "dialogical mechanisms" that, in his words, "produce 'deliberative uptake.' " See James Bohman, *Public Deliberation: Pluralism, Complexity and Democracy* (Cambridge, Mass.: MIT Press, 1996), 7–66.
63. Joshua Cohen and Joel Rogers, "Associations and Democracy," *Social Philosophy and Policy* 10 (1993): 282–312. The quoted passage is from 296–7.
64. Sunstein, *Democracy and the Problem of Free Speech* (and elsewhere), defends the claim that the U.S. constitutional structure is indeed animated by deliberative imperatives. But the very nature of his case, basically an exercise in retrieval, suggests that our political institutions do not at present function in a deliberative manner.
65. Knight and Johnson, "Aggregation and Deliberation," offers some initial work in this direction. See also David Miller, "Deliberative Democracy and Social Choice," *Political Studies* (special issue) 50 (1992): 54–67.
66. See William Riker, *Liberalism Against Populism*, (Prospect Heights, Ill.: Waveland, 1980).
67. David Austen-Smith, "Modeling Deliberative Democracy," unpublished manuscript, University of Rochester.
68. Note that this is a constraint on the form rather than the content of their preference orderings and that while this restriction makes a stable outcome possible it does not ensure one. Note also that I do not say "all we require here" lightly. In most political conflicts this would be a major and probably quite vulnerable accomplishment. See Knight and Johnson, "Aggregation and Deliberation," 282–3.
69. The quoted phrase is from Cohen, "Deliberation and Democratic Legitimacy," 17.

Joshua Cohen

Chapter Eight
Democracy and Liberty

1. Main Ideas

The fundamental idea of democratic, political legitimacy is that the authorization to exercise state power must arise from the *collective decisions* of the equal members of a society who are governed by that power.[1] That is a very abstract statement of the concept of democracy – as abstract as it should be. Democracy comes in many forms, and more determinate conceptions of it depend on an account of membership in the people and, correspondingly, what it takes for a decision to be *collective* – authorized by *citizens as a body*.

Consider two conceptions of democracy, distinguished by their interpretations of the fundamental idea of collective decision: I will call them *aggregative* and *deliberative*. Both views apply in the first instance to institutions of binding collective decision making,[2] and

I have presented parts of this essay to the Eastern Division Meetings of the American Philosophical Association, the University of Chicago Workshop on Deliberative Democracy, the Instituto Universitário de Pesquisas do Rio de Janeiro, the North Carolina Philosophy Colloquium, a seminar with the Graduate Fellows in the Harvard Program in Ethics and the Professions, in my Wesson Lectures entitled "Liberty, Equality, and Democracy" at Stanford University, at the University of Nebraska, Lincoln, Princeton University, and as the Wade Memorial Lecture at St. Louis University. I also discussed these issues in my Fall 1995 political philosophy seminar at MIT. I am grateful for all the comments and suggestions I have received, and want especially to thank David Austen-Smith, Zairo Cheibub, Alasdair MacIntyre, Carole Pateman, Adam Przeworski, John Rawls, Elisa Reis, Charles Sabel, T. M. Scanlon, Cass Sunstein, Iris Marion Young, and Judith Jarvis Thomson. Some of the main ideas are presented in "Procedure and Substance in Deliberative Democracy," in Seyla Benhabib (ed.), *Democracy and Difference: Changing Boundaries of the Political* (Princeton, N.J.: Princeton University Press, 1996, 95–119).

each interprets the fundamental ideal that such institutions are to treat people bound by collective decisions as equals. According to an *aggregative* conception of democracy, then, decisions are collective just in case they arise from arrangements of binding collective choice that give *equal consideration to* – more generically, are *positively responsive to* – *the interests of each person* bound by the decisions.[3] According to a *deliberative* conception, a decision is collective just in case it emerges from arrangements of binding collective choice that establish conditions of *free public reasoning among equals who are governed by the decisions*. In the deliberative conception, then, citizens treat one another as equals not by giving equal consideration to interests – perhaps some interests ought to be discounted by arrangements of binding collective choice – but by offering them justifications for the exercise of collective power framed in terms of considerations that can, roughly speaking, be acknowledged by all as reasons.

Because the requirements for free public reasoning among equals are not narrowly political – not only a matter of the organization of the state – democracy, on the deliberative view, is not exclusively a form of politics; it is a framework of social and institutional arrangements that

1. facilitate free reasoning among equal citizens by providing, for example, favorable conditions for expression, association, and participation, while ensuring that citizens are treated as free and equal in that discussion; and
2. tie the authorization to exercise public power – and the exercise itself – to such public reasoning, by establishing a framework ensuring the responsiveness and accountability of political power to it through regular competitive elections, conditions of publicity, legislative oversight, and so on.

Deliberative democracy, then, is not simply about ensuring a public culture of reasoned discussion on political affairs, nor simply about fostering the bare conjunction of such a culture with conventional democratic institutions of voting, parties, elections. The idea instead is manifestly to tie the exercise of power to conditions of public reasoning: to establish "all those conditions of communication under which there can come into being a discursive formation of will and opinion on the part of a public composed of the citizens of a state"[4] and to generate "communicative power"[5] – an institutionalized impact of that will and opinion on the exercise of political power.

In the large project of which this essay forms one part, I explore the deliberative conception and its implications. Assuming as background a plurality of comprehensive philosophies of life – the fact of reasonable pluralism, which I will explain shortly – I aim to show that democracy, on the deliberative conception, is a substantive, not simply procedural, ideal and that the substance comprises egalitarian and liberal political values. More specifically, I show the central role within a deliberative conception of democracy of religious, expressive, and moral liberties, political equality, and an egalitarian account of the common good. Egalitarian and liberal political values emerge, then, as elements of democracy rather than as constraints upon it.

In this essay, I focus on the liberties. After sketching the fundamental notions of reasonable pluralism (Section 2) and deliberative democracy (Sections 3 and 4), I discuss religious, expressive, and moral liberty, emphasizing their essential role in a democracy as conditions of *deliberative inclusion.* The conclusion – on political community and political legitimacy – explains how the deliberative conception presents a compelling interpretation of the democratic ideal.

2. Reasonable Pluralism

I begin with the fact of reasonable pluralism:[6] the fact that there are distinct, incompatible philosophies of life to which reasonable people are drawn under favorable conditions for the exercise of practical reason. By a "philosophy of life" – what Rawls has called a "comprehensive doctrine" – I mean an all-embracing view – religious or secular, liberal or traditionalist – that includes an account of all ethical values and, crucially, provides a general guide to conduct, individual as well as collective. Let us say that people are reasonable, politically speaking, only if they are concerned to live with others on terms that those others, as free and equal, also find acceptable. The idea of reasonable pluralism, then, is that good-faith efforts at the exercise of practical reason, by reasonable people thus understood, do not converge on a particular philosophy of life. Such philosophies are matters on which reasonable people disagree.

The fact of reasonable pluralism is just one of the many forms of human difference, others being differences of preference and ability, life chances and biological endowment, ethnicity and rhetorical style. These differences set a generic task for an account of democracy: to explain how people, different along so many dimensions, are to be recognized and treated as free and equal members of a political society (however we interpret those protean ideas). Though the task is generic, the solution varies according to dimension, and here – as a matter of focus, and not prejudging questions of importance – I concentrate on the dimension captured by the fact of reasonable pluralism.

I said that philosophies of life are matters on which reasonable people disagree, and I mean that as a platitude. But seeing it as such requires that we distinguish the fact of reasonable pluralism itself from various philosophical responses to it. Reflective moral divergence is, for example, commonly taken to provide strong evidence for the conclusion that no moral outlook is true, at least not objectively true,[7] or that moral truth transcends our cognitive powers. But persistent divergence of outlook among reasonable people does not require a nihilist or relativist explanation. Reasonable people may disagree about a singular truth. Nor does the absence of convergence command skepticism. For the purposes of political argument, all we should say in response to the fact of reflective divergence is that in matters of comprehensive morality the truth, if there be such, transcends the exercise of practical reason appropriate to expect of others, as free and equal.

Five considerations speak in support of the fact of reasonable pluralism and the force of this response to it. To start with, we observe persistent disagreements among familiar traditions of ethical thought, each with its own elaborate structure and complex history of internal evolution – disagreements, for example, about the relative importance of values of choice and self-determination, happiness and welfare, and self-actualization, and about the religious and philosophical background of these evaluative views. Second, in addition to the sheer fact of disagreement, the exercise of practical reason generates no apparent *tendency* to convergence on a philosophy of life. Furthermore, third, no compelling *theory* of the operations of practical reason predicts convergence of comprehensive moralities after sufficient evidence or reflection or argument is brought to bear. For moral deliberation, we have nothing comparable to the economists' proof of the existence of a general equilibrium of a competitive market economy with certain minimal optimality properties – much less an argument for convergence on such an equilibrium. Nor, fourth, are there any marginally attractive social or political mechanisms that might generate comprehensive agreement. Finally, we can identify natural explanations for the persistence of disagreement that do not require accusations of "unreason": the exercise of practical reason often proceeds within distinct traditions of thought with complex internal structures; personal circumstance and sensibility predispose people to different traditions; and empirical constraints (including the constraints of considered evaluative judgments) are typically too weak to swamp such differences, in part because evaluative concepts themselves are imprecise and their explications are contested.[8]

These considerations may appear to prove too much: to create troubles for the deliberative view, too. For the deliberative view, it will emerge, requires some agreement on political ideas. Why, then, don't the observations that support the fact of reasonable pluralism exclude that agreement, too? By way of response, I need to say something more about the fourth point: the absence of convergence-generating mechanisms in the case of comprehensive philosophies of life. Consider the difference on this point between comprehensive moral consensus and a narrower political agreement.[9] While it is implausible to expect agreement on political values to result from a convergence of practical reasoning conducted within different, independent moral traditions, it is not so implausible to expect important elements of political consensus to emerge from the acquisition of ideas and principles embodied in shared institutions. The acquisition of political ideals and values proceeds in part through participation in common, public institutions of various kinds – families, associations, the state. And the formation of moral-political ideas and sensibilities proceeds less by reasoning or explicit instruction (which may be important in the case of comprehensive moral views) than by mastering ideas and principles that are expressed in and serve to interpret these institutions. Thus, people living within institutions and a political culture shaped by certain ideas and principles are likely to come to understand those ideas and principles and to develop some attachment to them.

Take the idea of citizens as equal moral persons. This idea is, in several ways, manifest in the norms and traditions of interpretation associated with citizenship in a democracy (though practice often fails to conform to those norms) – for example, equality before the

law, and equal civil and political rights. We can understand how
citizens quite generally might acquire an understanding of one another as moral equals by holding the position of citizen and living
in a political culture in which ideas of equality associated with that
position play a central role in political discourse.[10] Different
comprehensive views that accept this political understanding of
equality will have different ways of fitting it into their broader conceptions. Some will accept political equality as following from a
fundamental religious conviction about human equality, or a general moral conception of human beings as equally intrinsically valuable; others will accept political equality as an important,
nonderivative value.[11] But what makes agreement possible in this
case is that citizens who grow up within a reasonably stable democracy will find this (self-) conception familiar and attractive: the
political ideas "expressed" in common, public institutions and appealed to in the culture to justify those institutions will shape the
moral-political education of citizens.

Of course, the acquisition of moral ideas does not proceed exclusively through institutions. So citizens will need to be able to
accommodate the political ideas and self-conceptions they acquire
through institutions within their different philosophies of life: to
find a way to combine, for example, a conception of human beings
as servants of God bound by natural duties with a political conception of citizens as free, equal, and self-governing. And many views
– religious, moral, philosophical – have sufficient internal flexibility
or openness to make such accommodations possible.[12] But while
this accommodation may take place when a comprehensive moral
or religious view is elaborated in ways that make it compatible with
a political conception, we have no reason to expect it to produce
agreement extending beyond political values; for no institutional
mechanism in a democratic society imposes pressure to reach
agreement in ways that would erase fundamental differences between moral, religious, and philosophical traditions. The pressure
of the shared institutions in explaining political agreement ends
even as considerable disagreement remains.

In short, political values are institutionalized in a democratic
society in ways that comprehensive moral (or religious, or philosophical) ideas are not. More precisely, comprehensive ideas are
sustained through more particular social associations that are not
shared: different churches, for example, advance different comprehensive views. So citizens acquire conflicting comprehensive views

through those associations. An account of how consensus might emerge on political values among citizens living in a political society, then, has resources unavailable to an account of a more comprehensive moral consensus.

Despite these considerations, one might still hold out hope for comprehensive moral agreement, and for a political community based on such agreement. In response to the observation that there is no tendency to reach agreement, we might, for example, take certain points of moral convergence – on the injustice of slavery or the value of religious toleration – as at least suggesting a broader tendency toward moral convergence.

Moreover, a political society with comprehensive moral agreement has at least four attractive qualities that might make it a society to be hoped for. In such a society, for example, members respect one another for their determinate, concrete commitments – for the values that animate their lives – and not simply for their abstract though perhaps unrealized human capacities, not merely for their inner but perhaps unexpressed dignity. Furthermore, all may believe the truth, whereas moral pluralism implies that some members are bound to endorse false moral ideas; even if we accept that false views have public rights,[13] still, endorsing the truth is an important human good; and endorsing it in common deepens mutual respect. In addition, agreement gives the members of a society a confidence in the bases of their conduct that is plausibly lacking under conditions of disagreement, thus mitigating pressures to reject the objectivity of ethical thought and embrace skepticism, nihilism, or simple alienation. Finally, as a practical matter, the absence of conflict on comprehensive views may ease communication and coordination.

In response to the proposed extrapolation from cases of convergence – slavery and religious toleration – it must be said that these are not cases in which people agree on comprehensive moral outlooks. Instead, people who belong to different moral and religious traditions come to agree on the injustice of certain especially injurious practices, despite persisting disagreement on other matters. Thus, the condemnation of slavery is common ground among Catholics, Muslims, Jews, and Protestants; and among Kantians and utilitarians. So the examples are not strong evidence for the thesis that practical reason generates a more general moral convergence among people working within different moral and religious traditions; rather, they are important cases of agreement on political values among people who have fundamental moral disagreements.

Moreover, let us suppose that comprehensive agreement has important virtues. Still, if the exercise of practical reason does not generate convergence among people who begin with very different outlooks, associated with different traditions of moral, religious, and philosophical thought and practice, then how is comprehensive moral agreement to be achieved? Perhaps through some form of common moral education in a comprehensive view. But how is such education – as distinct from education about requirements of civic responsibility and decency – to proceed in the face of different and competing forms of moral thought, each with its own associational life? Perhaps through the state's coercive means. But it is not so clear that the state can produce genuine moral agreement, as opposed to public spectacles of conformity; and if it could, the price seems unacceptable, despite the values associated with agreement.

I assume the fact of reasonable pluralism, then. And this fact gives shape to the conception of citizens as free and equal that constitutes part of the deliberative conception of democracy I want to explore here. To say that citizens are *free* is to say, inter alia, that no comprehensive moral or religious view provides a defining condition of membership or the foundation of the authorization to exercise political power. Not that religious or moral views are, religiously, morally, or metaphysically speaking, matters of choice. To someone who has a religious view, for example, believing the view is a matter of believing what is true and acting on it a matter of fulfilling obligations that are not self-legislated and are perhaps more fundamental than political obligations.[14] But politically speaking, citizens are free in that it is open to them to accept or reject such views without loss of status. To say citizens are *equal* is to say that each is recognized as having the capacities required for participating in discussion aimed at authorizing the exercise of power.

What, more particularly then, can we say about a conception of democracy suited to conditions of reasonable pluralism? By excluding a comprehensive consensus on values, the fact of reasonable pluralism may suggest that a procedural conception of democracy, limited to such values as openness and impartiality associated with fair process, is the only remaining option. After all, that fact deprives us of a background of shared moral or religious premises – shared reasons – that would give more determinate content to the idea of popular authorization. Without that background, we are left, it may seem, with no basis for agreement on anything more than fair procedures – perhaps not even that. Faced with disagreement on comprehensive views, what legitimate complaint can a person raise about a framework of collective decision, beyond the complaint that the framework fails to take her interests into account?

I think this conclusion is incorrect, and will sketch a view that combines an assumption of reasonable pluralism with a more substantive conception of democracy. I will suggest as well that this combination is a natural result of adopting a *deliberative* understanding of the collective decisions that constitute democratic governance.

3. Public Reasoning

A deliberative conception of democracy puts public reasoning at the center of political justification. I say *public reasoning* rather than *public discussion* because a deliberative view cannot be distinguished simply by its emphasis on discussion rather than bargaining or voting as methods of collective decision making. On any view of democracy – indeed any view of intelligent political decision making – discussion is important, if only because of its essential role in pooling private information, against a background of asymmetries in its distribution.

According to the deliberative interpretation of democracy, then, democracy is a system of social and political arrangements that institutionally ties the exercise of power to free reasoning among equals. This conception of justification through public reasoning can be represented in an idealized procedure of political deliberation, constructed to capture the notions of free, equal, and reason that figure in the deliberative ideal. The point of the idealized procedure is to provide a model characterization of free reasoning among equals, which can in turn serve as a model for arrangements of collective decision making that are to establish a framework of free reasoning among equals. Using the model, we can work out the content of the deliberative democratic ideal and its conception of public reasoning by considering features of such reasoning in the idealized case and then aiming to build those features into institutions.

Thus, in an ideal deliberative procedure, participants are and regard one another as *free:* recognizing the fact of reasonable pluralism, they acknowledge, as I noted earlier, that no comprehensive moral or religious view provides a defining condition of participation or a test of the acceptability of arguments in support of the exercise of political power. Moreover, participants regard one another as formally and substantively *equal.* They are formally equal in that the rules regulating the ideal procedure do not single out individuals for special advantage or disadvantage. Instead, everyone with the deliberative capacities – which is to say, more or less all human beings – has and is recognized as having equal standing at each stage of the deliberative process. Each, that is, can propose issues for the agenda, propose solutions to the issues on the agenda, offer reasons in support of or in criticism of proposed solutions. And each has an equal voice in the decision. The participants are substantively equal in that the existing distribution of power and resources does not shape their chances to contribute to deliberation, nor does that distribution play an authoritative role in their deliberation. In saying that it does not play an authoritative role in their deliberation, I mean that the participants in the deliberative procedure do not regard themselves as collectively morally bound by the existing system of rights except insofar as that system establishes the framework of free deliberation among equals. Instead, they regard that system as a potential object of their deliberative judgment.

In addition, they are *reasonable* in that they aim to defend and criticize institutions and programs in terms of considerations that others, as free and equal, have *reason to accept,* given the fact of reasonable pluralism and on the assumption that those others are themselves concerned to provide suitable justifications.

Which considerations count as reasons? Generically speaking, a reason is a consideration that counts in favor of something: in particular, a belief, or an action. Not an illuminating analysis: I doubt that illuminating analysis is available or that it would be helpful in answering our question.[15] What is needed is an account not of what a reason is, but of which considerations count as reasons. And the answer to this question depends on context. Whether considerations count in favor in the relevant way depends on the setting in which they are advanced. Applying this point to the issue at hand: a suitable account of which considerations count as reasons for the purposes of an account of democratic deliberation will take the form not of a generic account of what a reason is, but of a

statement of which considerations count in favor of proposals within a deliberative setting suited to the case of free association among equals, understood to include an acknowledgment of reasonable pluralism. This background is reflected in the kinds of reasons that will be acceptable – meaning, as always, acceptable to individuals as free and equal citizens.

I have already specified the relevant deliberative setting as one in which people are understood as free, equal, and reasonable and as having conflicting philosophies of life. Within the idealized deliberative setting that captures these conditions, it will not do simply to advance considerations that one takes to be true or compelling. Such considerations may well be rejected by others who are themselves reasonable – prepared to live with others on terms acceptable to those others, given their different comprehensive views – and endorse conflicting philosophies of life. One needs instead to find reasons that are compelling to others, where those others are regarded as (and regard themselves as) equals and have diverse reasonable commitments. How wide a range of commitments? Because we are addressing the institutional framework for making collective decisions and assume the participants to be free – not bound to their de facto commitments – the range of commitments is similarly wide: not exhausted by de facto commitments. Considerations that do not meet these tests will be rejected in the idealized setting and so do not count as acceptable political reasons. Let us say, then, that a consideration is an acceptable political reason just in case it has the support of the different comprehensive views that might be endorsed by reasonable citizens.

To illustrate these points about the role of the background – the conception of citizens as free, equal, and reasonable – in constraining the set of reasons, let us consider three implications; the first two will be particularly important in my discussion of the liberties.

First, people hold religious commitments on faith, and those commitments impose what they take to be overriding obligations. Such commitments are not, as such, unreasonable: though faith transcends reason, even as "reason" is understood within the tradition to which the commitments belong, citizens are not unreasonable for holding beliefs on faith. But beliefs held on faith – perhaps beliefs in what are understood to be revealed truths – can reasonably be rejected by others who rely only on the darkness of an unconverted heart, and so cannot serve to justify legislation.

Thus, it matters to our response to the case against abortion

stated in the recent encyclical, *Evangelium Vitae*, that Pope John Paul II claims that the gospel of life *"can . . . be known in its essential traits by human reason"* and that the "Law of God" that condemns abortion is "written in every human heart [and] knowable by reason itself" – in short, that the argument is presented as independent of a particular faith position.[16] Though I see no reason to agree with this claim about what lies within the compass of reason, our response to the argument must be different from what that response would be if the argument appealed openly to revealed truths or beliefs held on faith. We must show that the conception of reason it appeals to is itself sectarian and that the argument fails on a conception of reason that is not.

Second, the adequacy of a consideration as a political reason – its weight in political justification – will depend on the nature of the regulated conduct, in particular on the strength of the reasons that support that conduct. Thus, considerations of public order provide acceptable reasons for regulating conduct. Different views have different ways of explaining that value: utilitarians will found it on considerations of aggregate happiness, Kantians on the preconditions of autonomous conduct, others on the intrinsic value of human life and human sociability. Moreover, people are bound to disagree about the requirements of public order: that disagreement may extend to whether a state is necessary to secure the conditions of order. But it will not be acceptable to suppose that, as a general matter, the value of public order transcends all other political values. Except perhaps in the most extreme circumstances, for example, a state may not impose a blanket prohibition on alcohol consumption – including consumption in religious services – in the name of public order. The reasons that support such consumption include considerations of religious duty – more generally, considerations of fundamental duty, which are normally overriding. And those considerations will provide a suitable basis for rejecting a justification cast in terms of the value of public order, except in the most extreme conditions.

These first two points about reasons both generate pressure for liberty. The first point underscores that reasonable pluralism will lead to the rejection of some bases for restricting liberty as politically weightless; the second indicates that other bases of restriction will not be weightless, but insufficient to outweigh reasons that can be acknowledged, consistent with reasonable pluralism, as commending or commanding a course of conduct.

Finally, third, the fact that a policy is most beneficial to me arguably provides me with a reason to support that policy.[17] But this reason carries no weight in public deliberation of the relevant kind, because others, concerned with their advantage and willing to find mutually acceptable reasons, will not accept it as a reason; moreover, it is reasonable for them not to accept it, in part because they can dismiss it while at the same time treating me as an equal and giving my good the same weight in their deliberations that they insist I give to theirs. Thus, I may *prefer* the arrangement that gives me the greatest advantage, and so have a personal reason for promoting it. But in the context of ideal deliberation, I must find considerations in favor of the arrangement that do not neglect the good of others. Similarly, I may wish to reject an arrangement that leaves me less well-off than some others. But I cannot offer as a reason against it that it leaves me less well-off, because every arrangement will leave some people less well-off than some others. So if I need to find reasons acceptable to others, I cannot reject a proposal simply because it does to me what each arrangement must do to someone – and, again, every arrangement leaves some less well-off than others. I can, however, reject it on grounds that an arrangement leaves me less well-off than anyone needs to be.

In presenting the deliberative view in terms of an ideal deliberative procedure in which parties are required to find reasons acceptable to others, I may appear to be tying the deliberative conception to an implausible requirement of political consensus – to the view that "deliberation leads to convergence."[18]

I make no such assumption. Instead, I assume that different views will have different interpretations of the acceptable reasons and of how different reasons are to be weighted – for example, reasons of equality and of aggregate well-being. As a result, even an ideal deliberative procedure will not, in general, issue in consensus. But even if there is such disagreement, and a need to submit the decision to majority rule, still, participants in the ideal case will need to appeal to considerations that are quite generally recognized as having considerable weight and as a suitable basis for collective choice, even among people who disagree about the right result: agreement on political values is not agreement on the proper combination of them. But when people do appeal to considerations that are quite generally recognized as having considerable weight, then the fact that a proposal has majority support will itself commonly count as a reason for endorsing it. Even people who disagree may, then, accept the results of a deliberative procedure as legitimate.

4. Discussion, Deliberation, Motivation

I said earlier that a deliberative conception of democracy cannot be characterized by its emphasis on discussion, that any view of democracy will have an important place for discussion because of its essential role in pooling dispersed, private information. Of course, discussion is not always so helpful. As Przeworski puts it, "If people behave strategically in pursuit of their interests, they also emit messages in this way":[19] behavior does not lose its strategic character simply because it involves the use of language. And if people "emit messages" – that is, communicate – strategically, they may well have incentives to misrepresent private information, in which case discussion may play an essential role in deception and spreading misinformation. The mere fact that conduct is linguistically mediated does not, of course, imply that agents are prepared to constrain their conduct by reference to norms of honesty, sincerity, and full disclosure, rather than simply taking the most effective means to their ends. The use of language may, as a matter of conversational implicature, commit the speaker to such norms – to endorsing them as proper standards of guidance and criticism. But I don't propose to rest anything on this hypothesis.

Though the strategic use of language to advance one's aims always carries the potential of deviating from norms of honesty, the strength of incentives to engage in misrepresentation depends, inter alia, on the underlying diversity of citizen preferences. Intuitively, the more diverse the preferences of individuals – the more they disagree about the best outcome – the greater are the gains from strategically lying, misinforming, or distorting; the greater the gains, the greater are the temptations to undertake such manipulation.[20] The point is familiar in the setting of legislative decision making in legislatures with committee structures. The more extreme the preferences of committee members relative to median legislative preferences (the more they are outliers), the less informative the committees will be (more noise, less signal). For this reason, majoritarian legislatures will not – unless they have a collective preference for self-deception – want to leave important decisions in the hands of a committee composed of preference outliers: members will not expect the committee to provide truthful and complete information.

But – and this is the crucial point – the extent of preference diversity is not fixed, not given in advance of political deliberation. Not that the *aim* of such deliberation is to change citizen preferences by reducing their diversity: the aim is to make collective decisions. Still, one thought behind a deliberative conception is that public *reasoning* itself can help to reduce the diversity of politically relevant preferences because such preferences are shaped and even formed in the process of public reasoning itself. And if it does help to reduce that diversity, then it mitigates tendencies toward distortion even in strategic communication.

Two points are essential here, one concerning reasons, the other concerning connections between reasons and motives. First, the reasoning that figures in collective decisions need not be exclusively instrumental – only a matter of determining the most effective means for achieving settled aims, given perhaps by desires. Indeed, practical reasoning – understood as reflection on and discussion about what reasons for action agents have – may proceed along deliberative paths with only the most attenuated connections to the agent's current aims.[21] Citizens are capable of recognizing *as reasons* considerations that conflict with their antecedent preferences and interests, ranking alternatives in accordance with such considerations and acting on those rankings. I might now recognize that I have good reason to refrain from harming others, but not think that I have reason ever to help them, nor have any desire at all to help. Suppose, however, that reflection on *why* I have reason not to harm leads me to see that the explanation for that reason also implies that I have reason to help. Though I have no desire to help, a new reason emerges from a search for reflective equilibrium that, as in this example, proceeds by considering the justification for settled reasons and the implications of the justification for other reasons that agents have. To the extent that I also have preferences that conflict with these reasons, I will continue to have incentives – perhaps strong ones – to strategically misrepresent information. But, coming now to the second point, seeing that certain of my antecedent preferences and interests cannot be expressed in the form of acceptable reasons may help to limit the force of such preferences as political motives.[22]

To illustrate: assume a commitment to deliberative justification

– assume, that is, the shared belief that political justification requires finding reasons acceptable to others, understood as free and equal, who endorse that commitment. And assume, alongside that, a desire that others serve my aims, regardless of their own.[23] Though this desire may prompt me to advance a proposal, it does not count as a reason in public argument. To defend the proposal consistent with my commitment to finding justifications of the appropriate kind, then, I need to advance reasons independent of the desire – which I will be prepared to do only if I believe that there are acceptable reasons. And presenting such reasons may lead to the formation of a new desire, say a desire to coordinate with others on mutually beneficial terms. Merely believing that I have such a reason may suffice to refashion preferences, but the motivational force of that recognition is likely to be greater if I must state the reasons thereby lending greater salience to them. That desire, unlike the desire that others serve my aims regardless of their own, is naturally expressed in a reason that is acceptable to others. Moreover, if I develop the desire to cooperate on mutually beneficial terms, my incentive to strategically misrepresent private information will decline. And that means that even if my communications are in part strategically motivated, I will be more likely to provide information that is commonly beneficial.

It should be clear, but it is nevertheless worth emphasizing, that the preference changes with beneficial effects on strategic communication are not simply changes of *induced* preference that result from the acquisition of new information through discussion.[24] Of course, new information may well induce new preferences: I now prefer eating bread to cheese because I believe that bread is more nutritious and prefer more nutritious to less nutritious food; if I learn that cheese is more nutritious, and I am rational, I will prefer cheese to bread. And sometimes disagreement among preferences is generated by simple differences of factual belief. Reducing differences owing to lack of common information will often be a good thing. But the kinds of preference changes I am contemplating reflect a sensitivity of motivations – understood as behavioral dispositions – to reasons, understood as standards of criticism and guidance, and not simply a sensitivity of some preferences to information about how most effectively to satisfy other preferences.

Though these are not cases of induced preference change, they are also not cases (like hypnotism or suggestion) of preferences changing without rational explanation. In the kinds of cases I am considering, preferences change because a person comes to understand – through practical reasoning – that his current preferences lack an appropriate justification: not because new empirical knowledge is acquired that bears on the achievement of an aim (as in the bread to cheese example), but because the preference cannot be supported by reasons of a suitable kind, the agent recognizes that it cannot, and that recognition has sufficient salience to shape motivations. In the background is the view that the notion of a reason is essentially normative – a term of justification and criticism – and that a reason is not a kind of motivation. Practical reasoning, then, is a matter of reflecting on what one is to do, not what one is motivated to do, though the results of such reasoning can motivate.[25]

5. Religious Liberty

I have focused thus far on the structure of the deliberative view. I turn now to its substance, in particular to the thesis that democracy – on the deliberative interpretation of collective choice – must ensure religious, expressive, and moral liberties. This proposal departs from conventional understandings of the relationship between democracy and these liberties. To illustrate that understanding, I want to present a familiar dilemma associated with the idea of democratic legitimacy.

On the one hand, the value of democracy seems too procedural to provide a basis for an account of legitimacy; some democratic collective choices are too repulsive to be legitimate, however attractive the procedures that generate them. On the other hand, the idea of democracy appears to be the authoritative, sovereign requirement on collective decisions. That is because democracy appears to be the form of collective choice mandated by the fundamental political idea that citizens are to be treated as equals. Because the ideal of treating people as equals is so fundamental, and so intimately linked to democratic procedures of binding collective decision making, democracy is naturally identified not simply as one political value to be combined with others, but as the way we must settle the ordering of other political values – the way to ensure equal standing in settling the common environment. To put issues off the democratic agenda appears, by contrast, to establish objectionable spheres of privilege. Thus, Robert Dahl says:

It seems to me highly reasonable to argue that *no* interests should be inviolable beyond those integral or essential to the democratic process. . . . [O]utside this broad domain [which includes rights of political expression, participation, and association] a democratic people could freely choose the policies its members feel best; they could decide how best to balance freedom and control, how best to settle conflicts between the interests of some and the interests of others, how best to organize and control their economy and so on. In short, outside the inviolable interests of democratic people in the preservation of the democratic process [inviolable because of the roots of that process in an ideal of equal intrinsic worth] would lie the proper sphere for political decisions.[26]

Dahl immediately indicates some qualms about this view and explores ways to ensure that conventional democratic process might better protect fundamental interests that are not integral or essential to it.[27] But he has identified a genuine problem, whose most familiar expression arises in connection with what Benjamin Constant called the "liberties of the moderns" – religious liberty, liberty of conscience more generally, liberty of thought and expression, rights of person and personal property. These liberties lack any evident connection to conditions of democratic procedure: to borrow Dahl's words, they are not integral or essential to it. So their protection is commonly understood as constraining democratic process – limiting its appropriate scope. In that respect they differ from political liberties, including rights of association, of speech on political questions, and of participation. If a constitution disables a majority from restricting political participation or regulating the content of political speech, that constitution can be interpreted as safeguarding the essentials of democratic process. Assurances of such political liberties help to ensure a connection between popular authorization and political outcome – to preserve the continuing authority of the people, and not simply the majority of them.[28] Those liberties – the liberties of the ancients – are constitutive elements of democratic process.

The liberties of the moderns appear, then, to be based on independent values, separate from the ideal of treating people as equals in arenas of collective choice that underlies the appeal of democracy. And that may suggest that, from the perspective of democratic thought, these liberties have roots no deeper than contingent popular consensus. Though abridgments of nonpolitical liberties that emerge from a fair democratic process may be unjust, they face no problems of democratic legitimacy.[29]

On the deliberative conception of democracy, this conclusion is wrong: a deliberative view provides a basis for wider guarantees of basic liberties. The explanation of this feature is that the deliberative conception requires more than that the interests of all be given equal consideration in binding collective decisions; it requires, too, that we find politically acceptable reasons – reasons acceptable to others, given a background of reasonable differences of conscientious conviction. I call this requirement the *principle of deliberative inclusion*.[30]

To illustrate the roots and implications of this principle, I want to start with the case of religious liberty, one of the principal liberties of the moderns and the one that most sharply illustrates the analytical structure.

As I mentioned earlier, religious views set demands of an especially high order – perhaps transcendent obligations – on their adherents. Moreover, if we see these requirements from the believer's standpoint, we cannot see them as *self-imposed* – chosen by the agent. To put the point without benefit of ocular metaphor: if we believe about these requirements (say, as to day and manner of worship) what the adherent believes about them, then we do not believe that the adherent choose to place herself under these demands. The content and stringency of the demands are fixed instead by the content of the convictions, which the adherent believes true, not by the adherent's endorsement of those convictions. To be sure, if a believer did not endorse the convictions, then she would not believe herself to be bound by them: but given that she does endorse them, she thinks that she would then hold false beliefs and would be more likely to do what is wrong.

Liberal political conceptions are sometimes said to endorse, if only by way of implicit commitment, a conception of human beings as "bound only by ends and roles we choose," and correspondingly to deny "that we can ever be claimed by ends we have not chosen – ends given by God, for example, or by our identities as members of families, peoples, cultures, or traditions."[31] Liberalism, on this view, rests on moral voluntarism. And such voluntarism implies that religious moralities are false. It is difficult, I think, to find political conceptions that embrace uncompromising moral voluntarism – that conceive of human beings as, in Michael Sandel's compelling phrase, "unencumbered selves." In any case, that philosophy of life cannot possibly serve as common political ground. And once it is rejected as such, we see that reasonable adherents cannot accept, as sufficient reasons in support of a law or system of policy, considerations that would preclude their compliance with the fundamental religious demands or require that they treat those demands as matters of choice.

What, then, of citizens who do not share those views, who reject them as false – perhaps some elements as meaningless? (I will describe the issue from the point of view of a citizen who has fundamental moral convictions, but not religious convictions. Broadly parallel remarks could be made from the standpoint of different religious convictions.) They might respond in one of three ways.

First, they might regard all religious views that impose such stringent demands, whatever their content and foundation, as unreasonable. This response might issue from the conviction that all religious views are intolerant, and for that reason politically unreasonable, or that religious convictions cannot withstand reflective scrutiny. But neither of these views is acceptable. The first is simply false. Nothing in religious conviction itself – any more or less than in secular moral conviction – requires endorsement of the view that "error has no rights" or that truth suffices for justification. As to the second, there may be conceptions of "reflective scrutiny" on which religious views cannot withstand such scrutiny. But those conceptions themselves are almost certain to belong to comprehensive views (say, empiricist philosophies) that cannot be permitted to set the bounds on public reasoning, any more than can natural theology's conception of natural reason. Moreover, any account of reflective scrutiny that condemns religious conviction will almost certainly condemn secular moral ideas as equally unreasonable.

A second possibility is to treat concerns to fulfill religious obligations as intense preferences, to be given equal consideration along with other preferences of equal intensity. This response urges us to put aside the content of the convictions and their special role – as first principles of practical justification – in practical reasoning. The roots of this response lie, I believe, in a misinterpretation of the value of neutrality. Neutrality requires that political justification in a democracy not depend on any particular reasonable view. But it does not require that we neglect the content of views, treat all as matters of mere preference, and let the strength of claims be fixed by the intensity of those preferences.[32] Doing so indicates a failure to take into account the special weight of religious or fundamental moral convictions to the adherent, particularly the weight of requirements that the religious or moral outlook itself designates as fundamental demands: an unwillingness to see how the adherent's convictions, in virtue of their content, state or imply that the requirements provide especially compelling reasons, and not simply strong preferences.

But if we are not prepared to treat convictions as (without qualification) self-imposed, accept them as true, dismiss them as false, or – putting their truth or falsity to the side – let their weight be fixed by their intensity as preferences, what is left? The alternative is to take seriously that the demands impose what the adherent reasonably regards as fundamental obligations (paradigmatically compelling practical reasons), accept the requirement – associated with the deliberative view – of finding reasons that might override these obligations and acknowledge that such reasons cannot normally be found.[33] The result is religious liberty, understood to include freedom of conscience, which condemns disabilities imposed on grounds of religious belief, and free exercise of religion, which condemns in particular limits on public worship.[34] It emerges as the product of three elements. The first is the demanding character of religious requirements, which, from the point of view of those who are subject to them, are matters of fundamental obligation. It accepts the idea that free citizens, who accept that no comprehensive moral or religious view provides a defining condition of participation or a test of the acceptability of arguments in support of the exercise of political power, are, in a way, "encumbered": it proposes a rendering of the idea that such citizens have obligations and commitments that are not properly understood, for purposes of political argument, as matters of choice. Second, it draws on the shared concern – fundamental to the deliberative conception – to find reasons that citizens who are subject to what they regard as basic obligations can reasonably be expected to acknowledge. And third, it draws on the fact that citizens who are not religious have fundamental convictions that they take to impose especially compelling obligations.

The first two points are by themselves sufficient, but the third underscores the unreasonableness of failing to acknowledge religious liberty; for those who might be prepared to deny freedom of conscience and liberty of worship to others will typically want to claim freedom of conscience for themselves. And if they are unable to defend that freedom by appealing to the truth of their views, then they will need to defend it by reference to the stringency of the demands imposed by their fundamental and not unreasonable convictions. And then treating others as equals will require that they give similar weight to other demands belonging to that general category.

Suppose, then, that we prevent a person from fulfilling such demands for reasons the person is compelled to regard as insufficient: "compelled," because denying the sufficiency of these reasons follows from a religious or moral philosophy that not unreasonably commands the person's conviction. This is to deny the person standing as an equal citizen – to deny full and equal membership in the people whose collective actions authorize the exercise of power. And that, according to the deliberative conception, is a failure of democracy. We have denied full membership by failing to provide a justification for the exercise of collective power by reference to considerations that all who are members of the sovereign body that authorizes the exercise of power and who are subject to that power, and prepared to cooperate on reasonable terms, can accept. There are many ways to exclude individuals and groups from The People, but this surely is one.

To conclude, I want to make two observations about this account of religious liberty. First, my remarks are limited. I have not said anything directly about how to handle claims for religious exemption from general obligations with a strong secular justification (including obligations to educate children); or whether special provision is to be made for specifically religious convictions, as distinct from conscientious ethical convictions with no religious roots;[35] or about tolerating the intolerant. My aim here is not to resolve, or even to address, these issues: any view recognizing rights of free exercise will need to face those hard questions. I am interested only in making the more restricted point that a deliberative conception of democracy is not barred – by its emphasis on an ideal of democracy – from acknowledging a fundamental role for rights of religious liberty: indeed, that it must provide a place for such rights. The basis of such rights, on the deliberative view, lies deeper than contingent popular consensus. Like rights of political expression, they are founded on the idea of democracy itself.

Second, I emphasize that the rationale for the guarantees of religious liberty that fall under the requirement of deliberative inclusion is neither narrowly political nor antipolitical. It is not narrowly political, because those guarantees are not simply about enabling people to participate in normal politics (or to participate without fear), nor simply about improving public discussion by adding more diverse voices to it. It is not antipolitical, because they are not simply about ensuring the strength of organized associations (churches among them) that help to protect individuals from the state's power.[36] The argument does not deny the links between religious liberty and associational liberty. The idea instead is that abridgments of such liberties would constitute denials to citizens of standing as equal members of the sovereign people, by imposing in ways that deny the force of reasons that are, by the lights of their own views, compelling. The reasons for abridgment are unacceptably exclusionary, because they are unsuited to the ideal of guiding the exercise of power by a process of reason-giving suited to a system of free and equal citizens.

The view I am presenting might, then, be contrasted with an approach suggested by Roberto Unger's conception of empowered democracy, as well as the approach I sketched in an earlier essay, "Deliberation and Democratic Legitimacy."[37] According to Unger, a system of immunities – negative liberties – is one component of a democratic order because "[f]reedom as participation *presupposes* freedom as immunity." The mistake of "critics of traditional democratic theory" is to believe that "participatory opportunities [are] a more than satisfactory *substitute* for immunity guarantees." According to Unger, participation is no substitute; instead, immunity rights are necessary if a citizen is to have the "*safety* that encourages him to participate actively and independently in collective decision-making." I do not disagree with the claim that immunity rights are necessary, nor with the criticism of other views. But I now think that the deliberative conception of democracy provides the basis for a less instrumental, less strategic rationale for certain liberties, even when those liberties are not needed to ensure appropriate inputs to democratic procedure.

6. Expressive Liberty

The principle of deliberative inclusion extends naturally from religious liberty to a *wide guarantee* of expressive liberty. By a "wide guarantee," I mean a guarantee not confined to political speech, even on very capacious understandings of political speech.

Cass Sunstein, for example, defines political speech as speech that is "intended and received as a contribution to public deliberation about some issue."[38] I believe that a deliberative view supports stringent protections of expressive liberty, even when the expression falls outside the political, thus understood.

The deliberative view thus extends a more familiar democracy-based strand of free-speech theory, which defends stringent protections of *specifically political speech* as one prerequisite for a democratic framework of collective choice.[39] Alexander Meiklejohn's version of this theory locates the roots of a strong free-speech guarantee in the U.S. constitutional design of popular self-government. Because popular sovereignty requires free and open discussion among citizens, the government undercuts the constitution's defining principle – treats citizens as subjects of government rather than its sovereign masters – when it interferes with such discussion. Others who favor the democracy defense add three considerations that supplement Meiklejohn's constitutional argument: (a) because citizens have diverse views, regulation of speech owing to its content establishes a regime of political inequality by silencing certain views or topics that may be important to some citizens; (b) content regulation effectively restricts the flow of information, perhaps reducing the quality of democratic discussion and decision; (c) content restrictions might limit the range of views in the discussion, and limits on range might confine the capacity of discussion itself to challenge received views and preferences by presenting unconventional outlooks.

Each of these considerations – fairness, quality, and reflectiveness – plays an important role in a full treatment of free expression as essential to deliberative democracy. Here, however, my aim is to indicate how the deliberative view supplements these considerations, and thus extends stringent protections beyond political speech – and thus also forestalls the need to stretch the category of "political speech" to cover, for example, *Bleak House, Ulysses,* and Mapplethorpe's photographs (Sunstein's examples) so that they are stringently protected. Restriction to political speech may seem natural, once one has decided to found rights of expression on potential contribution as *input* to a discussion about the proper use of public power. But a deliberative conception must be cautious about accepting such a limit. Though the idea of reasonable discussion aimed at agreement is fundamental to the deliberative view, it does not follow that the protection of expression is to be confined to speech that *contributes to* such discussion. It may also need to extend to speech that cannot permissibly be regulated as an *outcome* of such discussion.

Consider, then, expression that is not part of any process of political discussion – not intended or not received as a contribution to public deliberation about some issue. But assume, too, that it reflects what a citizen reasonably takes to be compelling considerations in support of expression. Such expression advances what I will call an "expressive interest": a direct interest in articulating thoughts and feelings on matters of personal or broader human concern, whether or not that articulation influences the thought and conduct of others.[40]

As examples, consider artistic expression driven by a concern to create something of beauty; or bearing religious witness with no intention to persuade others; or giving professional advice out of a sense of professional obligation, with no intention to shape broader processes of collective decision making. In the case of bearing witness, an agent endorses a view that places him under an *obligation* to articulate that view, and perhaps urge on others a different course of thought, feeling, or conduct. Restricting expression would prevent the agent's fulfilling what she takes to be an obligation, thus imposing a burden that the agent reasonably takes to be unacceptable. To acknowledge the weight of those reasons, the deliberative view extends stringent protection to such expression. Given the background of reasonable pluralism, the failure to extend such protection represents a failure to give due weight to the reasons that support forms of expression that are not inputs to public discussion. As such, it constitutes a denial of equal standing, and decisions to deny protection are not suitably collective.

Or take expression on matters of political justice. Here, the importance of the issue – indicated by its being a matter of justice – provides a substantial reason for addressing it, regardless of how the message is received. The precise content and weight of the reason are matters of controversy. Aristotelian views identify public engagement as the highest human good; and Brandeis urged that "public discussion is a political duty."[41] But even if political expression is neither the highest good nor a matter of duty, still, it is a requisite for being a good citizen, sometimes a matter of sheer decency. Typically, then, such expression has support from substantial reasons within different moral-political conceptions.

Bearing witness; speaking out on matters of justice; creating things of beauty; giving professional advice: such cases suffice to underscore the importance of the expressive interest. They work outward from fully conscientious expression – the paradigm of expression supported by substantial reasons from the agent's point of view, and therefore expression whose protection is supported by the principle of deliberative inclusion. To be sure, different evaluative conceptions have different implications for what is reasonable to say and do. But all conceptions assign to those who hold them substantial reasons for expression, quite apart from the value of the expression to the audience, and even if there is no audience at all. For this reason, the deliberative view endorses a strong presumption against content regulation, but does not confine that presumption to political speech.

Other reasons may also support that presumption, understood as part of a wide guarantee of expressive liberty: for example, considerations of reflectiveness (discussed earlier) which suggest that all manner of speech helps to form values and beliefs that also figure in public deliberation. But we need not confine ourselves to considerations of this kind. Content regulation is to be rejected because of the reasons for speech that are captured in the expressive interest, and not simply because such regulations prematurely foreclose public discussion.

To illustrate the point about the deliberative framework, the expressive interest, and a wide guarantee of expressive liberty, let us consider the case of regulations of sexual expression: in particular, regulations of pornography. Part of the trouble with such regulations – for example, the pornography regulations urged by Catharine MacKinnon – lies in this area.[42] An example of such regulation is an Indianapolis ordinance, adopted in 1986, which defines pornography as

the graphic sexually explicit subordination of women, whether in pictures or in words, that also includes one or more of the following:

- Women are presented as sexual objects who enjoy pain or humiliation;
- Women are presented as sexual objects who experience sexual pleasure in being raped;
- Women are presented as sexual objects tied up or cut up or mutilated or bruised or physically hurt;
- Women are presented being penetrated by objects or animals;

- Women are presented in scenarios of degradation, injury, torture, shown as filthy or inferior, bleeding, bruised or hurt in a context that makes these conditions sexual;
- Women are presented as sexual objects for domination, conquest, violation, exploitation, possession, or use, or through postures or positions of servility or submission or display.[43]

In a nutshell, the regulation targets the graphic fusion of sexuality and subordination.

Turning, then, to the connections of sexual expression and the expressive interest, suppose that concerns about human welfare and the quality of human life prompt expression; the evident importance of those concerns provides substantial reasons for the expression. A paradigm is expression about sex and sexuality – say, artistic expression that displays an antipathy to existing sexual conventions, the limited sensibilities revealed in those conventions, and the harm they impose. In a culture that is, as Kathy Acker says, "horrendously moralistic," it is understandable that such writers as Acker challenge understandings of sexuality "under the aegis of art, [where] you're allowed to actually deal with matters of sexuality."[44] Again, in an interview, Kathy Acker says:

> I think you'd agree there are various things in us – not all of which are kind, gentle, and tender – readers of de Sade and Genet would probably agree on this point! But I think you can explore these things without becoming a mass murderer . . . without causing *real* damage, without turning to *real* crime. One way of exploring these things is through *art*; there are various ways of doing this. We have . . . to find out what it is to be human – and yet not wreak total havoc on the society.[45]

The human significance of sexuality lends special urgency to the explorations Acker describes. Moreover, and here I join the issue about pornography and the expressive interest, that urgency does not decline when, as in the case of pornography, sexuality mixes with power and subordination – when, as in materials covered by proposed regulations, it is not "kind, gentle, and tender." On the contrary, a writer may reasonably think – as Acker apparently does – that coming to terms with such mixing is especially important, precisely because, in the world as it is, power is so deeply implicated in sexual identity and desire. To stay away from the erotization of dominance and submission – as pornography regulations require – is to avoid sexuality as it, to some indeterminate degree, is.

The connections between pornography (materials covered by the regulation) and the expressive interest may actually be strengthened because, in a world of unequal power, it engages our sexual desires, categories, identities, and fantasies as they are – even if our aim is to transform them. Regulations targeted particularly on the fusion of sexuality and subordination – on the apparent extremes of heterosexual and phallic conventions – will cover too much. For it may be in part by working with that fusion and acknowledging its force, rather than by simply depicting a world of erotic possibilities beyond power, that we establish the basis for transforming existing forms of sexuality.[46]

One difficulty with the regulations, then, is that they make no provision for the importance of the expressive interest – for the weight of the reasons that move at least some people to produce sexually explicit materials that conflict with the regulations. Underscoring that lack of provision, MacKinnon criticizes the exception in current obscenity law for materials with "literary, political, artistic, or scientific value": "The ineffectualness of obscenity law is due in some part to exempting materials of literary, political, artistic, or scientific value. Value can be found in anything, depending, I have come to think, not only on one's adherence to postmodernism, but on how much one is being paid. And never underestimate the power of an erection, these days termed 'entertainment,' to give a thing value." Of course, the expressive interest may be overridden, but the conventional rationales for regulation fail to acknowledge it, and thus fall afoul of the requirement of deliberative inclusion. More particularly, though the connections with the expressive interest do not settle the issue, they do help to increase the burden of argument that must be carried in justifying such regulations: those connections mean that defenders of regulations must make a more compelling showing of the harms of pornography, and not simply advance the speculative arguments that are commonly proposed.

7. Moral Liberty

I want now to discuss the implications of the principle of deliberative inclusion in the area of moral liberty, what John Stuart Mill called the "liberty of tastes and pursuits."[47] I propose to concentrate in particular on the *enforcement of morality.*

My principal focus here will be on the permissibility of imposing criminal punishment on citizens for violating the ethical code shared by the majority in a society, even when that conduct is neither injurious nor offensive to others: Is it permissible for a political society to use its criminal law to force members to lead lives that are not, by the lights of the majority, immoral or perverse?[48] Criminalization is, of course, a special case, and problems of moral liberty extend well beyond it. Mill's defense of moral liberty was as much a criticism of intrusive collective opinion as of state regulation. And, confining attention to state action, we need to address the codification of morality through regulations that are not backed by criminal sanction: for example, bans on same-sex marriage. But because the issues have important affinities, and can be seen more sharply in the area of criminalization, I will focus on it here.

In two important cases over the past decade – *Bowers v. Hardwick* and *Barnes v. Glen Theatre* – the U.S. Supreme Court affirmed the constitutional permissibility of criminalizing immoral conduct. In the first, "the presumed belief of a majority of the electorate in Georgia that homosexual sodomy is immoral and unacceptable" was offered as a suitable rationale for a law imposing criminal sanctions on consensual homosexual sodomy.[49] To be more precise, the Georgia law itself imposed criminal sanctions on consensual sodomy quite generally, but was upheld by the Court only as applied to homosexual sodomy. In the second, the Court upheld an Indiana public indecency law requiring dancers to wear pasties and a G-string. As rationale for the law, Justice Rehnquist offers the public's "moral disapproval of people appearing in the nude among strangers in public places." Moreover, he notes traditional common law restrictions on public nudity and the view underlying those restrictions: that public nudity was an act *malum in se*. Writing in concurrence, Justice Scalia emphasizes that the conduct is prohibited because it is "immoral" – in conflict with "traditional moral belief" – not because it is offensive: "The purpose of Indiana's nudity law would be violated, I think, if 60,000 fully consenting adults crowded into the Hoosierdome to display their genitals to one another, even if there was not an offended innocent in the crowd." Rejecting Mill's harm principle – which requires a showing of harm to others as a necessary condition for criminal sanction – Scalia says, "Our society prohibits, and all human societies have prohibited, certain activities not because they harm others, but because they are considered, in the traditional phrase, *"contra bonos mores," i.e.* immoral" – and he goes on to mention "sadomasochism, cockfighting, bestiality, suicide, drug use, prostitution, and sodomy" as areas in which legal regulation of conduct is constitutionally permitted, though the rationale for the regulations is rooted in "traditional moral belief."

As Scalia's examples indicate, the debate about the enforcement of morals is not confined to issues of sexual morality. Still, that has been a central historical focus – as in *Bowers* and *Barnes*, as well as in disagreements about generic anti-sodomy laws, and regulations of prostitution and pornography. I will maintain that focus here.

The debate about enforcing morality implicates in especially profound ways the value of democracy. Indeed, the debate about the permissibility of enforcing conventional ethics is commonly presented as a conflict between democracy, which is said to support the enforcement of morals, and some other value – say, personal liberty or autonomy – which is seen to be compromised by and to condemn that enforcement. Ronald Dworkin, for example, says that the argument from democracy is "politically the most powerful argument against liberal tolerance."[50] And in his classical critique of Lord Devlin's defense of the enforcement of morals, H. L. A. Hart says, "It seems fatally easy to believe that loyalty to democratic principles entails acceptance of what may be termed moral populism: the view that the majority have a moral right to dictate how all should live."[51]

To state the views of the moral populist in more generous terms: on moral issues, the values of the majority ought to be decisive because no other basis for determining our shared "moral environment" is compatible with the equality of citizens – no other basis is fair to citizens as equals. Moral disagreements in the community ought, then, to be resolved by a procedure of decision making that treats citizens as equals – say, majority rule. Lord Devlin himself suggests this case for enforcement in an essay titled "Democracy and Morality": "Those who do not believe in God must ask themselves what they *mean* when they say that they believe in democracy. Not that all men are born with equal brains – we cannot believe that; but that they have at their command – and that in this they are all born in the same degree – the faculty of telling right from wrong. This is the whole meaning of democracy, for if in this endowment men were not equal, it would be pernicious that in the government of any society they should have equal rights."[52]

A first response to the moral populist argues that majority rule on moral questions – like majority rule decisions to establish racially segregated schools – does not treat citizens as equals, because it permits people to act on their view that some citizens are worth less than others. But we ought to resist acceding to this temptation too quickly. It is at least possible to condemn a way of life and the conduct it comprises without condemning those who lead it as worth less than others: that is, for example, the point of current Catholic doctrine on homosexuality. We may wish to argue, in the end, that this view is hostility barely concealed – that when it comes to matters sexual, moral traditionalism is homophobia and misogyny carried out by other means. Still, the means are different: a complex structure of religious and moral argument. We ought, then, to be cautious about simply *identifying* a willingness to punish conduct judged immoral with either racism or sexism – which are, on their face and without reinterpretation, about people, not ways of life. "Attempting to preclude the entire population from acting in ways that are perceived as immoral is not assimilable to comparatively disadvantaging a given group out of simple hostility to its members."[53] To be sure, regulating ways of life as immoral may in the end be as objectionable as condemning people as of lesser worth, but we need to distinguish the troubles.

A second response to the argument from democracy is to defend a Millian harm principle on the basis of the value of autonomy or utilitarian principles. But this strategy may unintentionally lend added force to Devlin-style arguments. Let me explain, concentrating on appeals to the value of autonomy.

The argument from autonomy takes two principal forms. According to the first, the autonomy protected by restrictions on the enforcement of morality is principally the autonomy of the agent whose conduct would otherwise be regulated. According to the second, moral toleration benefits others, whose autonomy is enhanced by a greater range of alternatives.[54] The first version is more familiar and I will sketch a version of it presented by Ronald Dworkin, who offers it as a reply to one kind of communitarian argument for the enforcement of an ethical code.[55] What matters here are not the details, but the central thesis: that we cannot make people's lives go better by requiring them to conform, through threats of criminal punishment, to an ethical code that they reject and would otherwise violate. Dworkin rests this thesis on a theory of the best human life in which the value of autonomy or self-government plays a central role. According to this theory, a person's life is good only if the person chooses the values that guide it – or, if choice conveys the wrong picture, reflectively endorses those values.[56]

Dworkin endorses an especially strong form of the requirement of reflective endorsement, though he needs just such a strong form to defeat the argument for enforcement.[57] Reflective endorsement, he says, has *constitutive*, not merely *additive* value.[58] In particular, no part of a life contributes to the value of that life unless it is reflectively endorsed. So, for example, the development of intellectual powers makes a life better only if that development takes the form of *self-development* – development guided by the reflectively accepted values of the agent. Altruistic behavior – saving the lives of others, say – makes the saver's life better only if she endorses the value of altruistic behavior.

Dworkin's conclusions about the importance of reflective endorsement closely parallel Locke's defense of religious toleration; indeed, Dworkin's defense of moral toleration might be seen as generalizing Locke's argument. According to Locke, "Although the magistrate's opinion in religion be sound, and the way that he appoints be truly evangelical, yet, if I be not thoroughly persuaded thereof in my own mind, there will be no safety for me in following it. No way whatsoever that I shall walk in against the dictates of my own conscience will ever bring me to the mansions of the blessed. . . . Faith only and inward sincerity are the things that procure acceptance with God."[59] Just as worship is of no value unless accompanied by inner conviction, by faith freely embraced, so, too, decent or socially beneficial conduct – a good impact on the world – adds nothing to the value of a life unless the behavior is accompanied by a freely embraced, inner conviction about the value of the conduct.

Reasoning from this premise about the dependence of salvation on inner faith, Locke argued that the state could not save souls through enforced religious rituals, and should not try. Similarly, premising the constitutive value of autonomy, Dworkin concludes that the state cannot make a person's life *better* by forcing that person to live according to an ethical code he rejects. The problem with moral paternalism, then, is not that it fails to be suitably skeptical about the good, or that it provokes civil conflict, but that it rests on an incorrect theory of the good life; it fails to appreciate the constitutive role of reflective endorsement in the value of a life.

If this is right, then we cannot defend the enforcement of morals by claiming to show equal concern for the true good of all citizens. Indeed, that argument is, in Dworkin's words, "self-defeating" because, according to the autonomy theory, a life of enforced moral conformity is not better than a life of chosen immorality.[60] On the contrary, the requirement of reflective endorsement supports freedom of personal choice under favorable conditions for considering how best to live (e.g., conditions in which people pursue different "experiments in living," to borrow Mill's phrase).

This argument has considerable force. The premise about autonomy serves as an axiom in a family of reasonable comprehensive moralities; and for the sake of discussion, I assume that the conclusions are well-supported by the premises. But as political argument, it has an important shortcoming: it depends on a comprehensive philosophy of life, and the deliberative view requires that, under conditions of reasonable pluralism, we free political argument from such dependence, particularly when such argument bears on the fundamentals of conduct.

Thus, the autonomy theory is a form of comprehensive moral liberalism, rejected by citizens who think, not unreasonably, that human lives are made good at least in part by their compliance with divine law, or their conformity to the order of the universe, or the quality of their impact on the world, or the extent to which they realize human powers. To be sure, citizens who endorse such views may themselves reject the enforcement of morality because they judge it worse or inappropriate to force lives to be as good as they can be. But just as the belief in religious toleration is not and should not be presented as contingent on a religious view about the sufficiency of inner faith to salvation, acceptance of moral toleration is not and should not be presented as contingent on the view that personal autonomy is the supreme moral value and comprehensive guide to conduct. I mentioned earlier that the autonomy argument for moral toleration generalizes a Lockean argument for religious toleration; whereas the latter rejects enforcement of a religious code because inner faith is required for salvation, the former, more abstractly, treats reflective endorsement as constitutive of the goodness of a life for the person who lives it. I think there is something right in this use of religious toleration as a model, but as I explain in some detail below, the deliberative view presents the parallel in a different way: it emphasizes in particular the weight of the reasons that lie behind the regulated conduct and the unacceptability for the purposes of political argument of the considerations that would justify the regulations.

The failure of this argument might suggest that majority rule ought, after all, to extend to moral issues. Precisely by underscoring moral disagreement – indeed, reasonable moral disagreement – the limits of the autonomy argument might suggest that treating citizens as equals requires that the majority be left free to fix the shared moral landscape. Lord Devlin makes just this point. Agreeing that moral differences often cannot be resolved through a good faith exercise of practical reason – that "after centuries of debate, men of undoubted reasoning power and honesty of purpose have shown themselves unable to agree on what the moral law should be"[61] – he concludes that the arbiter of social morality cannot be reason, but must instead be the people – "the ordinary man, the man in the jury box, who might also be called the reasonable man or the right-minded man."[62]

But the deliberative account of democracy rejects that conclusion. To see why, notice first that controversies about the *enforcement* of morality characteristically track moral controversies: when enforcement is controversial, so, too, is the moral question itself. The issue, then, is not whether conduct, assumed not to be injurious to others, can permissibly be regulated for moral reasons *on which there is general agreement.* Instead, the issue is whether conduct can permissibly be regulated for moral reasons, despite deep and apparently unresolvable disagreement about the morality of the conduct and the grounds for regulating it.

This point seems easy to miss. In his criticisms of Devlin, for example, Hart asks "why we should not summon all the resources of our reason, sympathetic understanding, as well as critical intelligence, and insist that before *general moral feeling* is turned into criminal law it is submitted to scrutiny of a different kind from Sir Patrick's? Surely the legislator should ask whether the *general morality* is based on ignorance, superstition, or misunderstanding. . . ."[63] Such questions are certainly in order. But in controversial cases of enforcement, the assumption that regulations enforce "general morality" or "general moral feeling" is typically not, unless by "general" we mean "majority," in which case a very large step needs to be filled in – the step that authorizes the majority to speak in the name of the community.

Take the case of homosexuality. It would be preposterous to say that the moral consensus of the community condemns homosexuality, but some people want nevertheless to practice it despite its accepted immorality. Instead, some citizens, for religious or perhaps other reasons, condemn it and perhaps wish to regulate it (though not all who condemn also wish to regulate). Putting aside concededly insufficient appeals to Scripture, two principal arguments have been advanced for condemnation and regulation.[64] First, procreation is the natural end of sexuality (the natural end being the end for which God established sexual desire), natural ends ought to be practically authoritative, and conduct that by its nature is disconnected from or contravenes those ends is base, perverse, and worthless.[65] Second, homosexuality violates a principle of "complementarity," warring against the differentiation – including sexual differentiation – that is essential to God's ordering of the universe: "Human beings are . . . nothing less than the work of God himself; and in the complementarity of the sexes they are called to reflect the inner unity of the Creator."[66]

These lines of argument are parts of philosophies of life that others reasonably reject (indeed, they are very much contested within the traditions of thought to which they belong).[67] Others believe that there is nothing sinful, immoral, or in any other way objectionable about being gay or lesbian. Some reject the view that procreation is *the* natural end of sexuality or, more generally, that human conduct has natural ends or that those ends, such as they are, ought to be authoritative in settling the best way to live. And some reject the particular metaphysics of creation that founds the principle of complementarity.

Parallel points can be made for the other disputes: about sodomy, pornography, or nude dancing. In each case, we ought not ask whether the state may enforce the *general morality of the community*: on these issues, though the majority may share a morality, the *community* does not – the democratic community, constituted by free and equal citizens. Disagreements are fundamental and deeply rooted in reasonable differences of outlook, associated with, among other things, different views about our bodies, about the role of our embodiment and the pleasures associated with it in the conduct of our lives, about how to respond to the independence from rational control characteristic of sexual pleasure. Some citizens find the law of sin in our members: they see in the body an obstacle to our highest purposes, or at least the source of temptation to do wrong. Others think, not unreasonably, that embodiment is essential to our nature, that bodily pleasures provide ways to break free

219

of conventional constraint, and that our capacity to transcend such constraints is fundamental to our nature as free agents. These are matters on which – I say this as platitude – people disagree, often profoundly, in thought, sensibility, and conduct: a public basis for justification is absent. The constraints of shared evidence and conceptual precision required for agreement are simply not in view. Law has no place here, not in a democracy committed to treating its members as equals. As Justice Blackmun said in dissent in *Bowers:* "That certain, but by no means all, religious groups condemn the behavior at issue gives the state no license to impose their judgments on the entire citizenry."[68]

Fundamental, reasonable disagreement, then, puts strong pressure against the enforcement of conventional ethics: the principles in the name of which such enforcement might be justified cannot be accepted by all who are subject to them. And that pressure is particularly strong when, as in the case of sexual conduct, the regulations impinge deeply on the lives of those who are regulated. Given the underlying moral division, some members of the community suppose that the regulated conduct is not only permissible, but an essential part of their good: that sexual intimacy is a fundamental human good and that – particularly in view of the facts of human diversity – its value is contingent in part on its being guided by the judgments, feelings, and sensibilities of the parties to it.[69] Regulations impinge deeply, then, because the reasons that support such intimacy are substantial and can be acknowledged as such by people who reject those reasons. And because the reasons are so substantial, there is a correspondingly strong case against regulating it in the name of considerations drawn from philosophies of life that some citizens reasonably reject.

At the same time, should regulations not impinge very deeply – should the reasons supporting the conduct be less substantial – then the case against enforcement is less compelling, even if the reasons come from conventional ethics. Thus, regulating boxing because it is immoral – or betting because it is – may be less deeply objectionable than regulating sexuality. Though some may reject the reasons used to support the regulations, they may nevertheless accept majority support as itself sufficient reason. More generally, I think it is very difficult to argue for a blanket condemnation of the enforcement of community morality – in particular, a principled condemnation that does not depend on the complexities of legal categorization and associated slippery slopes – unless we premise the autonomy version of moral liberalism. In any case, no such blanket condemnation is intended here.

I said earlier that the proponents of enforcement often appeal to the value of democracy, urging that the equality of citizens requires that majority values fix the moral environment. This point has considerable force when a collective choice is necessary, as, for example, in the area of security policy: there, we need to arrive at a common decision, so the majority may speak in the name of the community – the majority principle itself may be a matter of general agreement among people who disagree about the right policy.[70] But where regulation is unnecessary, as in the area of sexual morality, this rationale is unavailable.

The case for the majority as tribune of the community is not confined to issues on which collective choice is mandatory. It also has considerable force when regulations do not impinge deeply: when they do not cover conduct rooted in fundamental obligations or supported in other ways by substantial reasons. In such cases, even if a regulation is not required, it is permissible to adopt one with majority support. For example, taxing citizens to support research and development may be unnecessary, but it is unobjectionable: given differences of judgment and interest, it is to be settled by a procedure that treats people as equals. But fundamental interests and substantial reasons are at stake in the area of sexual morality (once more, the key issue of contest about the enforcement of morality). Given the reasonable rejection of the moralities in the name of which the regulations are imposed, the presence of such fundamental interests condemns the regulations.

In short, then, moral liberty – like religious and expressive liberty – is an ingredient in the democratic idea of collective choice by free and equal citizens. The decision to regulate cannot be collective, in a suitable sense: it cannot arise from free reasoning among equals. It is for that reason undemocratic.

8. Community, Legitimacy, Democracy

To conclude, I will sketch some remarks on a fundamental question that I have postponed for the end: What makes the deliberative conception of democracy compelling as an interpretation of the fundamental democratic idea – that the authorization to exercise state power is to arise from the collective decisions of those whose decisions are to be governed by that power?

The principal virtues of the deliberative conception are allied closely to its conception of binding collective choice. By emphasizing the importance of articulating shared reasons, the deliberative view expresses an especially compelling picture of the possible relations among people within a democratic order; moreover, it states a forceful ideal of political legitimacy for a democracy. I take up these two points in turn.

First, the deliberative conception offers a more forceful rendering than aggregative conceptions of the fundamental democratic idea – the idea that decisions about the exercise of state power are *collective*. It requires that we offer considerations acceptable to others, understood to be free, equal, and reasonable, and whose conduct will be governed by the decisions. It requires more than that we count their interests, while keeping our fingers crossed that those interests are outweighed.

This point about the attractions of the deliberative interpretation of collective decisions can be stated in terms of ideas of *political autonomy* and *political community*. If a political community is a group of people sharing a comprehensive moral or religious view, than reasonable pluralism ruins political community. But on an alternative conception of political community, deliberative democracy is a form of political community. To see how, notice first that by requiring justification on terms acceptable to others, deliberative democracy provides for political autonomy. Without denying the coercive aspects of common political life, it requires that all who are governed by collective decisions, who are expected to govern their own conduct by those decisions, must find the *bases* of those decisions – the political values that support them – acceptable, even when they disagree with the details of the decision.

Through this assurance of political autonomy, deliberative democracy achieves one important element of the ideal of community – not because collective decisions crystallize a shared ethical outlook that informs all social life generally, nor because the collective good takes precedence over liberties of members. Rather, deliberative democracy is connected to political community because the requirement of shared reasons for the exercise of political power – a requirement absent from the aggregative view – itself expresses the full and equal membership of all in the sovereign body responsible for authorizing the exercise of that power, and establishes the common reason and will of that body.

When I say that it expresses "full membership," not simply

equal membership, I mean membership in the collective sovereign that authorizes the exercise of power, and not simply membership as a subject of that power. To be sure, an alternative conception of full membership is available: persons might be said to be full members of a political society just in case the values their philosophy of life comprises coincide with the values that guide the exercise of political power. Under conditions of reasonable pluralism, the deliberative view rejects such full coincidence, even as an ideal of practical reason. It acknowledges a separation between, as Michael Sandel puts it, "our identity as citizens [and] our identity as persons more broadly conceived."[71]

But why this separation? Why, Sandel asks, "should political deliberation not reflect our best understanding of the highest human ends?" After all, when it does so reflect, we have an experience of political community unavailable from more truncated political argument, confined to common ground that can be occupied by alternative reasonable views.

The answer is contained in the idea of reasonable pluralism, and I will not repeat the details here. Suffice to say that if we take the fact of reasonable pluralism seriously, then we need to watch our third-person plurals as we move from "our identity as citizens" to "our identity as persons": our identity as citizens is shared, or identity as persons is not. Acknowledging this, what are we to make of "*our* best understanding of the highest human ends?" As citizens, we do not have – nor can we expect to secure – a common view about the highest human ends. So the request that *we* make "*our* best understanding" the basis of political deliberation is empty – or, in practice, gets content from the conception endorsed by a particular group of citizens. In contrast, as persons, we each may have such understandings, but they are plural – they are "our best understanding*s.*" Because those views are incompatible, we cannot fully incorporate them all into political justification, and to use any one in particular is unacceptable.

This suggestion about deliberative democracy and the value of community may seem strained in light of the role of religious, expressive, and moral liberties in the deliberative view. For such liberties are commonly represented as – for better or worse – the solvent of community. And that is especially true when we reject the enforcement of community morality.

But the deliberative view offers a reason for skepticism about that claim. Under conditions of reasonable pluralism, the protec-

223

tion of the liberties of the moderns is not a solvent of community. Reasonable pluralism itself may be such a solvent, at least if we define community in terms of a shared philosophy of life. But once we assume reasonable pluralism, the protection of the liberties of the moderns turns out to be a necessary though insufficient condition for the only plausible form of political community. For those liberties fall under the "principle of inclusion." As that term indicates, they are conditions required to ensure the equal standing of citizens as members of the collective body whose authorization is required for the legitimate exercise of public power.

Finally, the deliberative conception of democracy presents an account of when decisions made in a democracy are politically legitimate and how to shape institutions and forms of argument so as to make legitimate decisions.

Generally speaking, we have a strong case for political legitimacy when the exercise of political power has sufficient justification. But, as a conceptual matter, a person can believe that the exercise of power is well justified – therefore legitimate – while also acknowledging that others over whom it is exercised reject the justification. As a conceptual matter, legitimacy does not require that the relevant justification be acknowledged as such by those who are subject to the legitimate power: there need be no justification *to* them. But the background of democracy – the idea of citizens as free and equal – and the fact of reasonable pluralism are important in characterizing a more limited conception of justification: because of these conditions, the relevant justification must be addressed to citizens, by which I mean that its terms must be acknowledged as suitable by those subject to political power. Given that citizens have equal standing and are understood as free, and given the fact of reasonable pluralism, we have an especially strong showing of legitimacy when the exercise of state power is supported by considerations acknowledged as reasons by the different views endorsed by reasonable citizens, who are understood as equals. No other account of reasons is suited for this case.

Notes

1. "Governed by" rather than "affected by." Democracy is about justifying authority, not about justifying influence. See Michael Walzer, *Spheres of Justice* (New York: Basic Books, 1983); Christopher McMahon, *Au-*

thority and Democracy (Princeton, N.J.: Princeton University Press, 1995).

2. I am grateful to T. M. Scanlon for emphasizing the importance of this parallel.

3. See Robert Dahl, *Democracy and Its Critics* (New Haven, Conn.: Yale University Press, 1989). Dahl holds that the "principle of equal consideration" – which he attributes to Stanley Benn and which states that the good or interests of each must be given equal consideration – is the most compelling interpretation of the deeper "idea of intrinsic equality," according to which individuals are, for the purposes of collective decisions, to be considered equal (85–6). Dahl justifies democracy, as a process for making collective decisions, by reference to the principle of equal consideration, given a "presumption of personal autonomy": the presumption that individuals are the best judges and most vigilant defenders of their own interests. See *Democracy and Its Critics*, chs. 6–8.

4. Jürgen Habermas, "Further Reflections on the Public Sphere," in Craig Calhoun (ed.), *Habermas and the Public Sphere* (Cambridge, Mass.: MIT Press, 1992), 446.

5. Ibid., 452.

6. For discussion of this fact, see Joshua Cohen, "Moral Pluralism and Political Consensus," in David Copp, Jean Hampton, and John Roemer (eds.), *The Idea of Democracy* (Cambridge University Press, 1993), 270–91; John Rawls, *Political Liberalism* (New York: Columbia University Press, 1993); and Joshua Cohen, "A More Democratic Liberalism," *Michigan Law Review* 92, 6 (May 1994): 1502–46.

7. On the importance of moral diversity as a source of pressures toward relativism and nihilism, see Gilbert Harman, "Moral Relativism," in Gilbert Harman and Judith Jarvis Thomson, *Moral Relativism and Moral Objectivity* (Oxford: Basil Blackwell, 1996), 8–14.

8. See Rawls's discussion of the burdens of judgment in *Political Liberalism*, 54–8. Leif Wenar argues that these burdens are not widely acknowledged, that, for example, "a religious doctrine characteristically presents itself as universally accessible to clear minds and open hearts," and he cites the Vatican II statement on Divine Revelation in support. See "*Political Liberalism*: An Internal Critique," *Ethics* 106 (October 1995): 32–62. But to say that certain religious truths require revelation is to acknowledge that they, unlike truths of natural religion, are not simply available to clear minds and open hearts.

9. The remarks that follow draw on my "A More Democratic Liberalism."

10. Consider in this connection the virtually unanimous popular endorsement of political equality and equality of opportunity indicated in Herbert McClosky and John Zaller, *The American Ethos: Public Attitudes*

Toward Capitalism and Democracy (Cambridge University Press, 1985), 74, 83.

11. Thus, Dahl formulates the "principle of equal consideration of interests," as well as the "idea of intrinsic equality" on which it rests, to apply solely to processes for making binding collective decisions, and indicates that both might be adopted by adherents to religious moralities, as well as utilitarian and Kantian moral views. See *Democracy and Its Critics*, 85–7.

12. Consider, for example, the changes in the Catholic doctrine on toleration that emerge in Vatican II. The idea of human dignity, always a central element in Catholic moral and social thought, is developed along new lines as the basis for an account of political legitimacy with principled limits on the state's authority in matters of religious faith and practice. See "Declaration on Religious Freedom," 1.2. Dignity imposes an obligation to seek the truth and embrace it. But though the "one true religion subsists in the Catholic and apostolic Church," the pursuit and embrace of truth must comport with our nature as free beings "endowed with reason" and the dignity owing to that nature. And this requires immunity from "external coercion," as well as "psychological freedom." The introduction to the Declaration ties the force of the sense of dignity and an understanding of its implications to modern experience (the "consciousness of contemporary man"). In an interesting essay on modern Confucian humanism and human rights, Tu Wei-ming suggests a way to reinterpret Confucian doctrine as incorporating a conception of dignity, tied to obligations in social relationships, that could serve in turn as a basis for a conception of human rights. Here, too, the conception of dignity is tied to central Confucian notions, but its formulation is prompted by modern political sensibilities, as articulated through international institutions. See Tu Wei-ming, "A Confucian Perspective on Human Rights," unpublished, 1995.

13. For critical discussion of the idea of the "exclusive rights of truth," see John Courtney Murray, "The Problem of Religious Freedom," in J. Leon Hooper, S. J. (ed.), *Religious Liberty: Catholic Struggles with Pluralism* (Louisville, Ky.: Westminster/John Knox Press, 1993), ch. 2.

14. Michael McConnell says, "It would come as some surprise to a devout Jew to find that he has 'selected the day of the week in which to refrain from labor' since the Jewish people have been under the impression from some 3,000 years that this choice was made by God." "Religious Freedom at a Crossroads," *University of Chicago Law Review* 59 (1992): 115. The source of the quotation to which McConnell is responding is *Estate of Thornton v. Caldor, Inc.*, 472 U.S. 703, 711 (1985) (O'Connor, J., concurring).

15. Here I follow discussion in T. M. Scanlon's *What We Owe to Each Other*, ch. 1 ("Reasons"), unpublished manuscript, 1997.

16. Pope John Paul II, *Evangelium Vitae* (New York: Times Books, 1995), §§29, 62. For critical discussion of these claims and the argument based on them, see Judith Jarvis Thomson, "Abortion," *Boston Review* 20, 3 (Summer 1995): 11–15.

17. I say "arguably" because it might be said that reasons are essentially public and capable of being shared. If that is right, then the fact stated in the text would not constitute a reason.

18. See Adam Przeworski, *Democracy and the Market* (Cambridge University Press, 1991), 17.

19. Ibid.

20. See Keith Krehbiel, *Information and Legislative Organization* (Ann Arbor: University of Michigan Press, 1991), 81–4, 95–6. Apart from this dependence on preference diversity, the effectiveness of speech depends on the ease of verifying information, and whether discussion proceeds sequentially and in public. See David Austen-Smith, "Strategic Models of Talk in Political Decision-Making," *International Political Science Review* 13, 1 (1992): 45–58; on economic institutions that promote verification and sequential, public conversation, see Charles Sabel, "Learning by Monitoring: The Institutions of Economic Development," in Neil Smelser and Richard Swedberg (eds.), *The Handbook of Economic Sociology* (Princeton, N.J.: Princeton University Press, 1995), 137–65.

21. For discussion, see Christine Korsgaard, "Skepticism about Practical Reason," *Journal of Philosophy* 83, 1 (January 1986): 5–25; Scanlon, *What We Owe to Each Other*, ch. 1. For illuminating criticism of instrumental rationality, see Robert Nozick, *The Nature of Rationality* (Princeton, N.J.: Princeton University Press, 1993), ch. 5. Particularly important for purposes here are the remarks on the symbolic utility of acting on principles.

22. Using Nozick's terminology (see note 21), when I see that a proposal cannot be defended with acceptable reasons, its symbolic utility declines. Assuming that symbolic utility is motivationally important, the motivation for advancing the proposal declines.

23. I am not worrying here about distinctions between "desire" and "prefer" – in particular that the latter is a polyadic relation.

24. On the distinction between primitive and induced preferences, and a case for the view that deliberation-induced preference change is a matter of changes in induced preferences as a result of new information, see John Ferejohn, "Must Preferences Be Respected in a Democracy?" in Copp et al. (eds.), *The Idea of Democracy*, 236–7; David Austen-Smith, "Modeling Deliberative Democracy," unpublished manuscript, April 1995.

25. For suggestive discussion of the role nonstrategic reasons can play in constraining discussion and improving its effectiveness, see James Johnson, "Is Talk Really Cheap? Prompting Conversation Between Critical Theory and Rational Choice," *American Political Science Review* 87, 1 (1993): 74–86.

26. Dahl, *Democracy and Its Critics*, 182.

27. Dahl has long been skeptical about the role of courts with powers of judicial review in providing such protection. See his remarkable essay, "Decision-Making in a Democracy: The Supreme Court as a National Policy-Maker," *Journal of Public Law* 6 (Fall 1957): 279–95, and *Democracy and Its Critics,* chs. 12, 13.

28. See John Hart Ely, *Democracy and Distrust* (Cambridge, Mass.: Harvard University Press, 1980); Dahl, *Democracy and Its Critics;* and, more generally, on constitutional requirements as enabling democracy, Stephen Holmes, "Precommitment and the Paradox of Democracy," in Jon Elster and Rune Slagstad (eds.), *Constitutionalism and Democracy* (Cambridge University Press, 1988), esp. 195–240; and Samuel Freeman, "Original Meaning, Democratic Interpretation, and the Constitution," *Philosophy and Public Affairs* 21 (Winter 1992): 3–42.

29. This is, I believe, Dahl's view. Critics of Roberto Unger's conception of empowered democracy have (mistakenly, I believe) assumed that he endorses it. See his *False Necessity* (Cambridge University Press, 1987), 508–39. And it bears a strong family resemblance to the democracy-based interpretations of the U.S. Constitution advanced by Ely in *Democracy and Distrust,* and Bruce Ackerman in *We, the People* (Cambridge, Mass.: Harvard University Press, 1991), esp. ch. 1.

30. Of course, not all differences of conviction are reasonable. One implication is that the problem of toleration for the intolerant is a separate issue in an account of religious liberty. Religious liberty generally ought not to be treated as a response to a problem of unreasonableness.

31. Michael Sandel, *Democracy's Discontent* (Cambridge, Mass.: Harvard University Press, 1996), 322.

32. See Scanlon's suggestion that proponents of subjective criteria for interpersonal comparisons might defend those criteria by arguing that they "would be agreed on by people to the extent that they seek a principle recognizing them as equal, independent agents whose judgment must be accorded equal weight." T. M. Scanlon, "Preference and Urgency," *Journal of Philosophy* 72 (1975): 655–69.

33. On the encumbered self, see Sandel, *Democracy's Discontent,* 14.

34. On the distinction between these two aspects of religious liberty, and the connections between the arguments for them, see John Courtney

Murray, "The Problem of Religious Freedom," in Hooper (ed.), *Religious Liberty*, 141–4, 148–51.

35. On this last point: the key to the case for religious liberty is that the content of a view assigns stringent obligations to a person who holds it. But specifically *religious* content is not essential.

36. See the discussion of this rationale in Stephen Carter, *The Culture of Disbelief* (New York: Basic Books, 1993), 17–18, 35–9. As a general matter, Carter's defense of religious liberty seems too exclusively focused on the parallels between religious and associational liberty and, correspondingly, too dismissive of the continuities between freedom of conscience and freedom of public worship. On those continuities, see Murray, "The Problem of Religious Freedom," 148–51.

37. Unger, *False Necessity*, 525, emphases added; Joshua Cohen, "Deliberation and Democratic Legitimacy," in Alan Hamlin and Phillip Petit (eds.), *The Good Polity*, (1989), 17–34.

38. See Cass Sunstein, *Democracy and the Problem of Free Speech* (New York: Free Press, 1993), 130.

39. See Alexander Meiklejohn, *Political Freedom* (New York: Harper & Brothers, 1960); Sunstein, *Democracy and the Problem of Free Speech*; Robert Bork, "Neutral Principles and Some First Amendment Problems," *Indiana Law Journal* 47, 1 (Fall 1971): 1–35; Ely, *Democracy and Distrust*; Owen Fiss, *Liberalism Divided* (Boulder, Colo.: Westview Press, 1996).

40. For discussion, see Joshua Cohen, "Freedom of Expression," *Philosophy and Public Affairs* 22, 3 (Summer 1993): 207–63.

41. *Whitney v. California*, 274 U.S. 357, 375 (1927) (Brandeis, J., concurring).

42. The discussion that follows is taken from Joshua Cohen, "Freedom, Equality, Pornography," in Austin Sarat and Thomas Kearns (eds.), *Justice and Injustice in Law and Legal Theory* (Ann Arbor: University of Michigan Press, 1996), 99–139.

43. Indianapolis, Ind., City-Council General Ordinance No. 35 (June 11, 1984). The full text is cited in Catharine MacKinnon, *Feminism Unmodified*, (Cambridge, Mass.: Harvard University Press, 1987), 274 n 1. The regulation was overturned in *American Booksellers Ass'n. v. Hudnut*, 771 F.2d 323 (7th Cir. 1985), *affirmed without opinion*, 475 U.S. 1001 (1986).

44. See Kathy Acker, "Devoured by Myths: An Interview with Sylvere Lotringer," in *Hannibal Lecter, My Father* (New York: Semiotext(e), 1991).

45. Interview with Andrea Juno in Andrea Juno and V. Vale (eds.), *Angry Women* (San Francisco: Re/Search Publications, 1991), 184–5.

46. See Judith Butler, *Gender Trouble: Feminism and the Subversion of Identity* (New York: Routledge, 1990); Susan Keller, "Viewing and Do-

ing: Complicating Pornography's Meaning," *Georgetown Law Review* 81 (1993): 2195–228; Duncan Kennedy, *Sexy Dressing: Essays on the Power and Politics of Cultural Identity* (Cambridge, Mass.: Harvard University Press, 1993), 126–213.

47. See J. S. Mill, *On Liberty*, ch. 3.

48. Ronald Dworkin, "Liberal Community," *California Law Review* 77, no. 3 (1989): 479–504.

49. 476 US 186, 196 (1986).

50. Dworkin, "Liberal Community," 483.

51. H. L. A. Hart, *Law, Liberty, and Morality* (Stanford, Calif.: Stanford University Press, 1963), 79.

52. Lord Devlin, "Democracy and Morality," in *The Enforcement of Morals* (Oxford: Oxford University Press, 1965).

53. See Ely, *Democracy and Distrust,* p. 256. See also John Hart Ely, "Professor Dworkin's External/Personal Preference Distinction," *Duke Law Review* (1983): 985.

54. For an illustration of this strategy of argument, see Joseph Raz, *The Morality of Freedom* (Oxford: Oxford University Press, 1986), ch. 15. According to Raz, the duty of toleration is "an aspect of the duty of respect for autonomy." Autonomy requires a range of choices among different ways of life that include "distinct and incompatible moral virtues." People who endorse those ways of life tend, however, to be intolerant of one another. So ensuring the structure of alternatives required to foster autonomy requires guarantees against intolerance. But as this sketch indicates, the rationale for the guarantees lies not in the benefits conferred on individuals who receive protection, but in the preservation of a system of alternative possibilities for others.

55. Dworkin, "Liberal Community."

56. I take the term "reflective endorsement" from ibid., 485–6.

57. The argument closely resembles the "maximalist" strategies for defending freedom of expression that I discuss in my "Freedom of Expression." The difficulties are correspondingly parallel.

58. The roots of this claim about the constitutive value of reflective endorsement lie in what Dworkin calls the "challenge" model of value: the view that a good human life is a life that responds suitably to life's challenges. Dworkin appears to think that an agent's conduct counts as meeting a challenge if and only if the agent engaging in the conduct reflectively endorses it. See his "Foundations of Liberal Equality," in *The Tanner Lectures on Human Values 1990* (Salt Lake City: University of Utah Press, 1991), vol. 11. I don't find Dworkin's case very plausible, but will not pursue the reasons here. I am indebted to John Tully for discussion of Dworkin's view.

59. John Locke, *Letter Concerning Toleration* (Indianapolis: Bobbs-Merrill, 1955), 34.

60. See Dworkin, "Liberal Community," 487.

61. Devlin, "Democracy and Morality," 93.

62. Ibid., 90.

63. H. L. A. Hart, "Immorality and Treason," *The Listener*, July 30, 1959, 3, my emphases.

64. A third argument, advanced by Roger Scruton, claims that homosexuality exhibits an objectionable form of narcissism and obscene perception, that instead of "mov[ing] out from my body towards the other, whose flesh is unknown to me . . . I remain locked within my body, narcissistically contemplating in the other an excitement that is the mirror of my own." *Sexual Desire* (New York: Free Press, 1986), 310. Though Scruton presents the antinarcissism argument as an alternative to arguments from the natural end of sexuality and complementarity, it is not clear that it stands independently of the latter.

65. For a crisp statement, see C. H. Peschke, *Christian Ethics* (London: C. Goodliffe Neale, 1978), 2:379.

66. For discussion of the idea of complementarity, see Scruton, *Sexual Desire*, 309; Andrew Sullivan, *Virtually Normal: An Argument About Homosexuality* (New York,: Knopf, 1995); and especially Gareth Moore, *The Body in Context: Sex and Catholicism* (London: SCM Press, 1992), ch. 7. Moore rightly points out that, on natural interpretations, the idea of complementarity depends on the procreation-as-natural-end doctrine. The passage on complementarity comes from the *Letter on the Pastoral Care of Homosexual Persons* of the Catholic Church's Congregation for the Doctrine of the Faith.

67. See, e.g., Sullivan, *Virtually Normal*, and Moore, *The Body in Context*.

68. *Bowers v. Hardwick* 476 U.S. 186 (1986).

69. For suggestive remarks about the importance of sexual intimacy – connecting its value to the importance of individuality and imagination, while separating that value from concerns about procreation – see Stuart Hampshire, *Innocence and Experience* (Cambridge, Mass.: Harvard University Press, 1989), 124–31.

70. I borrow the example of security policy from the discussion of toleration in Thomas Nagel, *Equality and Partiality* (Oxford: Oxford University Press, 1991), 164–5. The general point – that the case for majority rule weakens when a collective policy is not necessary and that such policy is not required when it comes to moral issues – can be found in both Nagel and Joel Feinberg, *Harmless Wrongdoing* (Oxford: Oxford University Press, 1990), 51.

71. Sandel, *Democracy's Discontent*, 322.

Chapter Nine

Health–Health
Trade-offs

1. The Problem

U.S. constitutional government aspires to be deliberative as well as democratic. Government decisions are supposed to be responsive to public will; but public institutions are also designed to ensure an exchange of information, a degree of reflection, and exposure to diverse views. It is for this reason that the aspiration to achieve deliberative democracy is a defining feature of U.S. constitutionalism.[1]

In the past decade, much of the discussion of deliberative democracy has been highly abstract. That discussion has dealt primarily with competing conceptions of political autonomy, the nature of deliberation, the vices and limits of interest-group pluralism, the best conception of majority rule, and the kinds of reasons that are appropriately invoked in the public domain. My purpose in this essay is both more practical and more mundane. I hope to describe a set of serious failures in democratic deliberation – in the particular area of environmental risk – and to connect those failures with current institutional practices and potential institutional solutions. In the process it will be necessary to say something about individual and social rationality, and about the relationships among choices, preferences, and considered judgments. These claims will connect, I believe, with some of the more abstract issues raised by proponents of deliberative democracy.

Sometimes Americans seem obsessed with risks. The discovery of a new danger – in the air, in food, in the workplace, in consumer products – can provoke extensive media attention, produce congressional hearings, and even spur enactment of new legislation. It may not be too much to say that the diminution of social risks has

232

Table 9.1. Principal Death Risk Trends

| | Annual Rate of Increase in Death Rates | | |
Year	Work (per 100,000 Population)	Home (per 100,000 Population)	Motor Vehicle (per 100,000 Population)
1930–40	−1.8	−0.2	−3.3
1940–50	−2.3	−2.2	−4.0
1950–60	−2.8	−2.1	−3.5
1960–70	−1.2	−1.7	−0.8
1970–80	−1.6	−2.7	−3.4
1980–90	−3.2	−2.4	−4.3

Source: W. Kip Viscusi, *Fatal Tradeoffs* (Oxford: Oxford University Press, 1992), 285.

been the most novel and important task of the national government since the late 1960s.

To regulate risks sensibly, government needs to deliberate in order to compile information and to obtain differing perspectives, if only so that it can anticipate likely public reactions to whatever it ultimately does. To deliberate well, it needs to know a number of facts. For example, a basic question is whether risks are in fact increasing. Many people believe they are. But actually most risks are diminishing. It is disputed whether regulatory forces, market pressures, or technological developments are responsible for the encouraging results. But it cannot be disputed that, in many ways, things are getting better. Consider the data presented in Table 9.1.

The fact that risks are decreasing does not mean that current risks do not deserve governmental attention. Some risks are increasing; this is true for AIDS and for certain cancers. Resources for risk reduction are also badly allocated.[2] A recent study suggests that better allocations of existing expenditures could save an additional 60,000 lives at no increased cost and that, with better allocations, we could save the same number of lives we now save with $31 billion in annual savings.[3] This evidence is not decisive; as we will see, a deliberative democracy need not look only at lives saved. But the evidence is highly suggestive. There are also serious and apparently unjustified asymmetries in lifesaving expenditures, with a median per life-year saved, for transportation, of $56,000; for occupational regulation, of $346,000; and for environmental regulation, of $4,207,000.[4] There are enormous variations within each group as well. Of course, these numbers are of uncertain reliability, but it is clear that with better allocations and more deliberative judgments, much could be done to make things better.

There is, moreover, a pervasive problem in risk regulation, one that is only now beginning to receive public attention.[5] The problem occurs *when the diminution of one health risk simultaneously increases another health risk*. For example, fuel economy standards, designed to reduce environmental risks, may make automobiles less safe and in that way increase risks to life and health. Regulations designed to control the spread of AIDS and hepatitis among health care providers may increase the costs of health care, making health care less widely available and thus costing lives.[6] Government bans on the manufacture and use of asbestos may lead companies to use more dangerous substitutes.[7] Regulation may make nuclear power safer, but by increasing the cost of nuclear power, such regulation will ensure reliance on other energy sources, such as coal-fired power plants, which carry risks of their own. When government requires reformulated gasoline as a substitute for ordinary gasoline, it may produce new pollution problems. When government regulates air pollution, it may encourage industry to increase the volume of solid waste and in that sense aggravate another environmental problem. The general problem is ubiquitous.

In this essay I discuss the relation between health–health trade-offs and the law, in an effort to see how democratic judgments on this topic might be made more deliberative and also how deliberative judgments might be made more democratic. I develop a simple framework for deciding how regulatory agencies aspiring to achieve democratic deliberation should approach such trade-offs. I suggest that this framework must be complicated by reference to the nature of individual and collective rationality in risk assessment.

I also deal with how institutions might make democratic processes more deliberative. To this end I briefly discuss the respective roles of courts, Congress, and the president in managing health–health trade-offs. I urge that agencies should often be taken to have legal authority to make such trade-offs and that they ought to exercise that authority much more than they now do. I also argue for a modest but far from trivial judicial role in requiring agencies to consider aggregate rather than isolated risks. More generally, I urge that Congress amend the Administrative Procedure Act (APA) to require agencies to consider ancillary risks and to minimize net risks. I also argue that the Office of Information and Regulatory Affairs should make the reduction of overall risk one of its principal missions. Much more than it now does, it should undertake a coordinating function so as to ensure that this mission is carried out. In these ways I hope to connect the question of deliberative outcomes with the subject of institutional design.

The essay is organized as follows. In Section 2, I offer a conceptual map, designed to make some relevant distinctions. In Section 3, I offer a first approximation of an approach to health–health trade-offs; the first approximation is a simple effort to limit aggregate risks understood in "expected value" terms. I then suggest that this first approximation be qualified by reference to some complexities in ordinary citizen judgments about risk. People care not simply about "expected value," but also about whether risks are involuntarily incurred, especially dreaded, inequitably distributed, potentially catastrophic, faced by future generations, and so forth. Reflective judgments of this sort diverge from both expert and economic valuations, though in interestingly different ways. Those reflective judgments bear a great deal on how we think about the "rationality" of risk regulation.

Section 4 deals with existing law, urging agencies to undertake more health–health trade-offs than they now do and explaining how a judicial role could encourage this to happen. Section 5 deals with how Congress and the president might approach health–health trade-offs. It also offers some notations on the pervasive problem of *deliberative pathologies*.

2. A Conceptual Map

Regulated and Ancillary Risks

To get a handle on this problem, we need to make some distinctions. Call the risks that government is trying to control *regulated risks*. Call the risks that are increased by regulation *ancillary risks*. Ancillary risks take many different forms, depending on their relationship to the regulated risk. We might say that the increase in acid deposition is *not within the same domain* as the risks prevented by the regulation of nuclear power plants. This is true in two ways. First, and most important, the law does not consider it in the same domain, for the agency that regulates one of these risks has no authority to regulate the other. Second, the source of the risk of acid deposition (mostly coal-fired power plants), simply as a matter of fact, is different from the source of the risk from nuclear power plants. Compare a situation in which the regulation of sulfur dioxide emissions increases emissions of carbon monoxide. If this happens, we are dealing in any event with air pollution, indeed air pollution from largely the same technologies, and the Environmental Protection Agency (EPA) has the statutory authority to regulate both sources.

We can therefore imagine a complex continuum of relationships between regulated risks and ancillary risks. Of course there are differences of degree as well as differences of kind. And of course we might describe the domain of regulated risks in many different ways. Usually the best way to define the risk domain is through the relevant law, which, as we will see, sets constraints on the kinds of risk that might be considered.

A nation that aspires to achieve deliberative democracy might well seek a measure of coordination among agencies, so that an agency operating in one risk domain does not increase risks in another. In fact, coordination is a principal means of overcoming selective attention and in that way achieving deliberative outcomes. Certainly agencies should coordinate their efforts to reduce net risks. But a special problem in this connection is that agencies have quite different standards for deciding when risks require regulation.[8] The International Commission on Radiological Protection, for example, recommends that environmental factors should not cause an incremental cancer risk, for those exposed over a lifetime, of about 3 in 1,000. But U.S. agencies do not follow this recommendation, and their own practices vary widely. The Nuclear Regulatory Commission sees 1 in 1,000 as acceptable; the EPA's acceptable range varies from 1 in 10,000 to 1 in 1,000,000. The Food and Drug Administration (FDA) has tried to use a standard of 1 in 1 million, but under the Delaney Clause, courts have required a standard of essentially zero.[9] For the Occupational Safety and Health Administration (OSHA), the "significant risk" requirement found in its governing statute means 1 in 1,000; labor groups have sought an increase to 1 in 1 million.

These variable standards make health–health trade-offs quite complex. If one agency is using a standard of 1 in 1,000 for risk A, and doing so lawfully, how should it deal with an increase in risk B, when that risk is regulated by a different agency operating lawfully under a different standard? Matters become even more complex when risks from cancer are being compared with other sorts of risk.

There are many different mechanisms by which risk regulation may increase aggregate risks.[10] All of these mechanisms have a degree of complexity, and hence collective judgments that respond to them may well misfire. First, a regulatory ban may result in independent health risks coming from ancillary "replacement" risks. If we ban substance A, the replacement substance B may be dangerous too. If a carcinogenic substance is regulated, perhaps people will use a product that is not carcinogenic but that causes serious risks of heart disease. It is important for government to be aware of this possibility. Second, regulation may produce an offsetting risk that is qualitatively similar to or indistinguishable from the target risk. Perhaps regulation of some substances that threaten to destroy the ozone layer will produce greater use of other substances that also threaten the ozone layer. Third, regulation may force society to lose or forgo "opportunity benefits." For example, careful procedures for screening drugs and services may deprive people of certain health benefits at the same time that they protect people from certain health risks. This problem has received recent attention with respect to the FDA, especially its efforts to control the spread of AIDS. Fourth, regulated substances may have health benefits as well as health risks, and by eliminating the benefits, regulation may create health dangers on balance. Fifth, regulation of one risk may protect a certain group of people while imposing a new risk on another group. This may happen if, for example, a ban on a certain pesticide protects consumers, plants, and animals while increasing risks to farmers. Analogously, a ban on something with a certain risk may create another risk in a way that benefits a certain segment of industry. In this way, as in others, *risk redistribution* rather than *risk reduction* may be the purpose and effect of risk regulation; well-organized private groups may seek regulation precisely in order to obtain a competitive advantage. Sixth, economic costs imposed by regulation may create health risks as well, as we shall soon see.

237

"Richer Is Safer"

Regulations cost money – sometimes a great deal of money – and private expenditures on regulatory compliance may produce less employment and more poverty. People who are unemployed or poor tend to be in worse health and to have unusually short lives.[11] This point has been reflected in legal opinions, perhaps most prominently in Judge Easterbrook's suggestion that a fetal protection policy might "reduce risk attributable to lead at the cost of increasing other hazards," including the hazards stemming from less income, since "there is also a powerful link between the parents' income and infants' health."[12] The more general question is this: Would it be possible to connect governmentally required expenditures on risk reduction with shifts in unemployment and poverty?

An incipient literature attempts to do precisely this. A 1990 study attempted to develop a model in order to quantify the view that "richer is safer."[13] According to Kenney, a single fatality might result from an expenditure of from $3 million to $7.5 million. In a concurring opinion in a 1991 case involving occupational safety and health regulation, Judge Williams invoked this evidence to suggest that OSHA's refusal to engage in cost–benefit analysis might not be beneficial for workers.[14] Judge Williams reasoned in the following way. If a fatality results from an expenditure of $7.5 million, some regulations might produce more fatalities than they prevent. Many regulations, of course, cost more than $7.5 million per life saved. In Judge Williams's view, an agency that fails to measure costs against benefits might be failing to measure mortality gains against losses.

The claimed relationship between wealth reduction and mortality is controversial,[15] but a number of studies find such a relationship (Table 9.2).

This point leads to a broader one with considerable implications for law. Even if agencies are sometimes prevented, by law, from measuring costs against benefits, perhaps they could compare health losses with health gains, and conclude that some regulations are not worthwhile because they cost lives on net. In fact, it can be shown that some regulations fail "health–health analysis" whether or not they pass cost–benefit analysis. Consider Table 9.3.

The idea that "richer is safer" has started to affect public deliberations about risk. In a now-celebrated letter written in 1992, James McRae, the acting administrator of the Office of Information

Table 9.2. Regulation and Mortality

Study	Data	Implicit Income Gains Necessary to Avert One Death (Millions)	Comments
Keeney (1990)	Used income and mortality correlations from Kitagawa and Hauser (1960) data and others	$12.3	Cited in *UAW v. OSHA* as $7.25 1980 dollars; represents an upper bound
Joint Economic Committee (1984)	Aggregate U.S. income, employment, mortality, and morbidity, 1950–80	$1.8 to $2.7	Reflects income loss from recession of 1974–5
Anderson and Burkhauser (1985)	4,878 male workers over 10 years, 1969–79	$1.9 (wages), $4.3 (other income)	Older workers aged 58–63; measured effects of wages and of value of one's home on mortality
Duleep (1986)	9,618 white married male workers aged 35–64 over 6 years, 1973–8	$2.6	Controls for prior disability and educational attainment
Duleep (1989)	13,954 white married male workers aged 25–64 over 6 years, 1973–8	$6.5	Finds income effects at all income levels

(continued)

239

Table 9.2 (*continued*)

Study	Data	Implicit Income Gains Necessary to Avert One Death (Millions)	Comments
Duleep (1991)	9,618 white married male workers aged 35–64 over 6 years, 1973–8	$3.9	Controls for prior disability, educational attainment, and exposure to occupational hazards
Wolfson (1992)	500,000 Canadian workers, over 10–20 years	$6	Investigates longevity rather than mortality; finds income effects at highest quintiles of income
National Institutes of Health (1992)	1,300,000 Americans, all ages, 1979–85	$12.4	Estimate reflects effect of income changes on family mortality; study does not use multiple regression, does not control for prior health status or education
Chirikos and Nestel (1991)	5,020 men, aged 50–64 studied during 1971–83	$3.3	Uses two measures of health endowments

Table 9.2 (*continued*)

Study	Data	Implicit Income Gains Necessary to Avert One Death (Millions)	Comments
Chapman and Hariharan (1993)	5,836 older men over 10 years	$12.2	Uses four distinct controls for prior health conditions
Graham, Hung-Chang, and Evans (1992)	38 years of age-adjusted mortality and income data for the U.S.	$4.0	Distinguishes effects of permanent income from those of transitional income

Source: Randall Lutter and John Morrall, "Health–Health Analysis," *Journal of Risk and Uncertainty* 8 (1994): 43, 49.

and Regulatory Affairs (OIRA), wrote to the Department of Labor, questioning a proposed OSHA regulation involving air contaminants in the workplace. OSHA had estimated savings of between eight and thirteen lives per year, at an annual cost of $163 million. McRae suggested that there was a significant gap in OSHA's analysis: if a statistical fatality were produced by an expenditure of $7.5 million, the regulation could actually cause twenty-two additional deaths. McRae asked OSHA to investigate the relation between health, wealth, and safety. OSHA responded that existing data seemed speculative, but called for more comments from the public.

Eventually, a public outcry forced OIRA to retreat. Senator Glenn in particular complained of OIRA's "Alice-in-Wonderland type claim that health and safety regulations cause harm to workers" and objected that the "richer is safer" view "seems to stand logic on its head – to say that controlling a dangerous substance in the workplace makes an increased health hazard to the worker." Despite the public outcry, increasing research on the issue suggests that lives can indeed be lost through required regulatory expendi-

Table 9.3. Regulations Passing Health–Health Analysis versus Cost–Benefit Analysis

Budgeted Regulation	Year	Agency	Cost per Life Saved (Millions of 1992 $)
Steering column protection	1967	NHTSA	0.1
Unvented space heaters	1980	CPSC	0.1
Cabin fire protection	1985	FAA	0.3
Passive restraints/belts	1984	NHTSA	0.4
Fuel system integrity	1975	NHTSA	0.4
Trihalomethanes	1979	EPA	0.4
Underground construction	1989	OSHA-S	0.4
Alcohol and drug control	1985	FRA	0.7
Servicing wheel rims	1984	OSHA-S	0.7
Seat cushion flammability	1984	FAA	0.8
Floor emergency lighting	1984	FAA	0.9
Crane suspension platform	1988	OSHA-S	1.2
Children's sleepware flammability	1973	CPSC	1.8
Side doors	1979	NHTSA	1.8
Concrete and masonry construction	1988	OSHA-S	1.9
Hazard communication	1983	OSHA-S	2.4
Asbestos	1986	OSHA-H	2.8
Benzene/fugitive emissions	1984	EPA	3.8
Regulations failing cost–benefit analysis			
Grain dust	1987	OSHA-S	8.8
Radionuclides/uranium mines	1984	EPA	9.3
Regulations failing health–health and cost–benefit analysis			
Benzene	1987	OSHA-H	23.1
Ethylene oxide	1984	OSHA-H	34.6
Uranium mill tailings/inactive	1983	EPA	37.3
Acrylonitrile	1978	OSHA-H	50.8
Uranium mill tailings/active	1983	EPA	71.6
Asbestos	1989	EPA	72.9
Coke ovens	1976	OSHA-H	83.4
Arsenic	1978	OSHA-H	125.0
DES (cattle feed)	1979	FDA	178.0
Arsenic/glass manufacture	1986	EPA	192.0
Formaldehyde	1987	OSHA-H	119,000.0

Source: Randall Lutter and John Morrall, "Health–Health Analysis," *Journal of Risk and Uncertainty* 8 (1994): 43, 59.

tures and that there is reason for government to take the problem seriously.

Why Does It Matter?

We have now seen enough to know that an impressive body of work attempts to measure health gains from regulation against health risks from regulation. But why should we focus on this particular question? Would it not be better to attend to the overall gains from regulation and to the overall losses from regulation? Ought not public deliberation to focus on all of the relevant gains and losses? What is so special about health–health trade-offs?

Part of the answer lies in existing public judgments, taken as simple brute facts. People seem to think that regulation is bad if it causes more deaths than it saves; a demonstration to this effect counts strongly against regulation. But people do not always know how to compare health gains (fifteen lives gained, for example) with monetary losses (an expenditure of $15 million, for example). This uncertainty stems partly from the fact that lives and dollars cannot easily be aligned on a single metric and in this sense are not easily made commensurable – an issue I discuss in Section 3 – and partly from the fact that the appropriate amount to spend to protect a (statistical) life very much depends on context. A deliberative judgment on net health trade-offs is easier to reach than a deliberative judgment on other sorts of trade-offs. It may thus be impossible to obtain an *incompletely theorized agreement*[16] that a net mortality loss is bad – incompletely theorized in the sense that people from diverse theoretical perspectives can agree on that proposition. Incompletely theorized agreements on particular results are an important part of democratic deliberation; they are a distinctive solution to the problems of social pluralism and disagreement.

It would, however, be inadequate for present purposes to point to existing public judgments, which may be irrational or confused. Perhaps public uncertainty about cost – benefit judgments depends on an unwillingness to acknowledge that even (risk to) life has its price. But part of the answer lies in attending more closely to problems of incommensurability, which occur when no single metric is available by which to assess variables at stake in a social decision. In the area of risk regulation, a single metric is troublesome simply because it elides qualitative distinctions. To be sure, if all effects are reduced to the metric of dollars, it may be possible to make better assessments, in the sense that comparisons and hence trade-offs can become easier. But reduction of mortality and morbidity effects to dollars can erase important qualitative distinctions.

In the face of such distinctions – distinctions in *how*, not simply *how much,* things are valued[17] – participants in democratic deliberation often resist a metric of dollars. To say this is not to deny that trade-offs have to be made among qualitatively diverse goods. But perhaps people can make choices more easily when the trade-offs involve qualitatively indistinguishable things, like lives, rather than qualitatively diverse things, like lives and dollars. A judgment of this kind undoubtedly underlies the interest in "health–health analysis." When it is hard to trade off lives against dollars, the burdens of judgment might be eased when we are trading off lives against lives.

There is considerable truth to this suggestion. But it is a bit too crude. As we shall see, lives are themselves not commensurable, in the sense that a single metric – "lives saved" – is itself too crude to account for considered democratic judgments. Problems of incommensurability cannot be eliminated so easily. They play a large role in health–health comparisons too. But such problems might be reduced, if not alleviated, by focusing on number of life-years saved, or perhaps number of decently livable life-years saved, by a government policy.

3. Incorporating Health–Health Comparisons

First Approximation

Let us try, in a simple, intuitive way, to identify the factors that should enter into deliberative judgments about health–health trade-offs. Begin with a simple case in which the costs of information and inquiry are zero. If this is so, all agencies should investigate all risks potentially at stake. Agencies should always take account of ancillary risks and try to limit aggregate risks.

Of course, the costs of investigation and inquiry are never zero; in fact, they are often very high. We can readily imagine that agencies could spend all their time investigating ancillary risks, and never do anything else. (This is a potential problem with cost–benefit analysis: cost–benefit analysis may itself fail cost–benefit analysis. Deliberation may not be worthwhile for the same reason; to paraphrase Oscar Wilde, it may take too many evenings.) When the costs of inquiry are not zero, the obligation to inquire into ancillary risks might be a function of several factors. First is the cost of delay, understood as the cost of not regulating the regulated risk until more information has been compiled. To figure out this cost, it is necessary to explore the seriousness of the regulated risk and the length of time necessary to investigate the ancillary risk. Second is the cost of investigating the ancillary risk, where this cost is understood as a product of the cost of compiling and evaluating the relevant information. Third is the benefit of investigating the ancillary risk, with the benefit understood as the likelihood of uncovering information that might help to produce a better result.

Under this view, it is of course important to know something about the possible extent of the ancillary risks and the costs of discovering it. Before the actual investigation has occurred, there will be a good deal of intuition and guesswork here; the full facts cannot be known until inquiries have been completed, and the real question is whether it is worthwhile to complete the inquiries or even to embark on them. To know this one has to know something about the ancillary risk. But even at an early stage, it is possible to know that some ancillary risks are likely to be high, while others are trivial or low. Moreover, some ancillary risks can be investigated relatively inexpensively, while the investigation of others depends on scientific and predictive judgments that require an enormous investment of resources. Finally, an agency might be reluctant to inquire into ancillary risks on the theory that, if it does so, it will be unable to regulate the risk at issue before it is too late. Thus, it seems clear that the extent and nature of the regulated risk are crucial factors for those deciding whether to explore ancillary risks.

On this simple, intuitive view, we might think in the following way. If it would be enormously expensive to investigate whether fuel economy standards would really result in smaller and more dangerous cars, if the fuel economy standards would themselves do a great deal of good, and if the likelihood of high ancillary risks seems small, then it makes sense to proceed with the fuel economy standards without investigating the ancillary risks. On the other hand, it is easy to imagine a scenario in which investigation of ancillary risks is reasonable or when failure to investigate would be irrational. (As it happens, the position of the National Highway Transportation Safety Administration [NHTSA] with respect to fuel economy standards and safety is that the ancillary risks are worth investigating.)

245

Compare the question of how to handle ancillary risks created by the prohibition of asbestos. One ancillary risk arises from the fact that asbestos appears to be the best product for use in brake linings, and existing substitutes are worse. Whether this is true, and how serious the ancillary risk is, can be investigated at the present time. But other ancillary risks involve the substitutes for asbestos in products for which no substitutes are now available. In the view of the EPA, the ban on asbestos will force technological innovation, producing new substances that do the work now done by asbestos. This may be a reasonable view. If so, the government has reason to regulate asbestos now and to wait before evaluating any substitute risks.

Existing Law

How should we understand existing law in light of this first approximation? As we shall see, Congress has apparently forbidden health–health analysis in many settings, and questions therefore arise about what understanding, if any, accounts for the prohibition.

Some of the relevant statutes might be seen to reflect *categorical judgments* about calculations of the kind just discussed. Congress might think, for example, that the Nuclear Regulatory Commission (NRC) should not ask whether regulation of nuclear power will make for more acid deposition, because the problem of unsafe nuclear power is an especially serious one, because nuclear power regulation is unlikely to produce significant increases in acid deposition, and because it is very hard for the NRC, given its limited budget and expertise, to make the necessary extrapolations. Under the considerations I have discussed, the NRC might plausibly be exempted from the duty of exploring ancillary risks.

Alternatively, the problems posed by ancillary risks might be solved by the *division of labor*. Here difficulties in democratic deliberation are handled by allocating authority in a certain way. Any effects on automobile safety that come from air pollution regulation might be controlled by the NHTSA. Perhaps the NHTSA has the authority to make sure that ancillary risks do not come to fruition. Any adverse effects of EPA regulation could be prevented by the NHTSA. Perhaps the two agencies will coordinate their efforts to ensure that aggregate risks are minimized.

Or consider the health risks from regulation that induces employment and poverty. It might be thought that the disemployment effects of regulation are, or should be, addressed by other governmental institutions, including those entrusted with the power to reduce unemployment and poverty. Of course, there are problems with the division of labor strategy. Coordination of risk regulation is difficult to achieve, and in modern government it has not been pursued in any systematic way. In any case it would be surprising if a healthy division of labor accounted for existing practice, for there is no evidence that agencies systematically respond to increases in ancillary risks created by regulation.

Another explanation would point to the important role of *interest groups* in the regulatory process. On this view, the disparities in regulatory strategies are attributable to the fact that well-organized groups are able to obtain legislation in their interest or to fend off harmful regulation. It should not be surprising that the statute regulating agricultural practices allows for a form of open-ended balancing; agricultural groups are in a good position to fend off draconian legislation. Some environmental groups work very hard to obtain severe restrictions on carcinogenic substances. Here problems in governmental performance are a product of interest-group power that makes both deliberation and democracy less likely or less successful.

Yet another explanation would point to *myopia, selective attention, sensationalism, credit claiming,* and *random agenda selection* as important forces in the production of risk regulation. Some statutes stem from sensationalistic events, like the Love Canal scare, that encourage legislators to hold hearings and claim credit for fixing problems that are small or just part of a complex whole. Such statutes are likely to reflect myopia or selective attention. The result may well be a form of random agenda selection that does not adequately reduce risks, or that even increases some risks.

Finally, some statutes might reflect *public judgments* about how to conduct health–health trade-offs. Perhaps the public believes that an increase in a certain risk is not a relevant factor in the assessment of another risk. This could be a product of simple confusion, as in the well-established refusal, on the part of some of the public some of the time, to acknowledge any need for trade-offs. Such judgments should not be given any weight in law; but Congress, having its electoral self-interest at stake, appears to disagree with this proposition. Or public judgments might be based on gripping anecdotes or heuristics of certain kinds, productive of errors,[18]

247

that make draconian regulation of a certain risk seem quite sensible. In these ways, relevant judgments could be confused, and we might seek a form of expert judgment that would produce more in the way of regulatory rationality. Some such judgments might, however, result from something other than confusion. I take up this point in the next section.

Incorporating Complexities

Our first approximation has suggested that all risks be aligned along a single metric – expected annual deaths, aggregate benefits and costs – and hence measured against one another. Both expert and economic approaches attempt to do this, though in interestingly different ways. Experts tend to look at expected annual deaths and to assess risks accordingly.[19] But ordinary people base their judgments on something other than this. They look, for example, at whether the risk is faced voluntarily or involuntarily, whether it is equitably distributed, whether it is faced by future generations, whether it is potentially catastrophic, whether it involves a death that is especially dreaded, and whether it is new and poorly understood. Consider Table 9.4.

If aggravating and mitigating factors are taken into account, it might well be the case that people would find, say, 300 cases of cancer more acceptable than 350 cases of heart disease, given certain assumptions about what causes each. In contingent valuation studies, people purport to be willing to pay far more to prevent cancer deaths (from $1.5 million to $9.5 million) than they would to prevent unforeseen instant deaths (from $1 million to $5 million).[20] It is similarly possible that people might therefore accept a regulated risk involving 100 annual fatalities even if the ancillary risk involves 110 annual fatalities; perhaps the ancillary risk is less severe because it is voluntarily run, not especially dreaded, and well understood. The democratic decision to look at something other than quantity is easy to defend. It is also fully rational.

We come, then, to a complication for the initial approximation. In a deliberative democracy, risks should be evaluated in accordance with the various qualitative factors deemed relevant by ordinary people who are evaluating risk, at least if incorporation of those factors and the judgment that they are relevant can survive

Table 9.4. Risk Factors

Risk Characteristic	Aggravating Factor	Mitigating Factor
Nature of risk	Dreaded	Acceptable
Permanence	Irreversible/ uncontrollable	Reversible/ controllable
Duration	Faced by future generations	Faced by those now living
Equity	Unfairly distributed	Fairly distributed
Source of risk	Man-made	Found in nature
Freedom	Voluntarily incurred	Forced exposure
Existing understanding	Known to science	Unknown
Relation to status quo	New	Old

reflection.[21] Of course, it would be possible to assign numbers to these factors if this step aided analysis.

Economic approaches promise to avoid some of the problems of expert valuations. Most important, private willingness to pay should incorporate some or even all of the factors that underlie ordinary lay judgments. It might be possible to ascertain private willingness to pay from studies of actual market behavior and from contingent valuation studies.[22] And from these results it is possible to come up with diverse valuations of diverse social risks. Consider Table 9.5.

There are, however, enormous difficulties in the idea that officials can get, from private willingness to pay, an adequate sense of how to order the risks at stake in regulation. Health–health trade-offs cannot easily be based on surrogates for market valuation. Actual choices are geared to the context in which they are made; it is not clear that one can infer from actual choices in one context people's valuations about other choices in a different context. Contingent valuation studies can build in a sense of context, but the answers may not be at all reliable. In any case democratic choices should reflect a process of reason giving in which it is asked what

249

Table 9.5. Mortality Values by Cause of Death

Category (per Statistical Life)	Value Estimate ($ millions)		
	Low	*Medium*	*High*
Unforeseen instant death	1	2	5
Asthma/bronchitis	1.3	2.5	5.5
Heart disease	1.25	2.75	6
Emphysema	1.4	3.5	9
Lung cancer	1.5	4	9.5

Source: W. Kip Viscusi, *Fatal Tradeoffs* (Oxford: Oxford University Press, 1992), 342.

policies are best to pursue, rather than a process of preference satisfaction in which each person is asked how much he or she is willing to pay for a certain result. Deliberative outcomes should not be confused with aggregated willingness to pay.

Government officials must, in these circumstances, proceed pragmatically, perhaps by taking aggregate numbers based on expert judgments as a starting point and adjusting them with the supplemental considerations, involving democratic convictions, that I have described here. The starting point may reflect not "lives saved" but "decently livable life-years saved" by government regulation. It makes more sense to save one hundred children than to save one hundred people in their last years; it makes more sense, other things being equal, to save people who have decent life prospects than to save people who will, if saved, be condemned to lives of pain, distress, or hospitalization. Of course, these are judgments all other things being equal, and they might be countered by contextual considerations.

4. Courts and Existing Law

I now turn to existing law. If an agency takes account of ancillary risks, has it behaved unlawfully? If an agency refuses to consider such risks, should the courts require it do so?

Consideration of Ancillary Risks

Suppose, first, that an agency actually considers health–health trade-offs. Is it permitted to do so? Agencies have considerable flexibility here, since under existing law ambiguous statutes can be interpreted as agencies see fit.

Sometimes, however, statutes are unambiguous on this point, and ancillary risks are excluded as reasons for regulatory action or inaction. Under the Delaney Clause, for example, the FDA probably may not consider the possibility that the exclusion of foods with carcinogens will increase risks from (say) heart disease. The FDA is banned from considering this or any other ancillary risk. A similar problem arises under the toxic substances provision of the Occupational Safety and Health Act, which probably bans the OSHA from asking whether richer is safer, or even from balancing workplace risks against ancillary risks created by regulation.

But sometimes agencies are given sufficiently broad authority, and they may, if they choose, consider ancillary risks. One statute provides that agencies must ask whether pesticides produce "unreasonable adverse effects on the environment," and this term requires the agency to take "into account the economic, social, and environmental costs and benefits of the use of any pesticide."[23] This statute certainly authorizes the EPA to consider the possibility that any regulation would create aggregate harm. The Clean Air Act and the Federal Water Pollution Control Act allow government to consider a broad range of good and bad environmental effects in requiring technologies to reduce air and water pollution. Outside the context of toxic substances, the Occupational Safety and Health Act defines occupational safety and health standards as those "reasonably necessary or appropriate" to the goal of ensuring "safe or healthly employment and places of employment." The OSHA may reasonably decide that a standard is not "reasonably necessary or appropriate" if the effect of the regulation is the loss of aggregate lives. It is permitted to consider the effects of regulation on risks to life and health through poverty and unemployment.

Refusal to Consider Ancillary Risks

Now suppose that an agency refuses to consider, or to make decisive, the fact that its decision to reduce one risk increases another risk. Perhaps a new regulatory initiative from the NRC would increase the risks from coal-fired power plants. Is the NRC's refusal to consider such risks unlawful? The first question is whether the statute requires consideration of ancillary risks. The second question is whether, if the statute does not do so, the agency's decision is arbitrary or capricious.

As we have seen, many statutes do not require agencies to consider ancillary risks. In any case courts defer to reasonable agency interpretations of statutes, so in many instances the agency will have the authority to decide whether to consider ancillary risks. If the agency has the statutory authority not to consider ancillary risks, it is unlikely, under current law, to be found that its decision not to do so was arbitrary. The judgment about arbitrariness should and probably would be based on a framework like that set out in Section 2 of this essay. In an extreme case, failure to consider risks that are likely to be large, and that are not terribly costly to investigate, might be seen as arbitrary within the meaning of the APA. Indeed, I believe, for reasons to be elaborated shortly, that courts should be less reluctant than they now are to find agency action arbitrary on this ground.

A great deal, of course, turns on existing information. When the data about ancillary risks are speculative or unreliable, agencies are probably not required to consider such risks. The OSHA could lawfully conclude – as it has in fact concluded – that the evidence that "richer is safer" is too speculative to be used at this time. Its decision to this effect ought not to be found arbitrary or capricious unless it can be shown that the evidence is in fact solid and that the costs of incorporating it are reasonable. The relevant provision of the statute – the "reasonably necessary or appropriate" language – gives the OSHA discretion to do with this evidence as it chooses. Under the FIFRA, by contrast, an agency that fails to consider ancillary risks would probably be violating the statute, at least on a showing that the ancillary risks are real and the costs of investigation are not excessive.

Consider in this regard the principal case involving the issue of health–health trade-offs, *Competitive Enterprise Institute [CEI] v. NHTSA*.[24] The NHTSA establishes fuel economy standards; in doing so, it is required to consider the issue of "feasibility." In deciding the question of feasibility, NHTSA has taken account of passenger safety, including risks created by regulation, and while there is a possible statutory issue here, everyone in *CEI* accepted the NHTSA's views on this point. The question in the case was whether the NHTSA had acted lawfully in refusing to relax its fuel economy standards for certain model years. Automobile companies urged that relaxation was required in order to save lives – because the existing standards would lead to "downsizing" and hence to smaller and more dangerous vehicles – and they presented strong evidence to this effect.

The agency responded that this evidence was unconvincing and that "domestic manufacturers should be able to improve their fuel economy in the future by . . . technological means, without out-sourcing their larger cars, without further downsizing or mix shifts toward smaller cars, and without sacrificing acceleration or performance." The court held that this explanation was inadequate. The agency failed to claim or show that, in fact, manufacturers would fail to downsize their cars. In any case, downsizing would be costly, and that "cost would translate into higher prices for large cars (as well as small), thereby pressuring consumers to retain their old cars and make the associated sacrifice in safety. The result would be effectively the same harm that concerns petitioners and that the agency fails to negate or justify." The court therefore remanded to the agency for a better explanation or a change in policy.

On remand, the agency offered a somewhat better explanation. The NHTSA pointed to what it saw as the absence of clear indications that fuel economy standards had caused any manufacturer to price consumers out of the market for larger, safer cars. The NHTSA referred as well to an absence of manufacturer claims about the specific design standards that would result from the standards. The court found this explanation sufficient.[25] In doing so, it applied a highly deferential form of review.

In light of the record, however, and the predictable pressures on an agency like the NHTSA, the result in the case might well be questioned. The NHTSA may well suffer from a form of "tunnel vision," especially in dealing with fuel economy standards, for which there is a powerful constituency. The interests that call for attention to ancillary safety risks are typically poorly organized, and when the claims come from automobile manufacturers, the NHTSA may be too ready to distrust them. To say this is not to say that the NHTSA should be required to relax its fuel economy standards. But it is to say that a demonstration of the sort made by the automobile manufacturers might well serve as a kind of warning signal to the court, requiring a solid response from the agency. In *CEI*, the agency's response could not qualify as solid. A promising model for the future is provided by an important court of appeals decision holding that under a statute that required open-ended balancing of relevant factors, an agency was required to ask whether asbestos substitutes would lead to even greater risks.[26]

The point I am making here might well be generalized. In a government that aspires to be deliberative, agencies ought generally to be required to show that they are doing more good than harm. This does not mean that courts should engage in independent review of agency judgments on this score. But it does mean that courts should take a "hard look" at agency decisions failing to undertake health–health comparisons.

5. New Institutions

Congress

In its present form, Congress is ill-equipped to consider the problem of health–health trade-offs. Its committee structure ensures a high degree of fragmentation and does not allow for deliberation on such trade-offs. On the contrary, that structure makes ancillary risks difficult to evaluate or, much worse, even to see; often those risks are thought to be subject to the jurisdiction of another committee, which means, in practice, that coordination is extremely difficult. In these circumstances, I offer two simple suggestions for legislative reform.

The first is that Congress should create a new legislative body entrusted specifically with the power to assess aggregate risk levels, to compare risks, and to initiate the revision of statutes that increase net risks. This committee should have the power to introduce corrective legislation when a statute, or agency action under a statute, has been shown to increase aggregate risks.

My second suggestion is that Congress should address the problem of health–health trade-offs through a new directive in the Administrative Procedure Act. Notably, initiatives designed to require cost–benefit balancing say almost nothing about this problem. The principal exception is a House bill introduced in 1995, which contains a subsection entitled "Substitution Risks." This subsection says that "each significant risk assessment or risk characterization document shall include a statement of any substitution risks to human health, where information on such risks has been provided to the agency."

This is a strikingly modest initiative. It does not require agencies to investigate ancillary risks on their own. Nor does it say that agencies may not proceed unless the regulation yields net benefits. I suggest instead a proposed amendment to the Administrative Procedure Act: "Agencies shall ensure, to the extent feasible, that regulations do not create countervailing risks that are greater than those of the regulated risk." A modest forerunner of this idea can be found in the "clean fuels" provision of the Clean Air Act, which says that the administrator of the EPA may not prohibit the use of a fuel or fuel additive "unless he finds . . . that in his judgment such prohibition will not cause the use of any other fuel or fuel additive which will produce emissions which will endanger the public health or welfare to the same or greater degree than the use of the fuel or fuel additive proposed to be prohibited."[27] This idea should be generalized.

Executive Branch

The Office of Information and Regulatory Affairs (OIRA) has been entrusted with the power to coordinate regulatory policy and to ensure reasonable priority setting. In the Clinton administration, the OIRA appears to have become an advisory body, more limited in its power than it was in the Bush and Reagan administrations. In view of the absence of good priority setting, and the enormous room for savings costs and increasing regulatory benefits, this is highly unfortunate.

The OIRA should see as one of its central assignments the task of overcoming governmental tunnel vision, by ensuring that aggregate risks are reduced and that agencies' focus on particular risks does not mean that ancillary risks are ignored or increased. This is a more modest and particularized version of Justice Breyer's larger suggestion that the OIRA have the power to set priorities by diverting resources from smaller problems to larger ones.[28] No body in government is now entrusted with the task of ensuring that risk regulation is managed so as to ensure global rationality and coherence. The OIRA is well situated to take on that role, at least by attending to the possibility that the regulation of some risks may make risk levels higher on balance.

Notes on Deliberative Pathologies

These claims should hardly be taken to suggest that deliberation is a panacea or that more deliberation is always better. For one thing, it is entirely imaginable that more elaborate consideration of risk-related issues will simply perpetuate the status quo. Just as cost–benefit analysis may itself fail cost–benefit analysis, so too consideration of health–health trade-offs may actually impair human health. Thus, it is always necessary to consider whether extended consideration is worthwhile. We can generalize the point with the suggestion that deliberation takes time and in that sense tends to perpetuate existing practice; this possibility may argue against institutional reform that increases deliberation.

In addition, well-organized private groups or self-interested representatives may distort the deliberative process, partly because of greater access to information, partly because of political inequality more generally.[29] Of course, extended deliberative processes always create this danger. Whether greater political deliberation is desirable very much depends on what sort of information various actors hold and whether deliberation will reduce or aggravate existing political inequalities. Here too we have a general point about the risks of political deliberation, and in the abstract, the central questions are not susceptible to sensible answers. We can easily imagine an Office of Management and Budget in the control of a private faction, so that health–health trade-offs become simply another forum for risk redistribution and interest-group maneuvering rather than risk reduction. A greater congressional role could create equivalent risks.

Nothing I have said here is intended to deny the general problem of deliberative pathologies. I am assuming a degree of good faith and professionalism on the part of the relevant actors. If the assumption seems extravagant, it might be responded that the status quo is far from satisfactory, that interest-group pressures have very often succeeded in less deliberative systems, that risk reduction is all too infrequently the purpose and effect of regulation, and that it is at least reasonable to think that institutional change will make things better. No institutional judgments can be defended on an a priori basis; everything depends on facts, on what happens in practice. If the changes I have suggested do not work, then we should try something else. But in light of the problem at hand, it would be most surprising if nondeliberative institutions held out a great deal of promise.

6. Conclusion

Modern government suffers from failures of both democracy and deliberation. Sometimes outcomes are insufficiently democratic in the sense that they are not responsive to public judgments. Sometimes they are insufficiently deliberative in the sense that they reflect interest-group pressures, selective attention, inadequate concern for incentives, inadequate information, no real process of reason giving, and little regard for side effects. Among the principal side effects is the most ironic: the increased risks produced by risk regulation.

This is a significant problem, unaddressed (as far as I am aware) by any institution in any nation in the industrialized world. Through some simple steps, something can be done about it. Trade-offs among risks ought not to be based on a unitary metric, for reasons of both law and basic principle; but trade-offs must nonetheless be made. Institutions should be redesigned so as to ensure that such trade-offs can be made in a manner that entails more in the way of democratic deliberation. Under existing law, agencies should often be understood to have the authority to engage in health–health trade-offs, and they should exercise that authority more often than they do. Courts can play a modest role in encouraging agencies to increase aggregate risk reduction. Congress should add to existing legislation a general requirement that agencies consider all risks, to the extent that this is feasible. Finally, the OIRA should undertake the process of scrutinizing risk regulation to show that agency action does not suffer from the kind of tunnel vision exemplified by so much of modern risk regulation.

With this point, we can see that solutions to failures in democratic deliberation are in large part institutional. We can also see that, to be effective, institutional solutions must respond to predictable failures in collective rationality, involving selective attention, myopia, and incomplete information. We can see as well that the aspiration to achieve deliberative democracy reflects judgments and commitments that might well be brought to bear on concrete problems in modern governance.

257

Notes

1. I try to support this view in Cass R. Sunstein, *The Partial Constitution* (Cambridge, Mass.: Harvard University Press, 1993).
2. See S. Breyer, *Breaking the Vicious Circle* (Cambridge, Mass.: Harvard University Press 1992); Richard Pildes and Cass R. Sunstein, "Reinventing the Regulatory State," *University of Chicago Law Review* 62 (1995): 1.
3. Tammy Tengs et al., *Five Hundred Life-Saving Interventions and Their Cost-Effectiveness, Risk Analysis,* forthcoming.
4. Ibid.
5. See John Graham and Jonathan Weiner, *Risk vs. Risk* (Cambridge, Mass.: Harvard University Press, 1995), for the best general discussion. See also the valuable "Symposium on Risk–Risk Analysis," *Journal of Risk and Uncertainty* 8 (1994): 5.
6. See *ADA v. Martin*, 984 F.2d 823, 826 (7th Cir. 1993): "OSHA also exaggerated the number of lives likely to be saved by the rule by ignoring lives likely to be lost by it, since the increased cost of medical care, to the extent passed on to consumers, will reduce the demand for medical care, and some people may lose their lives as a result."
7. See *Corrosion Proof Fittings v. EPA*, 947 F.2d 1201 (5th Cir. 1991).
8. See M. Sadowitz and J. Graham, "A Survey of Permitted Residual Cancer Risks," *Risk* 6 (1995): 17.
9. *Public Citizen v. Young*, 831 F2d 1108 (DC Cir 1987).
10. See Aaron Wildavsky, *Searching for Safety* (Oxford: Transaction, 1987).
11. Ibid.
12. *Intl. Union v. Johnson Controls*, 886 F2d 871, 908 (7th Cir., 1989) (Easterbrook, J., dissenting), reversed, 499 US 187 (1991).
13. R. L. Keeney, "Mortality Risks Induced by Economic Expenditures," *Risk Analysis* 107 (1990): 147. See also R. L. Keeney, "Mortality Risks Induced by the Costs of Regulations," *Journal of Risk and Uncertainty* 8 (1994): 95.
14. *UAW v. OSHA*, 938 F.2d 1310 (DC Cir. 1991). See also *Building & Constr. Trades Dept. v. Brock*, 838 F2d 1258 (DC Cir 1988), suggesting that "leaning toward safety may sometimes have the perverse effect of increasing rather than decreasing risk." Ibid., 1267. See also *New York State v. Brown*, 854 F2d 1379, 1395 n. 1 (D.C. Cir., 1988) (Williams, J., concurring): "Extravagant expenditures on health may in some instances affect health adversely, by foreclosing expenditures on items – higher quality food, shelter, recreation, etc. – that would have contributed more to the individual's health than the direct expenditures thereon."

15. See Paul Portney and Robert Stavins, "Regulatory Review of Environmental Policy," *Journal of Risk and Uncertainty* 8 (1994): 11.
16. See Cass R. Sunstein, "Incompletely Theorized Agreements," *Harvard Law Review* 108 (1995): 1839.
17. See Elizabeth Anderson, *Value in Ethics and Economics* (Cambridge, Mass.: Harvard University Press, 1992).
18. See Pildes and Sunstein, "Reinventing the Regulatory State."
19. Ibid.
20. See George Tolley et al., *Valuing Health for Policy* (Chicago: University of Chicago Press, 1996), 341–42.
21. This proposition is defended in detail in Pildes and Sunstein, "Reinventing the Regulatory State," and in Cass R. Sunstein, "Which Risks First?" *University of Chicago Legal Forum*, forthcoming. A good critical discussion is Howard Margolis, *Dealing with Risk* (Chicago: University of Chicago Press, 1996).
22. See Tolley et al., *Valuing Health*; Viscusi, *Fatal Tradeoffs*.
23. 7 USC 136(bb).
24. 956 F.2d 321 (DC Cir 1992).
25. *CEI v. NHTSA*, 1995 WL 39252 (DC Cir 1995).
26. *Corrosion Proof Fittings v. EPA*, 947 F.2d 1201 (5th Cir. 1991).
27. 42 USC 7545(c)(2)(C).
28. Breyer, *Breaking the Vicious Circle*.
29. See Elster, *Sour Grapes* (Cambridge University Press, 1983); see also, in this volume, Chapter 2 by Fearon, Chapter 4 by Elster, and Chapter 5 by Stokes.

Chapter Ten

Full Representation, Deliberation, and Impartiality

How should we organize political systems in order to obtain impartial decisions?[1] In the United States, I will assume, the Founding Fathers gave an answer to this question that was both normatively interesting and politically very appealing. According to them, impartial decisions required careful deliberation among representatives of the whole society. In brief, their "formula" for securing impartiality was "full representation[2] plus deliberation."[3] In this sense, the two main obstacles to achieving impartiality in political measures were "hasty" decisions and "imperfect" or "incomplete" representation.

At the present time, I will also assume, the political system[4] seems to have problems reaching impartial decisions and – probably because of that – finds it difficult to earn the public's respect.[5] My guess is that these problems have at least one important cause: the political system (organized as it is) is unable to secure the full representation of society.[6] During the framing of the U.S. Constitution, I think, the framers assumed that they had adequately solved this problem of representation, something that we can no longer assume.

My suggestion is that if we want to fulfill the criteria of both deliberation and full representation, we need to introduce substantive changes into the present representative system. If not, we will be relying solely on deliberation to achieve impartiality. That is, we will be demanding from deliberation alone something that, by itself, it cannot give us.

As an introduction to my study, I will briefly discuss the ways in which deliberation and full representation may contribute to impartiality.

1. Deliberation and Impartiality

Deliberation may help impartiality in many different ways. First of all, it may be argued that decisions are often "partial" because of ignorance concerning the actual interests or preferences of others. Non-neutral decisions may be reached not because of the self-interest or partiality of the decision makers, but because of a misunderstanding of the way other people evaluate certain choices. The decision maker may ignore the fact that most people actually find unacceptable some option that he or she assumed to be universally acceptable.

Another important way in which deliberation may contribute to impartiality is by forcing each person to modify his or her argument in order to make it acceptable to others. So deliberation may help impartiality by forcing people to filter out mere self-interested arguments (Elster 1989; Sunstein 1993b). Proposals that have their foundation in proper names (this should be done because it benefits Mary) or particular interests (this should be done because it benefits the proprietors of this house) or in nonuniversal reasons (this should be done because I like it) are not likely to prevail in any genuinely deliberative assembly. When propositions like these are excluded, we may say, the resulting collective decision becomes more impartial.

Deliberation may also be important in "educating" people to act impartially. In effect, the process of deliberation, by which people exchange opinions, listen to others' arguments, and so on, helps people to improve their capacity to live with others (Pateman 1970: 42–4; Barber 1984; Cohen 1989).

Finally, deliberation may contribute to impartiality by helping each participant to clarify and "purify" his or her own position. In effect, deliberation may be useful by providing information and expanding the panorama of available alternatives (sometimes a person may disregard some possibilities just because of his or her restricted knowledge); and it may also be useful as a result of its "negative" function: helping people to discover factual and logical mistakes in their reasoning.

2. Full Representation and Impartiality

Full representation may contribute to impartiality in significant ways. First, it may help us to solve an *epistemic* problem, which is the following: impartiality requires us to treat others' preferences as if they were ours, but we may easily fail to satisfy this demand just because of the difficulties we have in putting ourselves in another's place. It is very difficult to know other people's interests (as well as the weight they attach to their own claims). In this sense, a fully representative system may help us to confront difficulties that are extremely hard to resolve just through individual or monological reflection.[7]

Second, full representation may help us to solve a *motivational* problem, which is the following: even if we knew perfectly the preferences of others, we might have no motivation to take these preferences into account. Full representation, in this sense, may force us to respect other people's claims. The "others" will be "there" to move us to respect them.

Will Kymlicka makes an argument related to the ones I have mentioned. According to this argument, what I call full representation could be important in terms of "trust." In this sense, Kymlicka says that "even if white men can understand the interests of women and blacks, they cannot be trusted to promote these interests." Quoting a work of Christine Boyle, he affirms that "[t]he reason is not necessarily that men do not understand women's interests, but rather that at some point members of one group feel that someone belonging to another group has such a conflict of interest that representation is impossible, or at least unlikely" (Kymlicka 1995: 139).

Although these types of arguments do not conclusively support full representation, at least they pose a difficult challenge to rival conceptions. In the following sections, I will demonstrate that this idea of full representation – as well as the aforementioned notion of deliberation – had an enormous influence on the justification of present institutions.

3. Deliberation and Full Representation in the Origins of Constitutionalism

In this section I will analyze the importance that this model of "deliberation plus full representation" acquired in the origins of modern constitutionalism. I will analyze, in particular, the way in which Edmund Burke, in England, and the Founding Fathers, in the United States, resorted to these ideas when they had to discuss and defend specific institutional arrangements.

Burke's Model

Edmund Burke was an important political thinker who defended – from a very conservative viewpoint – the ideas of both deliberation and full representation. His political actions and his writings helped to define the political history of his epoch.

First of all, I would say that Burke's ideas on these topics were not very clear or coherent. There is plain textual evidence, at least, of the confidence he had in deliberation as a means for achieving "correct" political decisions. According to him, the Parliament was the deliberative assembly of the nation and, in that forum, the representatives had the opportunity to define the real, objective interest of the community. The people, carriers of mere "opinions," had to be excluded from these debates (Pitkin 1967: 181).[8] According to Burke, "[The] representative owes you, not his industry only, but his judgment; and he betrays, instead of serving you, if he sacrifices it to your opinion . . . [because] government and legislation are matters of reason and judgment, and not of inclination" (Burke 1960: 115; Cone 1957: 274–5). Thus, the duty of the representatives was to act on behalf of the people's "real interests": "the judgment of those who [were] numero plures [had to be deferred] to those who were virtue et honore majores" (Burke 1960: 218). If the rulers did not act in this way, society would be condemned to catastrophe.[9]

Deliberation, then, was the key concept for explaining the correct political decisions of the rulers, and also the difficulties the common people would have, in achieving "right" political answers. Burke believed that the people were in a disadvantaged position to discern their real interests, mainly because they could not participate in parliamentary deliberations (Pitkin 1967). That is why he opposed any kind of measures aimed to make the representatives dependent on the people (i.e., the right to instruct the representatives).[10] Only with time and very slowly – he believed – would the people come to recognize the value of the principles that their representatives arrived at through their discussions. That is, after a certain time, the decisions of the representatives and those of the people would tend to converge (Burke 1960; Freeman 1980).

However, as Hanna Pitkin (1967) rightly defended, Burke stressed not only the deliberative function of the Parliament but also its representative function. According to Burke, rational deliberation requires information, sufficient data about the views, needs, and symptoms of society as a whole. That is why his deliberative model demanded an adequate representation of all the significant interests of the country.[11] Of course, since he was (what we could call) an "elitist" thinker, he had a very restricted view about the interests to be represented and how they should be represented.[12] In this sense, he made reference, basically, to the interests of merchants, landowners, and professionals, and he thought that the number of representatives was not really important; he was concerned not with votes but with arguments. The important thing was to have all the relevant arguments represented in the legislative forum (Pitkin 1967: ch. 8).

Having exposed Burke's elitist conception of "full representation," it is interesting to note that even he was ready to extend the notion of significant interests to other cases where legitimate, serious, and substantive interests were at stake. Clearly, he showed this attitude through his concern about the interests of the Irish Catholics, who were not represented in the Irish Parliament (Ross, Hoffman, and Levack 1949; Pitkin 1967).[13]

The Founding Fathers' Model

The Founding Fathers in the United States seemed to share many of Burke's political ideas. In particular, they also defended a political model of deliberation plus full representation. However, as I will show, their conception of this formula appeared to be slightly different from the one defended by Burke. In particular, the Founding Fathers' conception of "full representation" seemed less restrictive and somehow less "elitist." In this section I will try to develop these ideas.

On the one hand, although it is not obvious that the Founding Fathers were interested in designing a deliberative political system, there are some indications that suggest this claim. For example, most of the framers seemed to agree with Hamilton's opinion, according to which "[t]he oftener a measure is brought under examination, the greater the diversity in the situations of those who are to examine it, the less must be the danger of those errors which flow from want of due deliberation, or of those missteps which proceed from the contagion of some common passion or interest."[14] In fact, most of the institutional devices they proposed were defended by an appeal to their potential contribution to deliberation, and thus to impartiality.[15] For example, (a) they defended a representative system rather than a system of direct democracy, thinking that only the former would help reason to prevail over passions;[16] (b) they thought that indirect elections through a small body of representatives would be more judicious than general elections;[17] (c) they defended long-term mandates, stating – as Hamilton did in *The Federalist*, no. 71 – that the representatives would become "the guardians of [the community's interests and would give the people] time and opportunity for more cool and sedate reflection"; (d) they supported large districts in the belief that they would also favor more sedate reflection;[18] (e) they rejected imperative mandates and the right to recall, assuming that as a result of those devices the representatives would have "no will of their own" and would always be "obsequious to the views of the States";[19] and (f) they even decided to celebrate the Constitutional Convention behind "closed doors" in order to have "more open" discussions.[20]

On the other hand, the framers defended – as Edmund Burke had defended – a system of full representation. In general terms, they shared with Burke certain fundamental intuitions. Essentially, they agreed that the representative system had to embody the whole society, and that it could actually do so. Also, they shared with Burke a very restricted view of what it meant to represent the whole society. However, they tended not to use Burke's elitist language (at least, outside the closed doors of the Constitutional Convention) and, more important, they reserved a significant role for the "common people" (mainly, the "non-proprietors") within the political system.

To understand the Founding Fathers' view of full representation, it may be useful to consider certain assumptions about society that constituted the basis of their political doctrine. Principally, the framers presumed that society was basically divided into two groups, which were internally homogeneous, and that there were some institutional devices at their disposal that allowed them to incorporate members of both groups into the representative system. Let me say a few more words about these assumptions.

Society Divided into Two Primary Groups. Madison, in particular, emphasized this point in his primary works. In "Vices of the Political System" he affirmed the idea, which he also repeated in *The Federalist*, no. 10: society is divided, he said, between "those who hold, and those who are without property . . . those who are creditors, and those who are debtors."[21] Also, he reaffirmed these criteria in many letters he wrote before, during, and after the

Convention, in which he referred to an existing social distinction between "debtors and creditors" or "proprietors and not proprietors."[22] His speeches at the Constitutional Convention were particularly telling in this regard. On June 26, 1787, he replied to a speech that Charles Pinkney had made the day before, in which he distinguished three classes in U.S. society: the professional, commercial, and landed interests. Madison agreed that society was divided into many different groups (he mentioned the "creditors & debtors, farmers, merchts. & manufacturers"), but he emphasized that "[t]here will be particularly the distinction of rich & poor."[23] He then asserted that the framers were called upon to design "a system [which was supposed] to last for ages" and, for that reason, they should not "lose sight of the changes which ages will produce": in his opinion, the increase in population would deepen even more the twofold division of society, increasing the risk of power "slid[ing] into the hands of [those who will labor under all the hardships of life]." Alexander Hamilton, among others, shared this belief with Madison. According to him, "in each community where industry is encouraged, there will be a division of it into the few & the many. Hence separate interests will arise."[24]

External Heterogeneity, Internal Homogeneity. The Founding Fathers assumed that these two different groups were fundamentally homogeneous. Clearly, they recognized that the different states or regions could have particular claims. Nevertheless, they understood that majorities and minorities in each of the states possessed, internally, the same basic claims. Madison, for example, stated, "We cannot . . . be regarded even at this time, as one homogeneous mass, in which every thing that affects a part will affect in the same manner the whole."[25] There were debtors and creditors (the majority and the minority), and the institutional system had to give voice to these two main groups, and not necessarily to other possible minor interests. Resorting to Burkean criteria, in *The Federalist*, no. 56, he affirmed that "a few representatives . . . from each state may bring with them a due knowledge of their own state." The idea was that, for example, the institutional system had to give voice to the debtors and creditors of Virginia, the creditors and debtors of Maryland, and so on, but not necessarily to, say, the merchants, professionals, manufacturers, militia, and farmers of each of these states. Having representatives from the debtors and the creditors of the whole country would mean having the whole country adequately represented.

The degree of assumed homogeneity was, in fact, greater than what I suggested; the framers assumed that the creditors ("the few") would always defend the interests of the creditors ("the few"), no matter where they came from, and that the debtors ("the many") would always defend the interests of the debtors ("the many"), no matter where they came from. Because of this, the framers' main institutional concern was to "give an equal voice" to representatives of both the debtors and the creditors in general. Then, the representation of creditors and debtors from different states was an additional guarantee for securing the protection of more particular interests, but it was not the Founding Fathers' priority. In support of this statement it might be interesting to look to the system of "checks and balances," which probably constituted the "core" of the institutional design framed during that period. The main idea of the system of checks and balances was, in effect, to give equal power to both "the few" and "the many," as two separated and opposite groups. This view found expression, for example, in Hamilton's main political view: "Give all the power to the many, they will oppress the few. Give all the power to the few, they will oppress the many. Both therefore ought to have power, that each may defend itself agst. the other."[26] Madison stressed exactly the same point, stating that "[the] landholders ought to have a share in the government, to support the . . . invaluable interests [of property] and to balance and check the other [group]."[27]

Possibility of Including Both Groups in the Political System. The Founding Fathers assumed that it was actually possible to incorporate both the "majority" and the "minority" into the government, thanks to relatively simple institutional tools. Primarily, they thought about direct and indirect elections, and large districts (plus long mandates). Direct elections would permit the majority to be incorporated into the government, and indirect elections would allow the same for the minority. In this regard, for example, Madison assumed that indirect elections would "render the choice[s] more judicious,"[28] avoiding the selection of "demagogues" or populists, like those who tended to seduce the majority. E. Gerry was also explicit in this respect, showing existing connections between the direct and indirect character of elections and the selection of particular interests. He affirmed, for instance, that indirect elections would "refine" the electoral process, guaranteeing the representation of minority interests in society.[29] Rutledge also affirmed that indirect elections would make the "proper characters" (those of "the minority") "preferred."[30] In general terms, the framers assumed that the House of Representatives would express the interests of the majority, while the interests of the minority would be expressed and protected by the executive power, the Senate, and the judiciary (the members of which would be elected by indirect means).[31]

On the other hand, the framers also associated large districts with the election of very particular individuals. According to Madison, for example, large districts would be "manifestly favorable to the election of persons of general respectability, and of probable attachment to the rights of property, over competitors depending on the personal solicitations practicable on a contracted theater."[32] Large districts were clearly established to favor the presence of minority interests in the political system. Again, Madison was very explicit in this sense: "Should experience or public opinion require an equal and universal suffrage for each branch of the government, such as prevails generally in the U.S., a resource favorable to the rights of landed and other property, *when its possessors become the minority*, may be found in an enlargement of the election districts for one branch of the legislature, and an extension of its period of service."[33]

Self-interest. The Founding Fathers assumed that, among human motivations, the most important was that of self-interest. As Morton White (1987) put it, the farmers thought that "[t]he self-interest of an ordinary individual [was] more efficacious as a motive of his action than his moral belief that he ought to do what is in the interest of the nation" (126). And although they thought that they themselves – more "speculative men" – would not be subject to the same motives as ordinary individuals, they ended by recognizing that most public officials would be motivated mainly by self-interest. In fact, one of the keys of the institutional system they designed was – as Madison suggested in *The Federalist*, no. 51 – that "ambition had to counteract ambition": the government had to be prepared to resist these innate selfish tendencies.

On the basis of the foregoing beliefs, the farmers found it easy to arrive at certain important conclusions. On the one hand, they deemed that the majority would be more than adequately represented by the political system. In fact, they did not even consider the possibility of the majority being under-represented. On the contrary, their main concern was the opposite: they were afraid of giving too much voice to the majority. This could imply the enactment of partial laws or laws that did not defend more objective national interests.[34]

On the other hand, the farmers were convinced that the institutional system would provide sufficient protection for minority interests. This protection would come mainly, but not exclusively, from the judiciary. The reasoning behind this conviction, I think, was the following. If (a) judges are elected indirectly, (b) indirect elections guarantee the election of members from the minority sector (debtors, property owners), (c) the minority constitutes a homogeneous group, and (d) the members of this minority are fundamentally motivated (just like any rational person) by self-interest, then (e) the minority will be protected, since judges (members of the minority group) will be interested in protecting the group to which they belong.

In addition, the executive power and the Senate (also elected by indirect elections) would contribute to the protection of minority rights. In effect, according to the farmers, these powers would secure to the minority interests an actual voice, decision-making power, and, fundamentally, "veto" power over the majoritarian will.[35] In this respect, their idea was much less to secure proper deliberation among the different branches of government (or to avoid any hasty decisions in the enactments of laws) than to provide both groups – the majority and the minority – equal power within the political system.[36]

4. Achieving a Fully Representative System in Contemporary Societies

It is obvious that, since the framing period, things have changed dramatically. Modern societies are completely different from eighteenth-century societies. However, I think that in spite of the obvious changes, we may still find reasonable the idea that impartiality requires both deliberation and full representation: the formula is still normatively interesting and politically very appealing. In my opinion, the main thing that has changed, in this respect, is our concept of full representation.[37]

In effect, my intuition is that we still agree on the importance of having the whole society represented politically, but we have a different conception of what it means to represent "the whole society." In the following pages, I will try to defend this intuition, showing how different social changes have affected our conception of full representation.

In my opinion, the changes we have to consider when we study the present meaning of full representation are the following:

Pluralism. Modern societies can no longer be characterized as being composed of two different, fixed, and recognizable groups: one group that constitutes the majority of society and the other that forms the minority. Contemporary societies, instead, are characterized by a multiplicity of "comprehensive religious, philosophical, and moral doctrines" that would constitute "not a mere historical condition" but "a permanent feature of the public culture of democracy" (Cohen 1993; Rawls 1993: 36). These different groups, then, aggregate themselves in different coalitions with respect to different issues. As a result, we find changing coalitions of different minorities, and not a society clearly divided into two groups.

External Heterogeneity, Internal Heterogeneity. Presently, it seems reasonable to acknowledge a profound degree of social heterogeneity. This heterogeneity is reflected not only in the existence of many different groups, but also in the acute internal differences of each of these groups. For example, it is clear that we can no longer refer to the "women" or "blacks" as groups without acknowledging their internal differences. In fact, there have been plenty of dramatic demonstrations that it is not enough to have, say, a black person or a woman on the Supreme Court in order to protect the interests of blacks or women. People's identities are constituted by many different features that lead them to have multiple allegiances: for example, one and the same person might consider herself a woman, lesbian, liberal, lawyer, and so on, all these features being decisive for her identity.

Difficulties in Securing the Representation of All Groups. Given the aforementioned facts, it is currently unreasonable to rely on mechanisms such as direct and indirect elections or large districts for achieving the full representation of society. In fact, the "relevant" interests are so many and diverse that it might be difficult, if not impossible, to conceive of any institutional devices that might secure the representation of the whole community.

This new social context poses important questions with regard to the existent political system. Presently, it seems difficult to attribute to the representative system some of the virtues that were once associated with it. On the one hand, the system seems structurally incapable of taking into account the viewpoints of all those affected by the decision-making process. Thus, the epistemic virtue of the institutional system is dramatically impaired: there are infinite groups to deal with, these groups have no uniform positions, and it is almost impossible to provide them with an institutional voice. On the other hand, this absence of relevant viewpoints affects (what I called) the motivational virtue of the system. In effect, there are no good reasons for believing that those in power will have an incentive to protect the interests of common individuals as if they were their own interests.

These problems typically affect the Congress and its aim of being "fully representative": How could the Congress incorporate all the different viewpoints existing in society? How could it give voice to all those with legitimate claims? Moreover, it should be clear that the nonpolitical branch of government – the judiciary – is also affected by the aforementioned developments. Presently, we cannot be so confident as the American Founding Fathers were about the chances of minority interests being protected by the judiciary: the Founding Fathers had good reason to think that a very particular minority, the property owners, would receive protection from an institution consisting largely of property owners. But what reasons could we give in support of a similar claim today, when we have a very ample set of "minorities" (racial and ethnic minorities, women, gay groups, immigrants, etc.)[38] and a judicial system that is no longer composed of members of a particular minority? Presently, at least, we cannot harbor the same types of certainties that the farmers appeared to have had with regard to the protection of a (very particular) minority group, which was seen as "the" minority of society.

Surely, many people would not see the aforementioned facts as problems. Some would deny the existence of any kind of epistemic difficulties, by implicitly assuming an elitist or neo-Burkean conception. There would be, again, certain "objective" interests, on the one hand, and groups of politicians (or technocrats) especially well situated to recognize and protect their interests, on the other.

271

Let me say, in this respect, that I do not think that this renewed elitist position could be reasonably accepted by most people. In this context, I will consider this argument sufficient and will not pursue it further.

Other people would deny the existence of any motivational problem. Some, for example (dropping the assumption of general self-interest), might claim that most public officials act in an altruist way. An assertion like this is certainly true in many cases: some public officials actually defend the interests of those they represent as if they were their own. However, I will assume that, in modern societies, these cases are clearly the exception rather than the rule. Other people, believing in (something like) "the persuasive force of reason," could say that the important thing we lack, presently, is a clear theory capable of orienting public officials' behavior. Again, I will not consider this a serious argument. However, there is a much more interesting alternative to the two I have just mentioned – an alternative that does not require us to reject the assumption of self-interest. The idea is that representatives tend to be motivated to act impartially by (what has been called) the retrospective character of elections. In this sense, some authors state that representatives have an "incentive to anticipate the *retrospective judgement* of voters over the decisions they make at each point of time": rulers want to be reelected, and that is why they try to "avoid provoking, by their present decisions, future rejections by voters" (Manin 1994). The very self-interest of representatives, in this case, would move them to act impartially. The argument is interesting, but, I think, still misleading. To defend this objection I would mention the following. In the best case, what the retrospective-judgment argument proves is that representatives will try to be loyal to the interests of a majority – not necessarily to the "whole" community. In most cases, however, what actually happens is that, because political representatives have such long-term mandates, and are subject to so little control by the public between elections, they tend to feel free to act as they wish during most of their term. In addition, the periodic right to vote does not give people an opportunity to discriminate adequately between the good and bad acts of their representatives. Also, the large number of representatives and the lack of publicity given to most of their acts provide them with a remarkable degree of anonymity, behind which they can hide themselves, if they decide to do so.

So, if we recognize the persistence of the aforementioned problems, and still aim to fulfill the traditional goal of an institutional system that fully represents the whole society, what should we do to pursue that goal? In a very provisional and tentative way, I will say a few words in response to this question.

At least one important thing we should do is abandon the idea that politics begins and ends in Congress – that politics is reducible to parliamentary debates. Maybe we should start considering that extraparliamentary politics have the same importance as parliamentary politics, thinking, at the same time, about mechanisms for institutionalizing the politics that takes place outside congressional doors. Recently, there have been interesting theoretical developments along these lines.[39] Other studies have concentrated instead, on different ways to improve political representation within the existent parliament. They propose securing some seats for certain very significant groups or granting "veto power over certain important decisions to some or all of the major national groups" (Kymlicka 1995: chs. 6 and 7).

It may be interesting to explore the potential of this line of reform within the judiciary, and the Supreme Court in particular. It is interesting to note that, through informal means, the Supreme Court now tends to be composed of members of different minorities (a black judge, a woman judge, etc.), at least in countries like the United States and Canada. This rather awkward situation tends to reflect the Founding Fathers' reasoning: if we want our judges to be especially sensitive to the claims of minorities, and especially motivated to protect their interests, we need judges who are directly connected to these minorities. Of course, given what I called "internal heterogeneity," this solution is far from adequate: there are no guarantees at all that a woman judge or a judge of color will adequately protect the interests of the minorities they appear to represent (as seems to be confirmed by current examples in the U.S. Supreme Court). At the same time, it would be ridiculous, if not impossible, to incorporate representatives of all minority groups into the Supreme Court. However, the difficulties of designing a new and valuable institutional arrangement should not obscure the importance of this challenge, given its main alternative: an elitist system based on the idea that certain people can adequately recognize and understand, through their own monological reflection, the viewpoints of anyone else.[40] The implicit suggestion of this challenge is that we should seek institutional devices for making the Supreme Court (and/or organs like it) more open and sensitive to the viewpoints of the different and multiple minorities.[41]

5. A Few Conclusions

According to the ideas that I have defended in this essay, the present institutional system could be examined in the light of at least two important observations. First, the diverse groups that comprise society find it difficult to express and defend their particular claims. Second, the system does not provide sufficient guarantees for the protection of the interests of minorities. My opinion is that the present institutional system is structurally incapable of recognizing and attending to the diverse viewpoints that characterize modern multicultural societies. Then, if we defend, as I tried to defend, the notion that impartial political decisions require both deliberation and full representation, we should conclude that the problem of the institutional system in securing "full representation" will affect the impartiality of political decisions. I would like to suggest the implausibility of those studies that propose improving the impartiality of the decision-making process just by improving its deliberative character. I believe that deliberation is absolutely important, but at the same time it is far from clear that it is enough to guarantee impartiality: we need to know who deliberates, and we should be worried if most people are kept at the margins of political deliberation. Of course, there are many pertinent questions that I did not even try to answer here: How could we implement a deliberative system in which most of the people participated? What if such deliberation ended up promoting more conflicts than agreements? However, my aims were more restricted: I wanted to bring into question some widespread illusions about the potential of "mere" deliberation and to suggest the need for significant institutional reforms, aimed to achieve an ample – not an elitist – deliberation.

Notes

1. Here I will assume that the making of impartial (or not unjustly biased) political decisions is an important value of any institutional system.
2. I will assume that a "fully representative" political system is a system that represents "all those possibly affected" by its decisions (Habermas

1992). The conception of "plausible" representation that I will assume is a rather standard one: if we decide to have representatives, they should be open and sensitive to our demands; they should be neither completely independent of nor directly subordinated to our claims. See, e.g., Pitkin (1967).

3. Compare this "formula" with other suggestions for achieving impartiality, which appeared much later, among philosophers. For example, consider Richard Hare's (1981) formula (the "archangel's" method of "benevolence plus knowledge") or John Rawls's (1971) ("mutual disinterest plus the veil of ignorance").

4. By "the political system" I am referring mainly to the representative system at work in many modern Western democracies. I am thinking, primarily, of the U.S. political system and other political systems that mainly adopted the U.S. model (i.e., most Latin American countries).

5. I do not mean to say that in the past the decision-making process ensured impartiality, whereas it does not do so now. Perhaps it has just become more apparent that the decision-making process faces significant problems in securing impartiality among all potentially affected groups.

6. Will Kymlicka (1995: 129, 130) makes a similar point, stressing that the representative system in most Western democracies "fails to reflect the diversity of the population."

7. This is not to say that people are always the best judges of their own interests, nor that it is impossible to achieve impartiality through individual reflection.

8. This distinction between objective interests – defended by representatives – and mere opinions – maintained by the people – is parallel to the conservative distinction between reason and will. In Burke's words, "The will of the many, and their interest, must very often differ." See, e.g., MacPherson (1980: 44–7).

9. Burke openly acknowledged his fear of the popular will and asserted that government by the people actually meant rule by a small minority of the virtuous and the wise. See Freeman (1980: 124).

10. See Burke's famous debate with Henry Cruger on the right of the people to instruct their representatives, in Underdown (1958).

11. Burke explained this criterion with a clear metaphor: "[The people] are the sufferers, they tell the symptoms of the complaint [but only the representatives can recognize] the exact seat of the disease, and how to apply the remedy." See this opinion in, e.g., Freeman (1980: 124).

12. An interesting example of this attitude was his very definition of "the people." In effect, when he spoke of the people he was simply referring to those "of adult age, not declining in life, of tolerable leisure for . . . discussions, and of some means of information, more or less, and who are above menial dependence." Burke recognized that according to

this definition, no more than 400,000 such people could be found in England. See Freeman (1980: 125–6).

13. In other cases, Burke would have resorted to the idea of "virtual" representation. For example, the commercial interests from the south of England could not protest their lack of representation in the Parliament if some representative of the commercial interests from, say, the east of England was present in the National Assembly. The people from the South would have been "virtually" although not actually represented, and that would have been enough, according to Burke's standards. In the Irish case, by contrast, the Catholics were neither actually nor virtually represented.

14. See Hamilton, *The Federalist*, no. 73. Also see *The Federalist*, no. 70, where he affirms that "differences of opinion, and the jarrings of parties . . . , though they may obstruct salutary plans, yet often promote deliberation and circumspection."

15. On the connection between the ideas of impartiality and deliberation in the Founding Fathers' proposals, see Sunstein (1993a). The framers' commitment to a particular conception of impartiality is apparent in most of their writings and speeches. In fact, all their worries about designing an institutional system that could resist the pressure of factions seem a clear proof of this commitment. Among hundreds of texts that illustrate this point, see, e.g., Gerry, in Farrand (1966): 1:138; Butler, in ibid., 88; Wilson, in ibid., 119; Madison, in ibid., 3: 450–1; Hamilton, *The Federalist*, no. 35.

16. See, mainly, Madison, in *The Federalist*, no. 10. Hamilton shared Madison's enthusiasm for representation and affirmed that "[t]he republican principle demands that the deliberate sense of the community should govern the conduct of those to whom they entrust the management of their affairs; but it does not require an unqualified complaisance to every sudden breeze of passion, or to every transient impulse which the people may receive from the art of men, who flatter their prejudices to betray their interests" (*The Federalist*, no. 71).

17. Thus, in *The Federalist*, no. 68, Hamilton affirmed that "the immediate election should be made by men most capable of analyzing the qualities adapted to the station, and acting under circumstances favorable to deliberation and to a judicious combination of all the reasons and inducements, which were proper to govern their choice" (p. 345).

18. For example, Madison asserted that "although an ambitious candidate, of personal distinction, might occasionally recommend himself to popular choice by espousing a popular though unjust object it might rarely happen to many districts at the same time" (Farrand 1966: 3: 454).

19. Randolph, in Farrand (1966: 1:256). Similarly, Hamilton stated that "Congress, by being annually elected, and subject to recall, will ever

come with the prejudices of their States rather than the good of the union" (ibid., 298).

20. Hamilton, for example, stated that open procedures would have only implied accepting "the clamors of faction" and "propositions . . . made without due reflection." See Hamilton, in Farrand (1966: 3: 368), and Madison, in *The Federalist*, no. 37.

21. The Madisonian definition of factions ratifies rather than denies this view. Madison defined factions as a "majority or minority of the whole." However, he made clear that a minoritarian faction did not pose an important danger, given that "[i]f a faction consists of less than a majority, relief is supplied by the republican principle, which enables the majority to defeat its sinister views by regular vote" (*The Federalist*, no. 37). The real danger, according to him, was the one posed by "the majorities." Basically, he had in mind the majority of the debtors, threatening to control the legislature in different state assemblies. I defend this view with more details in Gargarella (1993).

22. See, e.g., his speeches of June 4 and June 6, 1787. Also, see his letters to Thomas Jefferson of October 24, 1787, and October 15, 1788.

23. Madison, in Farrand (1966: 1:421–3).

24. Hamilton, in ibid., 288.

25. Madison, in ibid., 422.

26. Hamilton, in ibid., 288.

27. Madison, in ibid., 431. Those who opposed the proposed constitution, the Antifederalists, disputed most of the assumptions shared by the delegates who defended it. Mainly, the Antifederalists believed that the institutions being created would not adequately reflect the whole society. Many Antifederalists proposed, for example, a larger number of representatives in order to improve the political representation of the people: the institutional system had to possess, through its representatives, the same interests, feelings, opinions, and views as the people themselves. They feared that the proposed constitution would concentrate political power in just a few hands. According to their view, the government would clearly be "aristocratic." See, e.g., the opinions of "A Federalist," "Montezuma," John Humble, "Aristocratis," John Mercer, "Philadelphiensis," and "A Farmer and a Planter," in Borden (1965). See also the opinions of G. Mason, R. Lee, "Centinel," and "John De Witt," in Storing (1981); Storing (1985); and Allen and Gordon (1985).

28. Madison, in Farrand (1966: 3: 330).

29. Gerry, in ibid., 1: 152.

30. Ibid., 359.

31. Pinckney, in ibid., 155; Madison, in ibid., 3:330, 617.

32. Madison, in ibid., 3: 454.

33. Ibid., my emphasis.

34. As a result of these beliefs, for example, during the Constitutional Convention E. Gerry proposed diminishing the power of the House of Representatives because "it might ruin the Country [by exercising its power] partially, raising one and depressing another part of it" (Farrand 1966: 2: 307); Wilson stated that "[the ideas of the House of Representatives and tyranny] were . . . properly associated (ibid., 300–1); Madison usually associated the House with "fickleness and passion" (ibid., 1:422); and Randolph objected to this organ, which constituted, in his opinion, the "democratic part" of the Constitution, because it represented the worst evil the nation had to confront (ibid., 27).

35. Clearly, for example, Madison stressed that the executive would be a barrier to "the strong propensity [of the legislature] to a variety of pernicious measures" (in ibid., 2:110; see also, ibid., 1:119, and 138; *The Federalist*, nos. 75, 76). With regard to the Senate, the framers recognized that it would be composed of "a portion of enlightened citizens, whose limited number, and firmness might reasonably interpose against impetuous councils" (Madison, in ibid., 422). As Dickinson put it, the senators would represent "the most distinguished characters, distinguished for their rank in life and their weight of property" (in ibid., 150).

36. Compare this position with that of Elster (1993). It is interesting that, in different contexts, Thomas Paine and Emmanuel Sièyes suggested that, if one of the aims of the political system was to avoid hasty decisions, the solution could be to divide the same assembly into three or more separate chambers, instead of giving veto power to the executive or creating a Senate, measures that would just give power to certain minorities. See, e.g., Paine, in Forner (1945: 389) or Sièyes (1789).

37. We have not changed – at least not so dramatically – our conception of deliberation.

38. I analyze the changes in our conception of "minorities" in Gargarella (1993, 1995).

39. For example, Joshua Cohen and Joel Rogers (1995) suggest promoting the organized representation of excluded interests where inequalities exist in political representation. This initiative should be promoted mainly by the state, which must encourage the emergence of these groups through the use of taxes, subsidies, and legal sanctions.

40. See, e.g., Phillips (1994), who stresses the difficulty of understanding or representing others' needs – of "jump[ing] the barriers of experience" – "no matter how careful or honest" we are. This should not be understood as an endorsement of the opposite idea, according to which we would be incapable of "putting ourselves in others' shoes." Anne Phillips also makes this point, recognizing that it is not necessary to be a member of a certain group to understand its interests (ibid.).

41. See, e.g., Nedelsky (1994), who suggests the idea of "a tribunal one-third of which would be composed of representatives of disadvantaged groups." See also Kymlicka (1995: ch. 7). Commenting on the famous Rodney King case, Amy Gutman (1993) connects this representation problem and the idea of deliberation. She states that cases like that of Rodney King reinforce "the claim that the multiculturalism of deliberations is often an indispensable aid to an adequate deliberation" (204–5). For a discussion of the epistemic problems behind these questions, see Phillips (1995).

References

Allen, W., and L. Gordon (eds.). 1985. *The Essential Antifederalist*. New York: University Press of America.

Barber, B. 1984. *Strong Democracy*. Berkeley: University of California Press.

Borden, M. (ed.). 1965. *The Antifederalist Papers*. East Lansing: Michigan State University Press.

Burke, E. 1960. *Selected Writings*. New York: Modern Library.

Cohen, J. 1989. "Deliberation and Democratic Legitimacy." In A. Hamlin and P. Petit (eds.), *The Good Polity: Normative Analysis of the State*. Oxford: Oxford University Press, 17–34.

1993. "Moral Pluralism and Political Consensus." In D. Copp, J. Hampton, and J. Roemer (eds.), *The Idea of Democracy*. Cambridge University Press, 270–91.

Cohen, J., and J. Rogers 1995. "Secondary Associations and Democratic Governance." In Erik O. Wright (ed.), *Associations and Democracy*. London: Verso, 7–101.

Cone, C. 1957. *Burke and the Nature of Politics*. Berkeley: University of California Press.

Elster, J. 1989. "The Market and the Forum." In J. Elster and A. Hylland (eds.), *Foundations of Social Choice Theory*. Cambridge University Press, 103–32.

1993. "Majority Rule and Individual Rights." In Stephen Shute and Susan Hurley (eds.), *On Human Rights. The Oxford Amnesty Lectures 1993*. New York: Basic Books, 176–216.

Farrand, M. (ed.), 1966. *The Records of the Federal Convention of 1787*, 3 vols. New Haven, Conn.: Yale University Press.

The Federalist Papers 1988. Ed. Gary Wills. New York: Bantam Books.

Forner, P. (ed.), 1945. *The Complete Writings of Thomas Paine*. New York, Citadel Press.

Freeman, M. 1980. *Burke and the Critique of Political Radicalism*. Oxford: Basil Blackwell.

Gargarella, R. 1993. *Irrationality and Representation: The Philosoph-*

ical Foundations of the Representative System. Doctoral dissertation, University of Chicago.

1995. *Nos los representantes.* Buenos Aires: Miño y Dávila.

Gutman, A. 1993. "The Challenge of Multiculturalism in Political Ethics." *Philosophy and Public Affairs* 22(3): 171–206.

Habermas, J. 1992. "Further Reflections on the Public Sphere." In Craig Calhoun (ed.), *Habermas and the Public Sphere.* Cambridge, Mass.: MIT Press, 421–61.

Hare, R. 1981. *Moral Thinking.* Oxford: Oxford University Press.

Kymlicka, W. 1995. *Multicultural Citizenship.* Oxford: Clarendon Press.

MacPherson, C. B. 1980. *Burke.* Oxford: Oxford University Press.

Manin, B. 1994. "The Principles of Representative Government." Unpublished manuscript, University of Chicago.

Nedelsky, J. 1994. "The Puzzle and Demands of Modern Constitutionalism." *Ethics* 104: 500–15.

Pateman, C. 1970. *Participation and Democratic Theory.* Cambridge University Press.

Phillips, A. 1994. "Dealing with Difference: A Politics of Ideas or a Politics of Presence?" *Constellations* 1(1): 74–91.

1995. *The Politics of Presence.* Oxford: Oxford University Press.

Pitkin, H. 1967. *The Concept of Representation.* Berkeley: University of California Press.

Rawls, J. 1971. *A Theory of Justice.* Cambridge, Mass.: Harvard University Press.

1993. *Political Liberalism.* New York: Columbia University Press.

Ross, J., S. Hoffman, and P. Levack (eds.). 1949. *Burke's Politics.* New York: Knopf.

Sièyes, E. 1789. *Dire de l'Abbee Sièyes sur la question du veto royal.* Versailles: Baudoin, Inprimeur de l'Assamblée Nationale, 1789.

Storing, H. 1981. *The Complete Anti-Federalist.* Chicago: University of Chicago Press.

1985. *The Anti-Federalist.* Chicago: University of Chicago Press.

Sunstein, C. 1993a. *The Partial Constitution.* Cambridge University Press.

1993b. "Democracy and Shifting Preferences." In D. Copp, J. Hampton, and J. Roemer (eds.), *The Idea of Democracy.* Cambridge University Press, 196–230.

Underdown, P. T. 1958. "Henry Cruger and Edmund Burke: Colleagues and Rivals at the Bristol Election of 1774." *William and Mary Quarterly* 15(1): 14–38.

White, M. 1987. *Philosophy, "The Federalist," and the Constitution.* Oxford: Oxford University Press.

Index

Printed in the United States
65228LVS00004B/145-162